7TH SEA
Heroes & Villains

JOHN WICK PRESENTS A SOURCEBOOK FOR 7TH SEA: SECOND EDITION "HEROES & VILLAINS"

LEAD DEVELOPER ELIZABETH CHAIPRADITKUL   CREATIVE DIRECTOR MARK DIAZ TRUMAN   SYSTEM LEAD MICHAEL CURRY

ART DIRECTION BY MARISSA KELLY   WRITING BY DALE ANDRADE   FLOOR COERT   ELIZABETH CHAIPRADITKUL   JAMES MENDEZ HODES

GARETH HODGES   BETSY ISAACSON   SHOSHANA KESSOCK   FELIPE REAL   STEFFIE DE VAAN

ADDITIONAL WRITING BY MICHAEL CURRY   RYAN SCHOON   ADDITIONAL CHARACTER DESIGN BY JEREMY ELDER   BRETT ZEILER

ART BY GIORGIO BARONI   MANUEL CASTANON   SHEN FEI   DIEGO RODRIGUEZ   EL TIO DRAKE

CHARACTER ILLUSTRATIONS BY ANNA KAY   HERO AND VILLAIN ICONS BY MEAGAN TROTT

GEOGRAPHY DESIGN AND MAP BY MARK RICHARDSON   GRAPHIC DESIGN AND LAYOUT BY THOMAS DEENY

EDITED BY MARK DIAZ TRUMAN   MONTE LIN   LAURA WALDHIER   JOHN WICK   AMANDA VALENTINE

PROOFING BY SHELLEY HARLAN   CARRIE ULRICH   STAFF SUPPORT BY J. DERRICK KAPCHINSKY

7TH SEA: SECOND EDITION DEVELOPED BY MICHAEL CURRY   ROB JUSTICE   MARK DIAZ TRUMAN   JOHN WICK

A note from John...

When Mark and I first talked about who we would bring on to write for **7TH SEA**, Liz was one of the first names we talked about. We handed her this book, gave her some guidelines, then told her, "Go." I'd worked so hard to make the core book a kind of guide: "This is what Second Edition is." I wanted others to read it and understand what we were trying to do.

And so, *Heroes & Villains* was a kind of experiment. We answered questions Liz and her writers threw at us, but otherwise left them alone. And when the writing started coming in, I was overjoyed. Yes, the book was a helpful guide, but even more than that, the writers blew our expectations out of the water. Not only did they maintain what Théah was—the themes and tone of the core book—but they expanded what Théah could be.

It's strange to say that I'm proud of this book because all the good work and creativity belong to others. So, let me say I'm proud to present this book. It's what I always wanted JWP to be: a medium for other creative folks to express their voices. I hope you enjoy it as much as I do.

—John Wick

Special thanks

When **7TH SEA: SECOND EDITION** made it to Kickstarter, I watched the campaign's progress in amazement and thought to myself...#lifegoals. When John and Mark asked me to work on **7TH SEA** with them, it took everything in my power not to write them back saying something along the lines of, "Yes, yes, a thousands times yes!" Luckily, I was able to maintain a modicum of professionalism. So my first shout-out goes to Mark & John—thank you letting me be part of this project and for everything you have taught me!

From start to finish, working on *Heroes & Villains* has been a crazy ride. I've never worked on a project with such a tight deadline or with a team so focused and dedicated to what they were doing. A huge thanks goes out to the writers who put their heart into every character they wrote and weren't afraid to push against what I originally thought out for the characters to make them truly unique. Thank you to all the amazing writers for really kicking ass and making this book great.

I also want to say a special thanks to Mike Curry and his brilliant mind. I wish I could secretly put you on every project I do. The way you think about games and the creative solutions you come up with for systems work are above and beyond.

To everyone reading the book, I hope you enjoy the stories we've collected in this book; thank you for your support!

—Elizabeth Chaipraditkul

Table of Contents

Chapter 1

Introduction

Heroism and Villainy

7TH SEA is a game of sorcery and swashbuckling, breathtaking adventure and daring duels. It takes you to a land far off yet familiar and plunges you into amazing stories you cannot wait to discover. At the heart of these stories are characters, both good and evil, who color the world, bringing it to life. The **HEROES & VILLAINS** book is about these characters.

Within these pages you will find essays on heroism and villainy, information about Villains' Brute Squads, a few new mechanics and most importantly, 80 character stories and stats to use in your game. The 40 Heroes in our book are true champions of Théah, each working in their own way to make the world a safer place. They come from far and wide, have adventures with one another and save innocent lives. As good and true as the Heroes are, the 40 Villains are dark and dastardly. Some come from broken pasts, others were born cruel, but all ruthlessly manipulate the world making it a worse place to live in.

Théah is unique and filled with a plethora of different Heroes and Villains. Many of these characters fall into different types. In this book, we have introduced different categories of Heroes and Villains to help you keep them all straight. The Heroes are split into five types: Indomitable, Deft, Tactician, Steadfast and Trickster. The Villains are also split into five types and are evil counterparts of the heroic types: Beast, Chameleon, Mastermind, Juggernaut and Deranged.

Each heroic and villainous type possesses its own flair and way of doing things. Some are more brutish, others sneak and some walk to the beat of their own drums. Each type has eight characters for you to sink your teeth into. The chapters also include an in-depth look at the type with suggestions for stats if you would like to make one yourself.

Explore ancient ruins with Bietrix de Veau. Recover the lost memories of the Schlammman. Infiltrate Luysio Barozzi's criminal organization and find out what plagues him at night. Overthrow the icy rule of Agafya Markova.

Now, it is time to explore Théah in the best way possible, through the eyes of its inhabitants!

The Good and the Bad

Within this book we have split Heroes and Villains into different types, to make your gaming experience easy and to add a fun aspect to the game. The reality of the world is that not everyone fits perfectly into stereotypes. In Théah this also holds true, but one thing is clear—Heroes are good and Villains are evil.

In the end, no matter how they do it, Heroes will make the right choice, the good choice when push comes to shove. Likewise, Villains will make an evil choice rather than a good one. This is not to say Villains cannot be sympathetic or have backstories or reasons to be filled with so much hate.

For example, a Hero who grows up destitute and bullied will turn the turmoil from her past into a productive future. She will find friends to strengthen her, learn all she can, and take the risks needed to better the lives of others. A Villain will take the strife he suffered and let it bring him down, twist his thinking and bring him to a dark place. He will grow up hating the world that put him in a bad situation and decide to take vengeance upon it.

Heroes and Villains deal differently with adversity and strife. When something bad happens to Heroes, they devise ways to cope, to change and to learn from their experiences. Heroism comes in many shapes and sizes: a maid who helps to smuggle slaves away from their owner is as much of a Hero as the swashbuckler dodging cannonballs and fighting evil pirates on the rigging of a ship. Heroes are dynamic, able to change, learn and grow. It is what makes them epic; it is what makes them champions of Théah.

In contrast, when something bad happens to a Villain, it reaffirms his dogmatic view of the world, closes his heart and drives them to hurt others. Villainy is sometimes born out of strife. However, villainy can also signify something simply broken in a person. With no tragic past, some Villains are terrifying creatures of malice who revel in the pain they cause for one simple fact—they enjoy it.

Thus, throughout this book you will be confronted with two very simple ideals—the good and the bad. Read through stories of the Théans included in this book and you will see what caused these characters to choose right from wrong or *vice versa*; decide whether or not there is hope for those who have committed horrendous acts, or if they are too far gone.

Types

There are five types of Heroes and five types of Villains presented in this book. Each type is unique and has its own quirks and weaknesses. The types are modeled after the five Traits: Brawn (Indomitable/Beast), Finesse (Deft/Chameleon), Wits (Tactician/Mastermind), Resolve (Steadfast/Juggernaut) and Panache (Trickster/Deranged). This is also how they are ordered in the book.

Heroes
Indomitable

The Indomitable are amazing warriors and strong souls. They are headstrong, bold and never back down from a fight. Their keen sense of honor and justice means they are the light in the darkness, leading the way into a brighter future.

Deft

The Deft are stealthy and quick on their feet. They are flexible and know in a tight spot to bend so not to break. This type has a strong heart and feels others emotions keenly, winning the day with fast moves and empathy.

Tactician

Tacticians are highly intelligent, masterful minds. They prize their tactics and wit above all else, sometimes blind to the people before them in favor of the outcome they constructed in their minds. Tacticians know battles can be solved in a debate or a war room, and they are willing to play the long game, because they know one day victory will be theirs.

Steadfast

The ultimate driving force behind any member of the Steadfast is hope. The Steadfast are unrelenting physically and mentally, knowing there is a better day to come just around the corner. When they have an idea in their minds it is nigh impossible to stop them from reaching their goal.

Trickster

Tricksters are a varied group of Heroes who interact with Théah in their own unique, quirky way. Each has their own brand of unorthodox problem solving tricks, which can confuse both allies and foes alike.

No matter how Tricksters ply their arts, one thing remains the same: they are true Heroes. And that, in the end, is all that matters.

Villains
Beast

Beasts are terrifying to behold on the battlefield. They are filled with a deep rage that colors their every action and drives them to depravity. These cruel souls extort, bully and murder, fueling their need for destruction.

Chameleon

Chameleons are shadowy people without identities. They switch from one role to the next depending on what suits them and what will allow them to get their way. While their mercurial nature could seem benign, Chameleons choose to attack from the shadows and terrorize, reveling in the chaos and pain they cause.

Mastermind

The counterpart to Tacticians, Masterminds enjoy mental games with a deadly twist. Surrounding themselves with underlings, they use their superior intellect to manipulate others. Masterminds always have a plan up their sleeve and know how to manipulate others to get it done.

Juggernaut

Juggernauts are unrelenting maniacs with a thirst for blood. Whatever scheme they have, they will not stop until it is met, and they do not care who they go through in order to do so. Juggernauts are singularly focused and deadly to anyone who tries to stop their success.

Deranged

The Deranged are insane villains with views so alien, most of their colleagues cannot understand them. They are utterly clear on what their worldview is, but it does not match the rest of society. Idealists at heart, the Deranged work to turn the world into their own sickly twisted vision of utopia.

REDEMPTION

The words "final victory" might seem ominous. In some cases a Hero's final conflict with a Villain might result in that Villain's death or permanent removal as a character in the game, such as via exile or imprisonment. It is important to never forget, however, that not all Villains are mindless monsters. Some may have strayed from an original path of righteousness, been driven mad by external forces or suffered from torture or cruelty their entire lives. Such Villains might be redeemed—turned away from a dark path and to a life of heroism.

There is no higher aspiration for a Hero than to transform a person of wickedness into a vision of good.

The Villains listed in this book have a section called "Redemption," meant to give both the GM and the player an idea of the requirements that would need to be met to turn a Villain away from a dark life. A Villain might not have suggestions, but rather reasons we feel he is too far gone for redemption, being too motivated by greed or dark ambition or having willingly shed any last vestiges of his humanity.

NEW ADVANTAGE, "SAVIOR"

Savior, 4 Point Advantage. Knack.
It is not enough to simply stop a Villain—you must change her. The greatest weapon against wickedness is to take an agent of evil and make her a force for good. When you take a Risk in the direct pursuit of redeeming a Villain and turning her toward a path of Heroism, you can spend a Hero Point in place of spending a Raise for any Action. If an Action would require multiple Raises (because of Improvisation, being Unskilled, being under Pressure, etc.) you only need to spend one Hero Point to accomplish it. Because you are not spending Raises for these Actions, it remains your turn—this means that, in effect, so long as you have Hero Points you can continue to take Actions back-to-back if every Action that you take is directly related to the redemption of a Villain.

How to Use this Book

HEROES & VILLAINS is a guidebook to Théah through the eyes of its people. As a GM, you can use the Villains as antagonists for your players and the Heroes as pre-generated characters so you can pick up and play a game of 7TH SEA no matter where you go. Each character has a plot attached to them, some of them even intertwining with one another, and so there is plenty of material for you to start a game with. As a player, you can pick out your allies and enemies, read about how to help other player's Stories come to fruition and delve into the shadowy depths of the Villain's evil motivations. In the end, this is your book. Use it as a guideline, a supplement, but most of all make it yours—Théah won't come alive unless you play in it.

In the Heroes Chapter there are tips and tricks for you to use when you create your character. There are suggestions on how to weave your Story in with those of other players and tips on getting the most out of a game session. Afterwards, we have included 40 Heroes from various Nations each with their own unique history.

In the Villains Chapter we have included advice to help you as a GM play a Villain and their underlings. We have also included new mechanics to advance a Villain's Schemes and an in-depth look into what a final duel with a Villain would look like. Finally, just as with the Heroes, there are 40 Villains with full stats to use in your game.

While reading this book, you may notice there have been a few new mechanics added into the game. These were born from the stories and lives these Heroes & Villains have led. All new mechanics have been included in an easy-to-use list at the back of this book as a quick reference in your games.

Chapter 2

Heroes

HEROES

Heroes of Théah

The life of a Hero isn't easy, especially in Théah. With Villains, monsters and myths at every turn, it takes an exceptional soul to answer the call to make the world a better place. The people who devote themselves to the common good are made of stronger mettle than most. They are fighters, philosophers and artists alike: people who always have their heart in the right place no matter the adversity they face.

Théan Heroes can be gentle and kind, brash and witty, somber and inquisitive, but each is cut from the same basic cloth. To them, the right action is clear and just, fair for all and instills hope in the hopeless. Heroes are willing to work and sacrifice because they know that there lies a better tomorrow beyond the conflicts of the day. Their work is unending but also deeply rewarding. After all, if they don't try and make a difference, who else is going to save the world?

While the Game Master (GM) is often considered the table's leader, engagement and crafting a epic story is something everyone at the table is responsible for. A good player pays attention to the mood at the table and does what she can to keep that mood positive and fun.

In many cases this is the easiest responsibility to fulfill. Stay off your phone, pay attention to what is happening at the table and keep distractions and off-topic side conversations to a minimum. This doesn't mean that you should stay completely silent when you aren't directly involved in play. If it helps, you can view your role as an excited audience member in these situations—react with enthusiasm, express your interest, congratulate other players and lament their failures.

Before we introduce the Heroes that fill this book, let's take a moment to talk about what it takes to play a Hero and what GMs should keep in mind about Heroics when they run 7TH SEA.

Playing a Hero

The responsibilities of a player and a GM at a gaming table are different. A player who adds value to the game takes an interest in the Stories of other players, makes a Hero who has ties to the world, expresses her goals and hopes for the game clearly to the GM and other players and is an active influence on the enjoyment of everyone who comes to the game.

In most cases, a player who detracts from the game believes that her responsibility ends at her own character sheet, that it is the GM's job to entertain and that she doesn't need to do anything except show up. That attitude is not particularly Heroic!

Playing a Hero starts by thinking about what kind of player you want to be, even before your character gets to dispatch a Brute Squad or stop an evil ritual. Here are a few of the ways that we've seen players succeed as Heroes both in and out of character.

Care About Other's Stories

Playing an RPG is a collaborative experience. Ideally, there should be a great deal of give and take at the table, as focus shifts between the Stories of various Heroes and the GM's Stories. A good player makes certain that he takes an interest in the Stories of other Heroes, helping them to accomplish their goals and building a sense of community and trust.

When you do this, you show others that you care about their characters. Heroes who work together are more likely to get what they want, and every Hero should have a chance to further his interests and his Stories. If you care about the Stories of others, you end up having just as much fun when they accomplish their goals as when you accomplish your own.

You can even begin to entwine your Stories with those of the other Heroes. If your brother is missing, and another Hero is looking for his lost lover…well, perhaps they are one and the same. If your Hero wants to find the assassin who murdered her father, and another Hero wants to expose his villainous uncle…perhaps they are one and the same.

You should avoid doing this without a discussion with the other player, but these are the sorts of things that make your GM smile. It creates less work for him, ensures more Heroes are interested in single Stories, and it creates wonderful roleplaying opportunities between the players.

Create Ties to the World

In most cases, the GM has an idea of what kind of game she wants to run, either in the sense of having a theme in mind or a Story she wants to tell. A good player asks questions about the game and what the GM wants to do, helping her create an atmosphere of fun, inclusion and immersion.

By taking an interest in the world and the stories that the GM is interested in, you send a clear message that you want to be a part of it. This encourages the GM to keep your character in mind as she writes, and makes the GM more likely to allow you to shape the Story's events and outcome.

If your GM wants to run a game set in a particular city, it is your responsibility to determine why your Hero takes an interest in that story. When the GM asks you why you want to overthrow the corrupt Baron, the worst thing you can do is to say, "I don't know, you tell me." If you honestly don't know, you should approach the question in such a way as to make it clear that you *want* to find a reason why.

Be Clear and Transparent

The GM's job is to engage the players by making judgements as to what is fun and interesting to them. This becomes impossible when the players purposefully withhold information, trying to catch the GM off guard. A good player makes his intentions clear, both in mechanical and narrative situations.

When you ask the GM a question—and you should absolutely ask questions—make certain that you are clear as to why you are asking it. If you want to know how a Sorcery and an Advantage interact, be explicit in what you are asking and what you plan to do if they interact in the way you interpret. If you ask a question about the information you get from an Non-player Character (NPC), don't be afraid to rephrase the information and repeat it back to the GM for the purpose of clarity.

If there is a miscommunication, the best course of action is to clear it up and make sure everyone is on the same page. Nobody wants to have a fast one pulled on them, and if you try to fool the GM or ask him leading questions in order to get the answers you want, he might resent you for it—and rightfully so. This sort of trickery promotes the notion that 7TH SEA is a game of players versus GM, and this couldn't be further from the truth.

Running a Game for Heroes

The Gamemaster might not be a Hero, but a great Gamemaster is a treasure.

As the GM, your job is to match the players' energy and excitement with exciting Stories, daring adventures and a play environment that works for everyone. In other words, you need to not only write the game: act as the *de facto* leader of the table, a referee and authority figure in matters of both story and mechanics and a curator of the game experience for all.

If those things sound intimidating, don't worry—we have a few more tips (beyond what you might find in the **7th Sea Core Rulebook**) to help you succeed.

Leading the Table

As the GM, it often falls to you to guide the others at the table both inside the game and otherwise. An easy example of this is at the start of a game—a session of **7th Sea** isn't going to even begin until you, the GM, say so.

It falls to you to manage the mood and pace at the table. If things are getting too intense, you can lighten the mood. If the players are spending time on their phones, it is your job to draw their attention back to the game at hand.

This doesn't mean you should rule your table with an iron fist. If your players are on their phone, it's entirely possible that they aren't interested in what is happening—and that could point to a failure on your part, meaning that you've missed the mark in your attempts to engage the players. It also means that you should be proactive in addressing these concerns. When you mess up it is on *you* to fix and address it.

You are the first among equals at the table. You aren't a dictator or queen or emperor, but the success or failure of the game starts with the tone you set at the table.

Challenging the Heroes

In traditional fiction, the hero of your story is typically the protagonist. This means that he is the one who changes, learns, evolves, adapts and overcomes the challenges laid before him. The story is *about* the protagonist changing, how and why he changes and in what way these changes and revelations are important.

In **7th Sea**, your Heroes are controlled by other people—your players. This means that the way Heroes evolve is collaborative. You have some control and influence over this decision, but your desires are far from the only factor. In many cases, the player tells you how he wants his Hero to change through his Stories.

In response, your job is to determine *how* those changes might take place. One of the most common vehicles for such change is in response to the actions of a Villain.

A Villain's job in the story is to ask the Hero why this change is important, usually indirectly. If your Hero is a former bloodthirsty pirate who wants to turn over a new leaf, his antagonist should either challenge or reinforce this notion. How will the former pirate respond when the Villain threatens his family? Or what if the Villain offers him a chance to get everything he ever wanted at a price he doesn't want to pay?

Once you know how you plan to change your Heroes, you decide how the Villain goes about it. This means the Villain acts upon the world to achieve her goals. A Villain may not be directly aware of a Hero, but your job as the GM is to make certain that your Villains are fulfilling these narrative objectives, even if the Villain doesn't know it.

In most cases, it is the Villain's job to *act* rather than *react*, especially in the early stages of the story. By being an active agent, the Villain forces the Hero to respond. This is how the Villain asks the questions the Hero must answer. Through this answer, the Hero confronts her own beliefs by reinforcing or changing them.

If your Hero believes all life is sacred, the Villain ruthlessly endangers or kills others to achieve his goals. When the Hero finally catches up, does she kill the Villain? All life is sacred…or is it?

If your Hero believes in a code of honor and ethics, the Villain exploits this code for personal gain. When the Hero finally confronts him, does he uphold his code or does she take matters into her own hands to mete out justice as she sees fit?

This is a very high-level, top-down way of approaching this tenet, but you can and should do this in small ways as well. A good goal is to seek to change at least one thing about each Hero every game session. Does she earn some new ability? Does she have a different opinion or a deeper appreciation for an important NPC? Does she find some valuable or unique treasure? Does she discover some long-lost secret?

If the Heroes in your game are not changing, they probably aren't the protagonists. If your Heroes aren't the protagonists of their own story, something has gone terribly wrong!

Acting as the Referee

When there are questions at the table as to rules interactions, game flow, continuity questions or narrative information, the others at the table look to you for rulings.

"Wait, how long ago did we leave Sandoval Island?" You're most likely the one that has the answer to that question. "Can I use the Slip Free Advantage here?" You're most likely the one who answers that question. "The rules don't specifically say this, but can I use my Sorcery to do something a little different?" You're most likely the one that has to answer that question. "So we've been asking around about this order of knights. Who is their leader?" That's right, you're most likely the one that must answer that question.

You should avoid flexing your authority on some matters, however, unless you are the one who is being asked. Matters about the motivations of the Heroes, what they think or feel, or how they "should" act should be reflected back at the players. "I don't know if you think this is the best plan—you tell me."

It is also okay to turn questions back to the table as a whole. If you're not sure if an Advantage applies or how a Sorcery would work in an extreme situation, ask the table for advice. Remember that you're here to tell a story *together*.

Final Thoughts

Overall, the most important thing that you do at the table is to ensure everyone is enjoying their experience. This is the guiding principle that should determine how you deal with all the other tenets.

This is a *game* and it should be fun. Sometimes that means drama or action or suspense or horror. Sometimes that means you need to build tension and sometimes relieve it. Sometimes you should give the players what they ask for, and for others you should put an interesting obstacle in their path.

Regardless, always take the time to talk to your players about the experience. They know if they are having fun much better than you do!

Indomitable Heroes

"I am the driving gale. I am the unquenchable flame.
I am the turning of the wheel. I am the unyielding hand of wyrd.
I am the right hand of justice...nothing can stop me."
—Olin Olle Olsen

A force of conviction and seething with confidence, the Indomitable rushes headlong into challenges long abandoned by even the boldest of Théans. She epitomizes the unstoppable force and has little time for immovable objects. No mountain is too tall, no feat of strength is too great and no foe is beyond defeat. Indomitables are often the physical embodiment of martial prowess and are near unbeatable when they set themselves to a task.

An Indomitable Hero is a throwback to an earlier time, a white knight come to defend the weak, a holy avenger sent to slay the dragon. She hungers for a worthy challenge and continually seeks greater and greater tests of her formidable physical abilities in her quest to defend what is right and good. Her hunger is only satiated by the most challenging duels, hardest fights and most grueling physical challenges. This Hero crosses deserts to right a wrong, climbs the highest cliffs to save innocents or fights armies single-handed to see justice done.

The Indomitable Hero is most readily defined by her awe-inspiring physicality and martial skill. Whether derived from a life of backbreaking labor in the field, swinging a hammer at the blacksmith's forge, constant practice at arms or raw talent, her ability is nearly unbeatable in a head-to-head confrontation. She always seeks the most difficult of quests and refuses rest until she is victorious.

People have a natural tendency to follow Indomitables, but Indomitables are not necessarily leaders. Many are lone wolves that need to be cajoled into joining a group. Some people mistake their supreme confidence for downright arrogance, while others think they are completely mad. From time to time, due to her formidable physical skills and boundless confidence, the Indomitable Hero may not recognize the need for a tactical withdrawal. In such instances, it may be nearly impossible to convince her not to charge headlong into danger, but the wise Indomitable realizes that those who follow her are not as resilient as she. Unlike the Beast, the Indomitable does not sacrifice her followers to achieve her objective, and she is guaranteed to fight a rearguard action while her allies retreat to safety.

Core Aspect: Might

Boundless physical prowess is the defining feature of the Indomitable, but this does not mean he is a bearsarker. The ranks of the Indomitable are filled with invincible duelists, fiery clerics, passionate nobles and intrepid explorers. What unites them is the strength they bring to their chosen cause and a willingness to personally brave any peril to achieve their objective.

The duelist faces an army of assassins to protect her beloved mistress. The noble leads his armies to defend his beleaguered nation. The explorer fights through alien jungles and deadly creatures to find a cure for her people. The humble cleric faces even Legion to defend the souls of his flock. The thread that unites them is a singular dedication to the defense of an ideal and a need to directly engage whatever foe they face.

The Indomitable relies on his physicality and combat skills to win the day, which often leads him into single combat with whomever (or whatever) his opponent may be. He is capable of tactical and strategic-level thinking, but revels in singular confrontation whenever possible, relying on his immense skill and Legion-may-care attitude to see him through.

A View of Villainy
Beast
Our dark reflections and most worthy adversaries. Their mindless savagery is their greatest strength and most exploitable weakness.

Chameleon
Unseen shadows of stealth and cunning, they draw power from darkness. Set their warrens ablaze and drag them into the light.

Deranged
Unstable and difficult to predict. Strike quickly and strike hard before their mood changes.

Juggernaut
Relentless foes of iron who never waver in the face of adversity. They provide meaning to life.

Mastermind
Deadly weavers of elaborate games. For all their genius, they forget that the shortest distance between two points is a straight line.

Playing the Indomitable

Nothing can stop an Indomitable Hero. She doesn't flinch from a fight, she doesn't break stride when faced with adversity and she certainly doesn't back down from a challenge. Indomitables pride themselves on being the first in and last out of any engagement and are always on the lookout for new challenges to test their mettle.

The Indomitable may not start a fight, but she definitely finishes it. She strides across the land with an unyielding sense of self-confidence that is rivaled only by her relentless dedication to the cause she espouses. She smiles in the face of adversity and sets her jaw in the face of impossible odds. She doesn't walk, she struts. She doesn't advance, she charges and she never, ever, goes to ground.

The Indomitable is kinetic energy in human form, always in motion, always seeking, always possessed of a near supernatural attraction to the most dire of perils, firm in the knowledge that her unequaled strength must carry the day. Even when this strength wavers, the Indomitable never lets it show. No matter how brutal her wounds become, the Indomitable always stands up, looks her foe in the eye and leaps back into the fray.

Creating an Indomitable Hero

An Indomitable Hero's main Trait should be Brawn, followed closely by Resolve. People who become this type of Hero are first and foremost excellent fighters and prefer to take the most direct approach to every situation. These people lend themselves to backgrounds such as Army Officer, Duelist, Hunter, Pirate and Soldier.

Important Skills for an Indomitable Hero are Brawl and Weaponry. Intimidate and Notice are also useful Skills for this person, depending on whether he prefers to brute force his way through situations or notice clues in his surroundings that leads to his goal.

Boxer, Bruiser, Large, Reckless Takedown and Strength of Ten are all fitting Advantages for an Indomitable Hero.

Ambroży Czyżyk

"Smell that? Formaldehyde and copper. She's here. Stay low and quiet, check your corners and exits and know your way back here. If you see her, don't engage. If she sees you, make some noise."

THE SARMATIAN COMMONWEALTH

Traits

Trait	
Brawn	●●●○○
Finesse	●●○○○
Resolve	●●●○○
Wits	●●●○○
Panache	●●●○○

Skills

Skill		Skill	
Aim	○○○○○	Perform	○○○○○
Athletics	●●●◐○	Ride	●●◐○○
Brawl	●○○○○	Sailing	○○○○○
Convince	●●○○○	Scholarship	●●◐○○
Empathy	●●○○○	Tempt	○○○○○
Hide	●○○○○	Theft	○○○○○
Intimidate	●○○○○	Warfare	●○○○○
Notice	●●●○◐	Weaponry	●●◐○○

Advantages
Brush Pass (151), Duelist Academy: Sabat (239), Reckless Takedown (150), Team Player (150), Together We Are Strong (155)

Quirks
Orphan. Earn a Hero Point when you put yourself in danger to ensure someone else doesn't have to be alone.
Winged Hussar. Earn a Hero Point when you and your steed plunge headfirst into a battle or conflict, heedless of the danger.

Virtue: The Witch
Intuitive. Activate your Virtue to ask the GM one yes or no question about an NPC. The GM must answer honestly and should be generous—for example, if there is a qualifier, he should tell you and explain more fully.

Hubris: The War
Loyal. You receive a Hero Point when your Hero goes back for a fallen comrade or refuses to leave a wounded ally.

Story:

Ambroży Czyżyk

History

Fleeing abusive parents, Ambroży Czyżyk lived on the streets until an orphanage took him in. Despite privation, he remained tough, smart, perceptive and optimistic; he was clearly bound for greatness. Ambroży's acceptance into the winged hussars surprised no one, but his return surprised everyone. The lowest-born hussar ever to achieve rotamaster rank, Ambroży returned from 13 years' service rich and popular. His knack for business made him even richer as a grain speculator. Yet high society bored him. He felt unmoored: too much time, too little purpose.

Ambroży rode through the streets at night, at first just to exercise the massive black destrier he'd brought home from the cavalry. But soon, his rounds forged a relationship with the homeless of Voruta. He surprised panhandlers with not only coin, but also tips on the warmest places to shelter or the restaurants that gave away the most food.

Ambroży was the first non-mendicant to notice street people disappearing. Sickness and exposure were the usual suspects, but such cannot hide bodies. He obsessively catalogued disappearances, clues and sightings of a phantom captor he nicknamed "the Ebon Doctor." His Army buddies thought him a conspiracy theorist…until he met the Doctor in battle.

As a hussar, Ambroży was used to cavalry charges. Here, he stumbled over boxes and trash in alleys as he chased down the Doctor. He barely caught up, his saber and shield just managing to save him from her preternatural strength. She ranted as they fought, impassioned but logical, something about Theus and Legion and sin that Ambroży, a liberal Vaticine, couldn't fathom. Still, in the end, she escaped. He'd stopped her from abducting a child.

When the newspapers found out about the incident, everything changed. Rotamaster Czyżyk and the Ebon Doctor loomed large in the public imagination, as everything from ideological figureheads in political debates to protagonist and antagonist in street theater. Young adventurers, with more bravery than sense, lined up outside Ambroży's door to help him pursue the Doctor. He has founded a City Watch, they're not hussars, but they have heart. Ambroży didn't plan this; he's not sure what comes next.

Goals

Find a home for the orphan he rescued.

The day he first came upon the Ebon Doctor, he stopped her from sweeping up a six-year-old homeless girl. Now, Svajonė lives with him, and as much as they enjoy each other's company, she needs a real home. Are her parents still out there? With the orphanage destroyed years ago, maybe it is time for a new one.

Appoint a better leader than he as Watch Captain.

Ambroży is awash in volunteers for his nascent City Watch. He excels at planning and martial arts, but not command or public relations. As the organization grows, Ambroży realizes it needs a charismatic, trustworthy public face. His often-scarred visage won't do.

Learn the source of the Ebon Doctor's superhuman strength.

A casual flick of the Doctor's wrist knocked Ambroży off his feet. A kick sent him flying through a door. How can so much power reside in such a small woman?

Playing Ambroży Czyżyk

Intimidating, affable, visionary. Rotamaster Ambroży Czyżyk has grown a great deal during his campaign against the Doctor. As a battle-scarred man with a far-fetched theory about a shadowy menace, he is practiced at describing weird things using ordinary, familiar language. But in moments of intensity or crisis, his words become dramatic and florid, like the protagonist in a Numanari tragedy.

Ambroży's relationship with the Ebon Doctor combines fear, fascination and hatred. He sometimes speaks quietly into empty rooms or at nothing, conversing with the Doctor even though she is not there. He will not easily admit it, but the theology that underlies her villainy, which he finds scrawled on scraps of paper at the site of each of her abductions, intimidates him. Even if it doesn't justify her means, it sounds to him like she's right. He fears that whatever she thinks is coming may be more dangerous than the Doctor herself.

Catalina Morta

"I was born dead and I am ready to die today. Are you? This is your last chance to surrender."

CASTILLE

Traits

Brawn	●●○○○
Finesse	●●●○○
Resolve	●●●○○
Wits	●●●○○
Panache	●●○○○

Skills

Aim	●○○○○	Perform	●○○○○
Athletics	●●○○○	Ride	○○○○○
Brawl	○○○○○	Sailing	●●●○○
Convince	●○○○○	Scholarship	○○○○○
Empathy	●●○○○	Tempt	●○○○○
Hide	○○○○○	Theft	○○○○○
Intimidate	●●●○○	Warfare	●○○○○
Notice	●●○○○	Weaponry	●●●○○

Advantages

Duelist Academy: Aldana (236), Fencer (151), Flawless Execution (see below), Leadership (149), Married to the Sea (150), Sea Legs (148)

Quirks

Ship Captain. Earn a Hero Point when you're the last one in your crew to safety.

Duelist. Earn a Hero Point when you resort to the edge of your blade to defend a noble ideal.

Virtue: The Emperor

Commanding. Activate your Virtue. The GM gives a Hero Point to all other Heroes in this Scene.

Hubris: Coins

Relentless. You receive a Hero Point when you refuse to leave well enough alone or quit while you're ahead, and it gets you into trouble.

Flawless Execution (2 Points)

Must have the ability to perform Duelist Maneuvers. Choose one Maneuver you know. You can spend a Hero Point instead of a Raise to perform this Maneuver. All other rules pertaining to Maneuvers still apply (you can still only perform some Maneuvers once per Round, you cannot perform the same Maneuver twice in a row, etc.). A Hero can only use this Advantage once per Round.

Story:

Catalina Morta

History

The crewmates of *La Morta's Espada* are all bound to the ship by oath—they vowed not to leave, save in death—a promise made to the Crown to redeem their past transgressions, crimes and regrets. All souls on this vessel are bound to their promise—that is, except the captain. Catalina Morta, child of two sailors that fell in love on the vessel of the damned, was born on the vessel and never took the oath.

The old captain offered to let Catalina go when her parents died, but she refused. *La Morta's Espada* was her home, and she fervently believed in its mission to protect Castille's merchant fleet. That steadfast loyalty, combined with a deft sword hand, saw Catalina rise through the ranks to captain the ship herself.

Cut off from land, Catalina thirsted for new experiences. Fresh arrivals to the ship were tasked with teaching her new knowledge and skills; she even learned Aldana from a Duelist who bound himself to the ship as payment for a life he took unjustly.

Catalina's dedication to Castille is absolute, even if she has never set foot on its shores, but she struggles with recent events. She questions if Castille is best served by the Council of Cardinals or by the young King, and where her own loyalty should lie. Being physically apart from court intrigue gives her some respite though, and she focuses on guiding Castille's merchant ships safely across La Boca de Cielo.

Politics isn't Catalina's only worry—she considers herself Vaticine, but adheres to the gentler faith of her parents rather than the judgmental path of the Third Prophet. As Catalina wrestles with her own conscience and sense of duty, she has made a small political decision: *La Morta's Espada* now prioritizes vessels that carry food and books, rather than weapons, to Castille. Catalina is determined to provide for Castillians, even if they don't know her name.

While Castillian ships rejoice when they see *La Morta's Espada*, other nations flee at the sight of the ragged black sails, fearing the ghostly rumors of the very real ship. Catalina doesn't just play defense for Castille—she pursues foreign ships to relieve them of their goods and coin. She especially relishes going after slave ships and freeing the slaves, as she believes no one should be bound into service against their will.

However, Catalina has realized that to truly captain *La Morta's Espada* properly, she must first enter the world of the living. Only one who has truly lived can welcome death. So, now from time to time, she leaves her beloved ship in the hands of her first mate and ventures onto land. She shall gain the experience she needs in order to serve Castille.

Goals

Rid the seas of Estallio, the giant serpent.

Some people claim that Estallio is a myth. Those people don't live on a barge of lost souls. To Catalina, there is no such thing as myth: Estallio is a threat to every Castillian vessel that crosses La Boca de Cielo. Catalina pursues any great shadow in the ocean's depth, hoping it will be Estallio or one of its spawn.

Gaze upon the cliffs of Avalon with her own eyes.

Catalina's heart still wanders. She would love to travel, and the cliffs of Avalon—as far from La Boca de Cielo as one can get—are the epitome of that longing.

See *La Morta's Espada* named flagship of Castille's merchant fleet.

The Cardinals are in it for their own enrichment. The Good King is too young to make tough calls. Meanwhile, the merchant fleet is Castille's lifeblood, and someone must place the needs of the fleet above all squabbles—Catalina is ready for that task.

Playing Catalina Morta

Catalina unwaveringly places Castille above herself. She will fight a thousand ships if that's what it takes to keep Castille safe. Catalina struggles with the customs of the living, but has forced herself into this new world for the glory of her beloved country.

Catalina rarely laughs, but in a rebuke to the cold darkness that surrounds her, she loves to sing shanties and tell rambunctious tales of her adventures. She's very proud of her scars as each is a token of her service to Castille and often recounts how she got each one.

Taking and dismissing lovers easily, the concept of jealousy eludes Catalina.

Eadric Croft

"I've come to help, if you'll let me. It won't be easy, but I'll keep fighting as long as you'll let me."

INISMORE

Traits

Trait	
Brawn	●●●○○
Finesse	●●○○○
Resolve	●●●●○
Wits	●●○○○
Panache	●●○○○

Skills

Skill			Skill	
Aim	○○○○○		Perform	○○○○○
Athletics	●●●○○		Ride	●○○○○
Brawl	●●○○○		Sailing	●●●○◐
Convince	○○○○○		Scholarship	●○○○○
Empathy	○○○○○		Tempt	○○○○○
Hide	○○○○◐		Theft	●○○○○
Intimidate	●●●○○		Warfare	●○○○○
Notice	●●○○◐		Weaponry	●●●○◐

Advantages

Bar Fighter (151), Direction Sense (148), Eagle Eyes (149), Reckless Takedown (150), Sea Legs (148), Sorcery: Glamour, Sorcery: Glamour, Sorcery: Glamour (210)

Quirks

Knight Errant. Earn a Hero Point when you uphold an ideal of knightly virtue in a way that gets you into trouble.

Sailor. Earn a Hero Point when you put aside your personal desires to ensure the safety and comfort of your allies.

Virtue: The Hanged Man

Altruistic. Activate your Virtue to suffer a Risk's Consequences in place of another Hero.

Hubris: Coins

Relentless. You receive a Hero Point when you refuse to leave well enough alone or quit while you're ahead, and it gets you into trouble.

Sorcery

Eadric is the embodiment of Wilfrith, The Knight of Will. His Major Trait is Resolve, and his Minor Trait is Brawn. He knows the Major Glamours Legend (Rank 1) and Reborn (Rank 2), and the Minor Glamours Stronger Than You (Rank 3) and Reduce the Brute (Rank 3).

Story:

Eadric Croft

History

Life on the Avalonian coast can be dangerous. If weather doesn't lash a village to pieces, raiding parties spell the end for unprotected locals. Few know that as well as Eadric Croft.

Born in the tiny village of Coldwater Bay in County Kilkenny, Eadric was only 12 when a raiding party decimated his village. Eadric awoke to the sounds of battle and his father holding off an armed raider. His father was killed, and Eadric was thrown into the fireplace while his mother picked up his father's sword to defend her son. The boy awoke to his dying mother putting him in a boat and sending him into the bay under cover of fog.

Wounded and lying in the bottom of the boat, Eadric Croft received his first vision. He saw a figure chained to rocks inside a half-drowned cave, singing sad, lilting tunes that echoed out over the water. When the boy awoke, his injuries were healed.

Coldwater Bay was not so lucky. Every inhabitant was slaughtered, their goods and livestock ransacked. Years passed, and people forgot about the massacre at Coldwater Bay. The Baron, Byron Kilkenny, ordered the village repopulated to ensure the key fishing village provided money to the county. The murdered villagers received paupers' graves overlooking the sea.

Nine years passed before the first stories of the Ghost of Inismore began to circulate County Kilkenny. Raiding parties had returned in force after years of relative peace. Only this time, someone was taking them on. Stories emerged about a dark-sided boat appearing out of nowhere during raids, sabotaging the raiders before they could even put to shore. They spoke about a quiet man with scars up and down his neck, face and arms who strode into battle against the marauders and defended the locals. One brave soul dared to ask the man's name after he rescued the village of Dalefell. "I'm no one," the stranger replied, "just a ghost." And so, the legend was born.

Eadric Croft is no ghost. The injured boy has grown into a hard but thoughtful man, drawn by his mysterious visions to places where the people are under threat. The rest of the time he lives alone on his boat, wandering the coast in search of the drowned caves that give him his visions.

His search has led him back home, towards the shores of Kilkenny, to his town renamed Redwater Bay. The people are once more in danger from raiders, and the Baron is unwilling to sufficiently defend his own people. Solitary by nature, Eadric knows he cannot fight the waves of raiders alone.

Goals

Foster good relations with locals.

Eadric's past and the visions that haunt him have caused him to lead a solitary life. Without friends and family, he runs the risk of becoming a true ghost or else losing himself to isolation and madness. Making connections with locals will also help head off the distrustful rumors being spread by Baron Kilkenny.

Organize locals against raiders.

No one can fight a war alone, and the constant raider attacks on the coastal villages isn't a problem Eadric can conquer by himself. He must gather the villagers and teach them to defend their homes or risk having his heroism undone the moment he leaves.

Learn the source of his visions in the Sea Caves of Kilkenny.

Terrifying visions haunt Eadric. He sees a drowned cave in the cliffs below Kilkenny and a figure bound to the rocks by iron chains. Eadric must discover the source of his visions, but fears that in doing so they just might come to an end and leave him powerless.

Playing Eadric Croft

Eadric Croft is a nomad, a restless soul driven to protect his people by an unknown source that provides him with his visions. He prefers the company of the sea to people and presents as uncomfortable and distracted when interacting with others. He speaks little, choosing action over words. Eadric would rather stay on his boat than on land and never looks anyone in the eye in everyday conversation. In a fight, however, Eadric is the epitome of a knight errant, direct, brave and true, his confidence and command restored.

Isaac Paige

"Dead sprint from here to the end of the roof, then a jump to that flagpole, kick forward...Then if I scale the gables on the pub roof, I can reach that line between the roof and the wrecked ship's mast. Then all I gotta do is swing into the rigging, and that part's easy. None of you better tell me the odds."

AVALON

Traits

Brawn	●●●○○
Finesse	●●●○○
Resolve	●●○○○
Wits	●●○○○
Panache	●●●○○

Skills

Aim	●●○○○	Perform	○○○○○
Athletics	●●○○○	Ride	○○○○○
Brawl	●○○○○	Sailing	●●●○○
Convince	●○○○○	Scholarship	○○○○○
Empathy	●○○○○	Tempt	●●○○○
Hide	○○○○○	Theft	●●○○○
Intimidate	○○○○○	Warfare	●○○○○
Notice	●●○○○	Weaponry	●●●○○

Advantages

Bar Fighter (151), Eagle Eyes (149), Fencer (151), Leadership (149), Perfect Balance (150), The Devil's Own Luck (155)

Quirks

Privateer. Earn a Hero Point when you defeat the enemies of the Crown of Avalon.

Sailor. Earn a Hero Point when you put aside your personal desires to ensure the safety and comfort of your allies.

Virtue: Coins

Adaptable. Activate your Virtue to take your first Action before anyone else in a Round.

Hubris: The Hero

Foolhardy. You receive a Hero Point when you're brash, cocky or reckless actions cause trouble for you and another Hero.

Story:

Isaac Paige

History

A young Isaac Paige joined the Sea Dogs rather than the Brotherhood of the Coast, because the Sea Dogs had no prohibition against gambling. Those who don't know Isaac well might describe him as addicted, but that's not quite true. Isaac is *in love* with gambling. The feel of dice in his hands. The satisfaction of an expertly shuffled deck. The math and science of probability. The challenge of card counting. The delight of learning a new game from a far-off land. The camaraderie and sportsmanship of gaming with friends.

An amazing warrior, good sailor and a capable captain, Isaac took many a prize for Avalon and earned a small fortune. He planned to retire early, marry his boyfriend Yves, hold on to his beloved frigate *Lady Luck* and sail from port to port seeing the sights and trading goods on the up-and-up instead of swapping violence for money. Isaac knew Yves' strait-laced mother would never speak to him again without an expensive wedding with the finest food, the best music and a guest list matching the population of a small country. So, Isaac did something he'd never done before: he gambled for money rather than fun.

Isaac overestimated his ability, as he often tends to do, and lost the second most precious thing in his life—his ship. He reasoned he could easily beat the pirate Captain Cormick McCormick in a game of dice, but dumb luck put him so far in debt, McCormick took *Lady Luck* as collateral.

Now, Isaac is a fixture of Wandesborrow's over-city. He has no ship, no crew and definitely no engagement until he can turn things around. The adolescent roof-runners—couriers and thieves and runaways—who spring and tumble from rooftop to rooftop, swinging on flagpoles and sliding down waterspouts, are baffled at the sudden appearance of a middle-aged pirate with a cutlass and pistol, racing alongside them and studying their tricks. They laugh every time he falls (and most of the time when he doesn't), but Isaac's a man on a mission. When the time comes to retake *Lady Luck*, Isaac will be in top fighting form, even more physically audacious than he was as a young man.

Goals
Assemble a crew of able privateers.

As bad as it felt to lose *Lady Luck*, telling the crew he lost the ship was worse. Every Sea Dog—in fact, every sailor in Avalon—knows Isaac's sad story by now, and most of them blame Isaac for it. To get a new crew, Isaac has to prove himself once again, as a leader, a sailor and a warrior.

Recapture *Lady Luck* while she rests at anchor.

Captain McCormick is a notorious pirate and an able commander. *Lady Luck* is both fast and well-armed. Isaac doesn't like his odds for recapturing her at sea. Sneaking onto the ship while she rests at anchor, with McCormick carousing in a tavern and only a skeleton crew aboard, might give him a chance.

Propose to Yves, with *Lady Luck* as an engagement present.

Isaac planned to ask his boyfriend of four years to marry him. *Lady Luck* was to be the engagement present. Yves was furious at Isaac and has only just gotten around to forgiving him—but Isaac needs to prove his reliability before Yves' family will let him settle down.

Playing Isaac Paige

Isaac tends to dress a little too formally for every occasion, and his most common expression is a charmingly nervous smile. He is self-effacing and has a tendency toward flattery, even to those he just met. He's so gentle and trusting that his ferocity in battle and tactical aptitude often come as a shock, though fighting is a necessary part of work for him rather than something he enjoys. He's made mistakes and fallen from grace, but he's ready to dedicate all his efforts to proving himself. One thing Isaac cannot resist is a bet. Gambling is his weakness and while he is desperately trying to change, it is difficult for him.

Isabeau Durpan

"A knight comes in many forms, but a pure heart is what unites us all."

MONTAIGNE • KNIGHTS OF THE ROSE & CROSS

Traits

Brawn	●●○○○
Finesse	●●●○○
Resolve	●●●●○
Wits	●●○○○
Panache	●●○○○

Skills

Aim	●●○○○	Perform	●○○○○
Athletics	●●○○○	Ride	○○○○○
Brawl	○○○○○	Sailing	○○○○○
Convince	●●○○○	Scholarship	●●○○○
Empathy	●●●○○	Tempt	○○○○○
Hide	○○○○○	Theft	○○○○○
Intimidate	●●○○○	Warfare	●○○○○
Notice	●●○○○	Weaponry	●●●○○

Advantages

Disarming Smile (149), Duelist Academy: Donovan (237), Fencer (151), Linguist (148), Team Player (150), Valiant Spirit (150)

Quirks

Duelist. Earn a Hero Point when you resort to the edge of your blade to defend a noble ideal.
Diestro. Earn a Hero Point when you best a trained duelist at her own game.

Virtue: The Thrones

Comforting. Activate your Virtue to cancel the effects of Fear on you and your friends.

Hubris: The Moonless Night

Confusion. You receive a Hero Point when your Hero fails to understand an important plot element and that misunderstanding leads to danger for herself or others.

Story:

Isabeau Durpan

History

Isabeau Durpan was never like other children. Born to Cordelia and Arnau Durpan in Surlige, Isabeau grew up wildly inspired by the stories of Bastion, the greatest warrior in all of Théah. She believed that surely the world must be a beautiful, perfect place already thanks to the good and kind Bastion. When her father told her that there was still inequity in the world, Isabeau vowed she would dedicate her life to becoming a warrior for good, just like her hero.

Isabeau focused all her efforts on becoming like Bastion. She received lessons in sword fighting as well as archery and tracking. She became an accomplished horsewoman and learned three languages. Isabeau grew proud of her martial accomplishments, until her mother reminded her that a warrior fought inequity through charity as well. Isabeau realized that she could serve others best as a gentle knight.

At the ripe age of 13, Isabeau left home and presented herself to the martial commander at l'Empereur's court. At first, Sir Callen Alberte scoffed at the idea of having the young lady as a squire, but Isabeau's dedication won him over. The old knight took Isabeau on himself, tutoring her in the ways of a knight. More importantly, Sir Callen educated her on the real needs of the people of Montaigne. For the first time, the noble-born girl saw how the peasantry lived and suffered under the burden of corrupt nobles and harsh living. She set to work helping wherever she could, and her passion impressed Sir Callen so that he willingly accepted her as his squire. They trained together for five more years.

Isabeau's greatest challenge came during the invasion of Castille, when she went into battle alongside Sir Callen. During the fighting, Isabeau witnessed the true horrors of war. She struggled to maintain her faith in the face of such bloodshed. It was Pierre, Sir Callen's son and fellow knight, who helped her through. The two fell in love and Isabeau believed they would marry at the war's end. However, Pierre was mortally wounded just days before peace was declared.

The trauma of Pierre's death nearly broke Sir Callen. He returned to court a shell of a man. Isabeau meanwhile was knighted for her bravery on the battlefield. But the ceremony was tinged with sadness due to her loss. She vowed before l'Empereur to carry on, not only for the sake of her hero Bastion, but for Pierre and Sir Callen and all those who need a defender in times of trouble. Now a Knight of the Rose & Cross, Isabeau rides wherever needed, assigned to l'Empereur's court.

Goals

Take Sir Callen Alberte on a quest to regain his confidence.

The death of Pierre hit Sir Callen very hard. Isabeau has heard of some Montaigne merchants in the north trapped in a mountain pass, supposedly by kobolds. This quest might be what Sir Callen needs to remember his vows.

Uncover the plot to undermine the Knights of the Rose & Cross from within.

Over the last few months, someone has been using courtly political intrigue to turn Knights assigned to the court against one another. Hurt feelings are turning into grudges, and there are fights breaking out. Find the heart of the machinations and bring them to light.

Win the title of Inheritor of Bastion at court.

L'Empereur has set aside a new title, the Inheritor of Bastion, and any hero of the court may try to impress His Majesty to earn the name. Find a challenge worthy of the title and prove to l'Empereur that Bastion only has one true inheritor.

Playing Isabeau Durpan

Isabeau is a woman of intelligence and noble breeding. Having set aside the pampered life for one of battle and sword, her kind smile reveals a woman with wisdom far beyond her years. Isabeau works to carry herself with nobility and poise. She speaks softly, quotes church texts often and would prefer to live simply while giving away what she has to those more in need. Isabeau also has a quiet sense of amusement about her choices in life and a self-deprecating humor that disarms even the most venomous opposition.

Lorenzo Caravello

"You fight for pride, or honor. I have three girls who need me. They are all the inspiration I need."

VODACCE • SOPHIA'S DAUGHTERS

Traits

Brawn	● ● ● ○ ○
Finesse	● ● ● ● ○
Resolve	● ● ○ ○ ○
Wits	● ● ○ ○ ○
Panache	● ● ○ ○ ○

Skills

Aim	○ ○ ○ ○ ○	Perform	● ○ ○ ○ ○
Athletics	● ● ○ ○ ○	Ride	● ● ○ ○ ○
Brawl	○ ○ ○ ○ ○	Sailing	○ ○ ○ ○ ○
Convince	● ● ○ ○ ○	Scholarship	○ ○ ○ ○ ○
Empathy	● ● ○ ○ ○	Tempt	● ● ○ ○ ○
Hide	● ● ○ ○ ○	Theft	○ ○ ○ ○ ○
Intimidate	● ● ● ○ ○	Warfare	○ ○ ○ ○ ○
Notice	● ○ ○ ○ ○	Weaponry	● ● ● ○ ○

Advantages

Duelist Academy: Ambrogia (237), Hard to Kill (153), Learned Duelist: Aldana (see below), Poison Immunity (150), Reputation: Heroic (150)

Quirks

Bravo. Earn a Hero Point when you put yourself in danger to defend the life of the person you've sworn to protect.

Duelist. Earn a Hero Point when you resort to the edge of your blade to defend a noble ideal.

Virtue: The Hanged Man

Altruistic. Activate your Virtue to suffer a Risk's Consequences in place of another Hero.

Hubris: The War

Loyal. You receive a Hero Point when your Hero goes back for a fallen comrade or refuses to leave a wounded ally.

Learned Duelist (3 points)

A Hero must have the Duelist Academy Advantage in order to purchase this Advantage. Choose another Duelist Academy Style to learn.

Story:

Lorenzo Caravello

History

Lorenzo Caravello was destined for great things. A skilled swordsman and an almost unparalleled duelist, Lorenzo left home at an early age to make his name in the world as one of Vodacce's greatest sword masters. He gained distinction with the nobility as a heroic figure and married a lovely merchant's daughter named Antonia. The two settled in a beautiful villa inside a vineyard while Lorenzo traveled through Vodacce as part of the Duelist's Guild. The happy couple had two daughters, Louisa and Estelle, who quickly became the apple of their father's eye. Still, Lorenzo was so caught up in his life as a daring swashbuckler, he spent little time at home with his wife and children. He always believed there would be time for that when his adventures were done.

Then tragedy struck. An urgent message sent Lorenzo racing back to his villa in time to hold Antonia's hand as she died in childbirth. Luckily, the doctors were able to rescue the infant and the grieving Lorenzo welcomed his little daughter Marienne into the world. Though he was nigh inconsolable, he realized how much precious time he'd squandered away from his family. Lorenzo vowed that he would not miss out on the important moments with his daughters. He retired from his life of adventure.

Lorenzo became the doting father that his girls needed, especially little Marienne. While her elder sisters became lively, intelligent young women, Marienne grew up sullen and sad. She blamed herself for her mother's death and withdrew from everyone around her. Because of her isolation, it took Lorenzo some time to discover Marienne was hiding magical abilities, similar to her sisters.

At the same time, the townspeople approached him with a new problem. Someone was kidnapping young women across the countryside, stealing them from their bedrooms, girls nearly the same age as his own daughters. Though his family needed him, Lorenzo realized few others would stand up for these girls and women, so he decided to take up his sword once more. Splitting his time between caring for Marienne and finding the culprits, the old swordsman is off to the rescue, not knowing that the kidnappers have set their sights on his own family.

Goals

Protect Marienne against suspicious locals.

Magic is viewed with a great deal of suspicion and hatred by the people of Vodacce, and Marienne's newly manifested powers have begun attracting attention. Lorenzo must help protect Marienne while guiding her to keep this magic under control. The little girl is prone to fits of sadness and anger, which can trigger the magic, making her quite hard to hide.

Find a new magic teacher for his girls.

Due to the hatred in Vodacce for magic, there are so few people who publicly display their powers. Lorenzo must find a teacher who can help Marienne control her powers and hone her older sisters' magic so they can truly protect themselves. Lorenzo is not the wealthiest man and worries that the price for this aid may be more than he can afford. But for his girls, the proud father spares no expense.

Uncover the kidnapper stalking young women across the countryside.

The locals around Lorenzo's town asked him to help find several young women who were kidnapped from local villages. Hot on the trail of any clues, Lorenzo must discover what connects these young women to one another. His only clue so far is the local church and a good deed's charity where they all volunteered their time, run by Father Antonio Guellemaine.

Playing Lorenzo Caravello

Lorenzo is a handsome Vodacce man just past his prime. Fit, though with a little paunch around the middle, he walks with the charismatic but slightly weary grin of a man with three rambunctious daughters. A pious man, Lorenzo is often given to prayer and believes in kind words but bold, decisive action. Though he can be stern in professional matters, that sternness all but melts away in the presence of his daughters. Around them he is a proud papa, all affection and loving attention. It's not unusual to see Lorenzo walking through town on his way to a sword lesson with his three daughters hanging all over him, the beaming example of parental pride.

Marrok

"Sometimes the wolf can protect the sheep."

USSURA

Traits

Brawn	●●●○○
Finesse	●●○○○
Resolve	●●●●○
Wits	●●○○○
Panache	●●○○○

Skills

Aim	●●●○○	Perform	●○○○○
Athletics	●●○○○	Ride	●○○○○
Brawl	●●●○○	Sailing	○○○○○
Convince	○○○○○	Scholarship	○○○○○
Empathy	●●○○○	Tempt	●○○○○
Hide	●●○○○	Theft	●○○○○
Intimidate	●●○○○	Warfare	○○○○○
Notice	●●○○○	Weaponry	○○○○○

Advantages

Boxer (151), Got It! (149), Perfect Balance (150), Sniper (152), Sorcery: Mother's Touch, Sorcery: Mother's Touch (217), Survivalist (148)

Quirks

Touched By Matushka. Earn a Hero Point when you teach someone a lesson in a way that would make Matushka proud.

Hunter. Earn a Hero Point when you use your hunter's acumen to save someone from danger.

Virtue: Reunion

Exemplary. Activate your Virtue and choose another Hero in the same scene to pool your Raises for the round, spending Raises to take Actions from your shared pool.

Hubris: The Devil

Trusting. You receive a Hero Point when you accept someone's lies or lopsided deal.

Sorcery

Marrok has the Gifts Command, Purify, Regeneration and See. His Restrictions are Forgiveness and Honesty.

Story:

Marrok

History

The early story of the man who would become Marrok started with an illicit affair in the heart of rural Ussura. A peasant woman named Irina lived in a village in Veche. She married Boris Ivanovich, a wealthy landowner whose prospects to move up in the world were high. Their marriage soured and Irina secretly pledged her love to the son of a Novgorov family traveling the province. When Irina discovered she was pregnant, she wrote her lover about the baby. Her husband intercepted her letters, locking her away until the birth, then took the child out into the woods and left him to die in the freezing winter night.

Perhaps, it was the baby's Novgorov ancestry. Maybe it was Ussura taking care of its own. Whatever the case, the baby did not perish in the elements. Instead, the little boy was rescued by a pack of wolves and raised as their own. Locals told stories about a pack of huge wolves running with a small child strong enough to keep up with even the most powerful pack members. Anyone who caught a glimpse of him described a handsome if desperately filthy boy with intense green eyes and long, matted hair.

For Marrok, life was dangerous, exciting and fairly innocent. It wasn't until he was 23 winters that things changed. Hunters from Veche believed these wolves were descended from the Leshiye and that bringing home the pelts would give them everlasting strength and luck in battle. Although the locals forbade them from hunting the animals, the men disobeyed. Marrok doesn't remember most of what happened, aside from the fighting. He remembers his pack dying as he fought over the injured form of his wolf mother. Then, there was nothing.

A day later, Marrok wandered into a farm, naked, covered in blood and clutching the torn shirt of one of the hunters. The kind farmer Alexi Natalova took the feral man in, tended his wounds and taught him the basics of language and the human world. Through Alexi, Marrok discovered the good in mankind and learned how the strong could protect the weak.

Months passed. Once Marrok was able, he explained about his pack's slaughter. He showed the farmer the hunter's shirt and swore he would track down the murderers of his adopted family. Leaving his only friend Alexi behind, he took to the road to track down the killers. Now Marrok is on the trail, looking for clues to link the torn shirt and the crest on its breast to the vengeance he so desperately seeks.

Goals

Find a human pack to travel with and protect.

Marrok posses the heart of a wolf, but has no pack—a situation he finds nearly intolerable. Living so closely with others for so long, Marrok needs companionship and camaraderie to survive and must find a human pack to fill the gap.

Bring the murderers of his wolf pack to justice.

Marrok must find the people who killed his wolf family and take vengeance. His only clue is the direction the killers came from and the bloody, torn shirt of one of the lead hunters. His friend Alexi was concerned and said the crest on the shirt was from the Vestenova family, loyal to the powerful Riasanova family of the Knias Douma.

Reclaim his birthright by learning his true father's name.

Once he rejoined the world of man, Marrok had many questions about his origins. Though he is dedicated first and foremost to finding the murderers of his pack, Marrok can't help but wonder where his human family must be. His only clue is the rock where he was found by the wolves and his startling resemblance to the well-known political prince, Aleksi Novgorov.

Playing Marrok

Marrok, or sometimes The Marrok as he's known by reputation, walks the line between feral beast and animalistic warrior. The mountain of a man walks with shoulders hunched against the cold under layers of shaggy fur attached to thick leather hides. He moves with animalistic grace and is nearly as fast on all fours as he is on two legs. Marrok speaks in low guttural noises and short sentences. His tone is always gruff, and he meets everyone's gaze, a clear challenge for dominance in his eyes and stance.

Olin Olle Olsen

"You may be wondering why I called you here today. Well, that rumbling sound you hear coming from your left is a moose stampede the village kids have started a little ways uphill. If any of you are left at the end of that, maybe we can fence."

VESTENMENNAVENJAR

Traits

Brawn	●●●○○
Finesse	●●○○○
Resolve	●●●○○
Wits	●●●○○
Panache	●●○○○

Skills

Aim	○○○○○	Perform	●○○○○
Athletics	●●●○○	Ride	○○○○○
Brawl	●●●○○	Sailing	●○○○○
Convince	○○○○○	Scholarship	○○○○○
Empathy	●○○○○	Tempt	○○○○○
Hide	○○○○○	Theft	○○○○○
Intimidate	●●●○○	Warfare	●●○○○
Notice	●●●○○	Weaponry	●●●○○

Advantages

Able Drinker (148), Duelist Academy: Leegstra (238), Hard to Kill (153), I'm Taking You With Me (154), Reckless Takedown (150)

Quirks

Duelist. Earn a Hero Point when you resort to the edge of your blade to defend a noble ideal.
Bearsark. Earn a Hero Point when you let the Game Master choose your character's next action.

Virtue: The War

Victorious. Activate your Virtue the first time you Wound a Villain during a fight to make him take a Dramatic Wound in addition to the Wounds you normally deal.

Hubris: The Emperor

Hot-Headed. You receive a Hero Point when your Hero flies off the handle and loses her temper, causing trouble.

Story:

Olin Olle Olsen

History

While other Vesten were raiders, the Olsung clan has always been farmers. It's less exciting than raiding for plunder, but in a hard and frosty land, it is harder to raise a healthy crop of carrots, turnips or parsnips than it is to run someone through with a sword.

One day, many years ago, a crew of pirates stormed on shore and met Olsung shieldbearers outside the village. The Olsungs were victorious after a farm girl made a suicidal charge and struck down the pirate captain with a single lucky axe blow that sent the pirate crew scattering in consternation. Her chieftain lambasted her for her ill-advised charge, but applauded her for winning the battle for them. She was the first Olin Olle Olsen, a symbol, a normal member of the clan who through sheer dumb luck and heart protected her lands.

It is each Olin's duty to choose a successor, passing the title on when a worthy warrior performs an act of distinction. (The clan chooses if the Olin dies before finding a nominee.) There was the Olin who orchestrated a pony cavalry charge below decks in a pirate ship. The Olin who trained a dog to retrieve her javelins. The Olin who put horns on his helmet so he could gore enemies like a bull. Olin Olle Olsen has always stood on guard against any threat to the clan, using deadly and bizarre fighting methods that can repulse an outnumbering force ten to one.

Only the clan skald and the previous Olin know this hero's true identity, lest the clan's enemies hunt down the Olin's loved ones. Olins wear armor to conceal their identity from the world. Representing martial fighters at peak ability, the Olin's title has come far since the first foolish girl charged into battle to protect her family. Yet, the current Olin's spirit still matches that of the original Olin so many years ago, fierce of heart and with an honor-bound duty to protect the Olsung clan's home.

New warriors of the clan can only hope to see the current Olin in action, to see their hero dance through enemy lines with a sword in each hand, a deadly spinning storm of swords, never stopping until every foe is routed. They have heard the tales of how the Olin always has a master plan to confuse enemies until the perfect moment to strike.

Goals
Find the next Olin through a martial tournament.

Olin Olle Olsen's life expectancy is predictably short. Protecting Vestenmennavenjar interests against violent threats from within and without is a matter of luck more than of skill. But as the Vendel League's influence turns Vesten country into a peaceful place, talented martial artists get harder to find. The current title-holder has planned an epic weekend of martial contests and traditional Vesten strategy board games to find someone worthy of the title.

Reclaim the ancient Stormbreaker Helm, sold off as an *objet d'art*.

The last clan matriarch sold the legendary Stormbreaker Helm, worn by the first Olin ever, to the Atabean Trading Company in exchange for enough food to last a winter, which was a good deal all things considered. The clan now needs the damn thing back for honor.

Defeat the trolls in Olsungs' ancestral hills.

Olsungs and trolls used to have a healthy relationship. The Olsungs brought offerings of food and liquor a couple times a month, and the trolls did not storm out of their highland lairs bringing frost and wind, smashing houses and eating people. The current troll chieftain, though, is a nationalist warmonger (apparently trolls have those too) who wants to reconquer the trolls' ancestral lands, including the Olsungs' ancestral lands.

Playing Olin Olle Olsen

Mysterious, dedicated, eccentric. Like the Scarlet Pimpernel, the Dread Pirate Roberts or Zorro, Olin Olle Olsen is a local hero who wears a concealing and inspiring costume. Olins speak little and affect a gruff, growling voice so enemies can't identify the hero. The Olin is alert and inquisitive, always checking the environment for exits, high ground and interesting ways to get the drop on foes. The Olin places duty to family and friend above all else, making sure all loved ones are kept safe.

Deft Heroes

*"Fear not, my friend, we may only be two steps
ahead of the prince, but we are at least seven ahead
of his men. Fortune conjures no peril that cannot
be avoided with a quick wit and fleet step."*

- Kaius de Bello

The Deft, the embodiment of flexibility, knows that triumphs require a swift victory. A Deft Hero is lightning fast on his feet, relying on a combination of quick thinking, quicker reflexes and an "always take the initiative" philosophy to win the day. He loves a challenge, and his foes seldom see him coming.

The Deft Hero is a creature of passion. Whether winning a duel with a dizzying display of swordplay, nimbly dodging traps in an ancient Syrneth ruin or ambling across the roof of a Vodacce prince's palazzo, speed is always on his side. The Deft is fully cognizant of his natural ability to seize the initiative, embracing it as a lover. He has supreme confidence in his alacrity and willingly pits himself against all comers, allowing his superior agility to see him through.

A master of stealth, the Deft uses his superior speed and quick thinking to quietly infiltrate the deadliest Syrneth ruins, best guarded Crescent harems and most secure Vodacce vaults without detection.

A Deft Hero is ideally suited to martial careers, but is not limited to them. While the Deft are well represented by songs of their ready rapier, drawn pistol or blinding fists, they are equally suited to life as a messenger, explorer, spy or merchant. Quick reflexes and fast thinking are just as valuable to an Eisen explorer crossing a monster-haunted ruin or a Castillian sailor climbing the rigging of a storm-tossed galleon as they are to the Montaigne musketeer or Vodacce duelist.

If a Deft Hero has a weakness, it is his impulsive nature and natural tendency to rely on his superior reaction time to get out of harm's way. While quick thinking is often his shield, it can be a liability when faced with a foe employing long-term planning or an overpowering display of raw strength. The Hero must also be careful to marshal his endurance when faced with a foe patient enough to outlast him before striking.

Core Aspect: Flexibility

Flexibility is the defining aspect of a Deft Hero, and this flexibility takes many forms. Always savvy and sharp, she finds it easy to translate quick thought into quicker action. This often manifests as an aptitude for combat styles that favor speed over brute strength, and the fencing academies and dueling squares of Théah are replete with legends of Deft duelists.

The Deft are masters of adaptation and flow like water around a problem, able to decide between a quick attack or a quick retreat at a moment's notice. A master of nonlinear thinking, she is highly reactionary, capable of changing her plans at a moment's notice. When a defender is too strong, she adopts stealth. When stealth is not an option, she strikes in the blink of an eye. The Deft's truest passion lies in frustrating her foes.

While world renowned as people of action, not all Deft Heroes are necessarily impulsive. The wise Deft waits to unleash her superior speed at just the right moment. It does not pay to simply strike one's foe. That strike must be executed at exactly the right moment, in exactly the right way.

A View of Villainy

Beast
Living avatars of brutality. Speed is our greatest ally.

Chameleon
They move as quickly and as quietly as we do. Strike quickly, for you will only get one chance at victory.

Deranged
Well deserving of our charity, but feared if left unchecked. Move very quietly about them and be ready for anything.

Juggernaut
Never strike second and always press your advantage until they finally succumb. Continue to press them until you are absolutely sure of their defeat, for they never relent.

Mastermind
Masters of long-term planning, they may predict your arrival, but seldom quickly. Trust your reflexes and their carefully laid schemes will come tumbling down.

Playing the Deft

A Deft Hero is not one to sit idly by and let the world pass without note. He is a person of action and what better moment to act than now? Long-term planning has its place for others and is not entirely offensive to him, but only if that plan ends in rapid and decisive actions that win the day. This Hero always seizes the initiative and never lets go until the moment of victory is at hand. Failure isn't the product of poor planning; it is always the product of indecision and poor reflexes.

Continually in motion—though not necessarily forward—a Deft Hero's fast thinking and flexibility opens up a vast range of opportunities that seldom reveal themselves prior to the moment of action. The Deft does not think in terms of days, weeks or months, but in individual moments containing infinite possibilities. Like a coiled spring, he feels that moment and explodes into a flurry of action, whether a deluge of rapier thrusts or the soundless padding of feet on tile roofs. If fury or soundless steps fail to prevail, he simply changes strategy and falls back to fight another day.

Creating a Deft Hero

As a Deft Hero, your primary Trait should be Finesse or Panache. Wits can be a close second, but being a member of the Deft is all about speed and agility. Backgrounds such as Assassin, Criminal and Spy all lend themselves to this type of Hero, but Deft duelists are not unheard of.

Aim, Athletics and Theft are important Skills for the Deft. She is at the peak of physical condition and counts on doing things right the first time. Skills such as Convince and Tempt are also good for the Deft to possess, just in case her quick reflexes fail.

Quick on her feet and able to hide well, a Deft Hero considers Fencer, Got It!, Opportunist, Perfect Balance and Psst, Over Here! all fantastic Advantages.

Bietrix de Veau

"I think it would be best to preface this with an apology. We sincerely did not mean to accidentally (and quite coincidentally) discover the entrance to a secret library, by awakening the sleeping ghosts guarding the entrance in your wine cellar. It was really just a happy discovery."

MONTAIGNE

Traits

Brawn	●●○○○
Finesse	●●●○○
Resolve	●●●○○
Wits	●●●○○
Panache	●●○○○

Skills

Aim	○○○○○	Perform	○○○○○
Athletics	●●●○○	Ride	●○○○○
Brawl	●○○○○	Sailing	●○○○○
Convince	●●○○○	Scholarship	●●○○○
Empathy	●●○○○	Tempt	○○○○○
Hide	●●○○○	Theft	●●●○○
Intimidate	○○○○○	Warfare	○○○○○
Notice	●○○○○	Weaponry	●●○○○

Advantages

Camaraderie (151), Eagle Eyes (149), Got It! (149), Linguist (148), Quick Reflexes (152), Second Story Work (150), Signature Item: Syrneth Puzzle Box (152)

Quirks

Archæologist. Earn a Hero Point when you turn an artifact of value over to a university, museum, or a publicly displayed site.

Explorer. Earn a Hero Point when you set your eyes upon a sight few, if any, Théans have ever seen before.

Virtue: The Hanged Man

Altruistic. Activate your Virtue to suffer a Risk's Consequences in place of another Hero.

Hubris: The Fool

Curious. You receive a Hero Point when you investigate something unusual, especially if it looks dangerous.

Story:

Bietrix de Veau

History

Bietrix's first memory was a hospital bed. She spent most of her childhood sickly. Her days consisted of doctor's visits and trying to occupy her bored mind, which yearned to be outside. The younger of two siblings, Bietrix was never going to inherit her family's fortune, so while her parents cared for her, she was for the most part forgotten about.

So, on the day of her 13th birthday, when her family was much too busy with her sister's upcoming nuptial to remember Bietrix's birth, it came as a great surprise to them when she came down for afternoon tea. "I am better," Bietrix announced to her family, grabbing a soft roll from the table and marching out the front door. She had no idea where she was going that day, but Bietrix knew one thing—it was going to be an adventure.

From that moment onwards, Bietrix's family was happy to forget her once more, and that suited the young woman just fine. Traipsing through her house covered in dirt, nicks and bruises from her most recent explorations of the tunnels under Charouse, Bietrix was like a ghost in the de Veau household, leaving a trail of dirt and unearthed artifacts everywhere she went. While Bietrix's explorations seemed prone to accidents, these unfortunate events turned up the most miraculous finds—a mysterious puzzle box, a gemstone necklace and even a chest filled to the brim with coins.

A turning point in Bietrix's life came when she was 18 and borrowed her father's riding coat when leaving the house. Too lazy to fetch her jacket upstairs, Bietrix was sure nothing bad would happen if she just borrowed her father's for a few hours. One cave-in and two fights later, Bietrix came home covered in soot and with a giant tear in her father's coat.

The next day, Bietrix walked past her father's study to see him beating one of the servants. When she asked him what he was doing, her father explained that his favorite riding jacket had been ruined. Horrified, Bietrix admitted to her father what happened, but the man simply laughed at her. The jacket should have never been out in the first place.

Storming away from her father's office, it became abundantly clear what she was meant to do with the multitudes of treasures she had pulled from the ruins. Bietrix sold her first artifact the very next day and gave the money to the servant's family so they could free themselves from her father's yoke. Bietrix has been using her wealth and adventures to help the people of Montaigne ever since.

Goals
Solve and open the Syrneth puzzle box she found.

The first and most precious treasure Bietrix ever found was a Syrneth puzzle box. It is one of the only treasures she keeps for herself and to this day she has not been able to open it.

Join the Explorer's Society.

Bietrix dreams of being made member of this amazing society. The only problem is she may have caused a few problems for the agents of the Society, totally by accident. These incidents have not gone a long way toward smoothing her way into the organization.

Make amends for getting Leonore Favre trapped underground.

When she was returning an ancient puzzle key she "borrowed" from the Tanguy's mansion, Bietrix met their maid, Leonore Favre. The two became instant friends and Bietrix convinced Leonore to come on an expedition with her. Deep within the catacombs underneath Charouse, Bietrix accidentally caused a cave-in and Leonore was trapped. By the time Bietrix came back with help, Leonore was rescued by the city guard and in trouble with her employers. Leonore has not spoken to Bietrix since.

Playing Bietrix de Veau

Bietrix is honest to a fault and tends to babble on, oblivious to the world (or people) around her. If and when she does realize she has hurt someone's feelings, she goes out of her way to make them feel better, often to the chagrin of the offended party. Bietrix spent much of her childhood in a bed and now spends most of her adulthood outside or in dusty old catacombs. Unlike many of her jaded peers, Bietrix is excited for adventure and lusts after mystery. She's a woman hungry for life and all it has to offer.

Eberhardt Fischer

"I should have the world's most boring job, but Eisen has a way of turning simple tasks into deadly adventures. In here, in the dark and the damp, the land itself is your enemy."

EISEN

Traits

Brawn	●●○○○
Finesse	●●○○○
Resolve	●●●●○
Wits	●●○○○
Panache	●●●○○

Skills

Aim	○○○○○	Perform	○○○○○
Athletics	●○○○○	Ride	●●○○○
Brawl	●○○○○	Sailing	●●●○○
Convince	●●○○○	Scholarship	●○○○○
Empathy	●●○○○	Tempt	●●○○○
Hide	○○○○○	Theft	○○○○○
Intimidate	●○○○○	Warfare	○○○○○
Notice	●●●○○	Weaponry	●●○○○

Advantages

Bar Fighter (151), Eagle Eyes (149), Indomitable Will (149), Lyceum (153), Quick Reflexes: Sailing (152), Time Sense (148)

Quirks

Merchant. Earn a Hero Point when you sell an item for far less than it's worth to someone who desperately needs it.

Sailor. Earn a Hero Point when you put aside your personal desires to ensure the safety and comfort of your allies.

Virtue: The Glyph

Temperate. Activate your Virtue to prevent any magical effect (Sorcery, Artifacts, Monsters, etc.) from affecting you.

Hubris: The Hanged Man

Indecisive. You receive a Hero Point when your Hero takes an Action to pause in hesitation, doubt, or uncertainty before he makes a move.

Story:

Eberhardt Fischer

History

Five years ago, Eberhardt Fischer returned to his village from a business trip, just in time to watch the Living Wave drag it under the swamp. The lurching, groaning mass of animated plant matter with giant, glittering stone eyes drowned everyone he'd ever loved.

Ever since, Fischer has lived with an ailment common in Eisen, named "battle fatigue" because it most often afflicts soldiers who have experienced extreme violence and stress. The condition is poorly understood and its symptoms are irregular between sufferers. Eberhardt feels overwhelming dread and panic when close to large bodies of water. The panic pushes him to the point of distraction and despair, making it difficult for him to speak or act.

Nevertheless, the Fischer business forces Eberhardt into contact with the swamp. His "simple merchant" cover disguises his real job as a transporter of dangerous, magical or priceless goods, whether it glows, screams, rattles, hops around on its own or whispers untold riches. He never looks in the boxes he transports and he never asks questions, though his clients sometimes volunteer the information. It's all he knows, and his ties to certain clients go back generations.

Despite his battle fatigue, Eberhardt still travels the swamp with his distinctive cargoes—and a long list of calming and focusing rituals to keep him operational even when his fears overwhelm him. Sometimes they are not enough and for about an hour, he grows very quiet, his eyes focused blankly on the horizon. While he is aware of who, where and when he is, he finds it difficult to speak or move under these circumstances.

Fear has given him a sort of sixth sense about the dangers of the swamp. What began as hypersensitivity to noises or motion has, with practice, allowed him to identify monsters at great distance, poling his craft away before they can close.

Eberhardt realizes the life he lives, focusing his weaknesses into extraordinary abilities, might help others with similar ailments. Now, he hires battle-fatigued soldiers, locked out of their profession, as guards for his boats. Eberhardt Fischer has inadvertently laid the groundwork for the return of many former heroes to heroism.

Goals

Map the swamp's most dangerous sector.

The region surrounding Eberhardt's village is called des Teufels Abfluss, or the "Devil's Mire." It's crucial to trans-Eisen trade. He knows a few routes through the area, but much of his navigation is by feel. If he can survey the sector, the maps will let him expand his business and move goods to regions in need. But he needs someone to cover him and his surveyors while they work.

Defeat whoever controls the marsh ghouls.

Eberhardt has noticed the marsh ghouls sometimes display a weird kind of organization when they attack, moving in a loose lurching formation or tactically cutting off victims' escapes. He suspects that they're reporting to some higher authority. What science or sorcery could turn an undead horde into an army?

Transport a Dracheneisen panzerhand to Kreuzritter agents in Freiburg.

Eberhardt isn't a full Kreuzritter, but they do trust him to transport important items. The swamp provides an excellent deterrent for the usual gang of enemies and bandits who would prey on Kreuzritter agents. Dracheneisen is a different story. Eberhardt has spotted shady characters lurking around the warehouse where he is keeping the panzerhand.

Playing Eberhardt Fischer

Eberhardt Fischer speaks quietly and politely, with the conversational rhythms of a lifetime merchant, always asking about his customers' well-being, keeping them at ease while avoiding too much talk about himself. He doesn't often smile, and he glances around constantly, checking his surroundings and exits in case he needs to make a quick getaway.

Trauma changed Eberhardt's life, possibly permanently, but it does not define him. To manage his battle fatigue while he is on the job in the swamp, Eberhardt relies on rituals such as rhythmic breathing, repeated phrases he whispers to himself and conversation with others about relaxing subjects like his dog or the weather.

Inés Maldonado

"My muse opened my eyes to love and through her I have found a new passion for my beautiful Castille. I will paint its vibrant colors with my brushes and defend it against the corruption of the Inquisition with the point of my rapier."

CASTILLE

Traits

Brawn	●●○○○
Finesse	●●●○○
Resolve	●●○○○
Wits	●●●○○
Panache	●●●○○

Skills

Aim	○○○○○	Perform	●●○○○
Athletics	●●○○○	Ride	●○○○○
Brawl	○○○○○	Sailing	○○○○○
Convince	●●○○○	Scholarship	●●●○○
Empathy	●●●○○	Tempt	●●○○○
Hide	●○○○○	Theft	○○○○○
Intimidate	●○○○○	Warfare	○○○○○
Notice	○○○○○	Weaponry	●●●○○

Advantages

Disarming Smile (149), Fascinate (149), Fencer (151), Friend At Court (149), Patron (152), Student of Combat: Feint (see below)

Quirks

Diestro. Earn a Hero Point when you best a trained duelist at her own game.
Artist. Earn a Hero Point when you make a sacrifice in the hope of making Théah a more beautiful place.

Virtue: The Lovers

Passionate. Activate your Virtue when another Hero takes Wounds to prevent her from suffering those Wounds. You take one Dramatic Wound instead.

Hubris: The Devil

Trusting. You receive a Hero Point when you accept someone's lies or lopsided deal.

Student of Combat (3 points)

You learn the Slash and Parry Maneuvers, as well as one non-Style Maneuver of your choice, and can perform these as a Duelist does. The Duelist Academy Advantage is considered a 3 point Advantage for you.

Story:

Inés Maldonado

History

Although the lifestyle of the Castillian nobility may sound glamorous to the farmer who toils in the dirt to feed his family, this is not how Inés Maldonado experienced it. Inés grew up a child of landless nobles who had taken residence in the estate of a better-off uncle. Inés was never one for sitting still and talking, but with no lands to oversee, those activities seemed the only thing expected of her. To find an outlet for her energy and creativity, she took up an apprenticeship with the master painter Domingo Tomás Aldana.

One night, Inés found herself at yet another stifling social obligation trying to instigate a harmless duel between the host and his brother, in the hopes of bringing some excitement to the sleep-inducing affair. Inés instantly forgot her silly scheme when Francisca entered the room. The pale, slender woman was dressed in the tantalizing brightly colored garb of a Vodacce courtesan, a black mask hiding her features except her soft grey eyes and fiery red lips. Inés gathered up all the confidence she could muster, briskly walked over and asked her to dance. They danced all night.

When she walked into Master Domingo's studio the morning after with large black circles under her eyes and a face pale with exhaustion, he merely gave her a knowing wink, pushed a brush into her hands and left her alone with a blank canvas. When he returned at dusk, he found Inés asleep in a chair next to her first true masterpiece.

As their frivolous escapades blossomed into a strong and intimate bond, Francisca confided to Inés that she was by birth a Fate Witch, not a courtesan. The identity had been a clever and necessary ruse provided by the secretive group, Sophia's Daughters. With their help, Francisca had escaped Vodacce and the clutches of her in-laws-to-be after they blamed her for the unfortunate death of her betrothed. Fearing that the courts may be too dangerous a place for them, the lovers left everything behind to start a new life in the Castillian countryside.

There in a cottage in a small village, Inés found her love for Castille. The peasants of Castille are her people in a way that its nobles could never be, a people so dynamic that even their siestas are filled with a hustle and bustle of activity. When the Inquisition came to threaten her glorious new life, Inés took up her sword to defend it. She has lately come into contact with an organization called Los Vagabundos. She is drawn to their cause, but she has not worn the mask…yet.

Goals

Find the great Master Ulises' magic brush.

Domingo used to speak reverently about a magical brush he owned. Sadly it was stolen from him during the War of the Cross. With the help of Francisca's Sorte, Inés might have a chance of finding and returning it to him.

Reveal the fiend reporting local Objectionists to the Church.

Inés has grown incredibly fond of the villagers in her small town and will not see them harmed or threatened, regardless of their religious convictions. And besides, such a malicious tattletale might also report on Francisca if the fiend knows she practices Sorte.

Unearth the Inquisition agent called "The Prophet's Fist."

Lately frightening stories have been going round about an Inquisition agent that is terrorizing the region. The Inquisitor who calls himself "The Prophet's Fist" is one of the nobles who lost his lands after the War of the Cross. So far he has kept the hangman busy in every town he visits. It is rumored that the confiscated possessions of the heretics wind up in the Inquisitor's own coffers, not those of the Church.

Playing Inés Maldonado

Inés can be outspoken, but if her frankness has upset someone she tries to lighten the mood with a joke. Her high energy can be contagious, and if something interesting is happening, she can be found in the center of it. When Inés paints, she focuses that same feverish energy on her canvas. She greatly values her community and protects it any way she can. When confronted with a threat, she tries to observe and gather information before taking up arms.

Kaius de Bello

"And then the three-legged kobold said... Okay, they stopped listening. So here's my plan to rob the tax collector's cart and give the money back to the people."

VODACCE

Traits

Trait	Rating
Brawn	●●○○○
Finesse	●●●○○
Resolve	●●○○○
Wits	●●●○○
Panache	●●●○○

Skills

Aim	●●○○○	Perform	○○○○○
Athletics	●●○○○	Ride	●○○○○
Brawl	○○○○○	Sailing	○○○○○
Convince	●●○○○	Scholarship	●○○○○
Empathy	●●●○○	Tempt	○○○○○
Hide	●●●○○	Theft	●●○○○
Intimidate	●○○○○	Warfare	○○○○○
Notice	○○○○○	Weaponry	●●●○○

Advantages

Camaraderie (151), Disarming Smile (149), Reputation: Oaf (150), Rich (152), Streetwise (150), We're Not So Different... (155)

Quirks

Aristocrat. Earn a Hero Point when you prove there is more to nobility than expensive clothes and attending court.
Criminal. Earn a Hero Point when you break the law in the pursuit of a noble endeavor.

Virtue: The Hanged Man

Altruistic. Activate your Virtue to suffer a Risk's Consequences in place of another Hero.

Hubris: The Prophet

Overzealous. You receive a Hero Point when your Hero strongly defends one of his opinions when the time or place is inappropriate.

Story:

Kaius de Bello

History

Kaius is the bastard son of Marcus de Bello. He is also the *only* son of Marcus de Bello, who spent seven years in a childless marriage and numerous affairs, before his wife died. Marcus officially adopted Kaius after the untimely death of Lady de Bello—after all, raising a bastard is better than having no heir at all. Kaius, who was five at the time, never saw his mother again and was left with only memories of her soft lullabies and warm embrace. Marcus told him his mother was a courtesan and that she died. Kaius suspects the latter is a lie and he still misses her.

Though Kaius was supposed to make Marcus proud, he did the opposite: Kaius drinks, entertains many lovers and gambles. His ill reputation has quickly spread through noble circles, and Marcus would struggle to find his son an honorable job even if Kaius wanted one, which he doesn't. This disgrace caused Marcus to turn away from his son, leaving Kaius the freedom to work on causes of his own.

Kaius is a fervent egalitarian who uses his lofty position to protect Vodacce's common folk from the capricious nobility. He warns indebted workers of impending creditors' visits so they can be elsewhere, smuggles courtesans out of the city when they've angered the wrong people and slips the poor plenty of coin (from his own winnings and family stipend) to pay their rent. He even takes up arms to protect them as "the Masked Crusader."

Outrageous as it may sound, he really does wear a mask, and the common folk do call him by that name. The Masked Crusader is a popular figure in folk song, stories and a series of romance novels in which he saves a string of disenfranchised men and women. Kaius takes special pleasure in the latter and reads the raunchier bits out loud to those friends who know of his secret identity.

Kaius has a young son of his own, Amadeo, with a courtesan named Catarina. Though their courtship ended long ago, the pair remain fast friends and tend to the toddler's needs together. Catarina does the actual parenting, for which Kaius is far too irresponsible, while he provides coin for clothes, books and tutors. Kaius visits whenever he can, but hides the child's existence from Marcus, lest he snatch Amadeo from his mother as he once did with Kaius. Catarina knows about the Masked Crusader, but has no desire to use this against Kaius even if he should stop supporting Amadeo.

Goals

Persuade the Vestini Merchant Prince to allow citizens' representation.

Kaius believes that a share in the decision process and profits makes workers more loyal and therefore more productive. He has even argued this with the Vestini Prince, who remains unconvinced, but his fourth son Calero is swayed by Kaius. Kaius and Calero have appealed the Prince to let them run a trial with a small group of workers.

Become the greatest Ambrogia master Vodacce has ever seen.

Kaius takes pride in three things: his lovemaking, tolerance for liquor and sword skill. Already a good swordsman, Kaius seeks to train with Veronica Ambrogia herself. She steadfastly refuses to train such a "buffoon" though, and Kaius must decide if he can risk telling her the truth about himself.

Seek true love in a noble heart that accepts his son.

Kaius is a hopeless romantic who wants to fall deeply and madly in love, settling down with that love of his life. Men and women are both considered for the part, but they must be a good parent to Amadeo.

Playing Kaius de Bello

Kaius is rarely in public without a drink in his hand and a handsome consort on either arm. Although, his drinking problem *is* real, he likes to play it up so enemies underestimate him as a drunken fool; he is deliberately loud, boastful and borderline stupid. Kaius drops the oafish act around allies, speaking eloquently about the need to revolutionize Vodacce society and abolish inequality. Spending most of his time around well-educated and independent-minded courtesans, Kaius has a blind spot for the gender inequality in Vodacce—he genuinely believes that bridging the class divide solves everything.

Lilly Ó Tuama

"I'm sorry, but I'm actually not the best person to handle the Sidhe–Wait. Is that your child I hear in the backroom? Yes, I'll help."

INISMORE

Traits

Brawn	●●○○○
Finesse	●●●○○
Resolve	●●●○○
Wits	●●●○○
Panache	●●○○○

Skills

Aim	○○○○○	Perform	●●○○○
Athletics	●○○○○	Ride	●●○○○
Brawl	●●○○○	Sailing	○○○○○
Convince	●●●○○	Scholarship	●○○○○
Empathy	●●●○○	Tempt	○○○○○
Hide	●●○○○	Theft	○○○○○
Intimidate	●●○○○	Warfare	●○○○○
Notice	○○●○○	Weaponry	●○●○○

Advantages

Barterer (149), Brush Pass (151), Direction Sense (148), Reckless Takedown (150), Small (148), Sorcery: Glamour, Sorcery: Glamour (210), The Devil's Own Luck (155)

Quirks

Knight Errant. Earn a Hero Point when you uphold an ideal of knightly virtue in a way that gets you into trouble.

Orphan. Earn a Hero Point when you put yourself in danger to ensure someone else doesn't have to be alone.

Virtue: The Glyph

Temperate. Activate your Virtue to prevent any magical effect (Sorcery, Artifacts, Monsters, etc.) from affecting you.

Hubris: The War

Loyal. You receive a Hero Point when your Hero goes back for a fallen comrade or refuses to leave a wounded ally.

Sorcery

Lilly is the Embodiment of Cenhelm, The Keen. Her Major Trait is Finesse, her Minor Trait is Wits. She knows the Major Glamours Legend (Rank 1) and First (Rank 1), and the Minor Glamours Heroic (Rank 2) and Summon Sidhe (Rank 2).

Story:

Lilly Ó Tuama

History

Lilly's story began long before she was born. As Vesten raiders followed on the heels of a harsh winter, Eva was left with an impossible choice: let her family die, or make a devil's bargain. A færie offered to help defend against the approaching raiders, but only if Eva gave her second-born child to the færie. Eva thought she could avoid paying her dues by having only one child.

Years passed, and Eva had her first child—only to have the babe die in infancy. Desperately wanting another child, and hoping the Sidhe had forgotten, Eva had the fated second born. Mere days later, a Sidhe came under the cloak of rain and darkness. She took the babe from her mother's arms and left a changeling in her stead marked with a crescent moon.

Lilly, a changeling left with a family who was not truly her own, grew up confused and angry. For many years, Lilly was convinced she was not human, but she had none of the weaknesses of a fæ and had no idea what she could be. Her parents loved her, but Lilly's soul was restless.

The lands of her birthright called to her when she slept, and her dreams were spent under the eternal twilight skies of the Sidhe. She ran away repeatedly, traveling with vagabonds and snake-oil salesmen before wandering back home. One night, she came to a crossroads where an impossibly tall man was held in an iron cage. He begged, "Release me, cousin"—and that's when Lilly knew. She hasn't been home since, afraid her family will read the truth in her eyes.

Lilly is terrified of herself. The Sidhe are stalwart protectors of Inismore, but they are also fiends and child-stealers. What if she is the latter? This fear drives her to cling to goodness, and Lilly never lies (though she might omit information) or steals. She has an exceptional singing voice and travels as a bard. Preferring to avoid fights and never having raised arms against another Inish, she instead relies on stealth and quickness to solve problems. While many people underestimate the small, unarmed woman, Inismore's peasants have come to rely on her. They send word to the Green Stag Inn when threatened, and Lilly always comes to their aid.

Lilly has a special reputation for dealing with the Sidhe. She's not sure how, but she always finds herself in the midst of their schemes. It's gotten so bad that her girlfriend Rhoswen jokingly calls her a "fæ magnet"—something Lilly doesn't find funny at all. Lilly is an expert at negotiating favorable bargains with the Seelie, while repelling the Unseelie.

Goals

Probe rumors of a Sidhe adviser to Hugh Monaghan.

Lilly suspects a nefarious scheme between a Sidhe and Hugh Monaghan, a local brigand who is quickly rising in power. She doesn't know the Sidhe is actually Monaghan's prisoner and Lilly's Sidhe parent—Monaghan deliberately leaked the information to lure Lilly and use her as leverage.

Open a gate to Bryn Bresail to learn about the Sidhe.

Lilly met a Seelie Sidhe, who invited her "home" to Bryn Bresail. She had choice words for him then, but now considers it. She could learn more about the Sidhe and what exactly Bryn Bresail is—but only on her own terms.

Discover the meaning of the crescent birthmark on her hand.

Lilly long sensed something off about her birthmark. She doesn't know it, but her Sidhe mother marked her as a protector of the Graal. Even now, Lilly feels the call to Elaine's side. Should Queen Elaine die, Lilly must take the Graal and see it safely to the hands of Avalon's next true ruler.

Playing Lilly Ó Tuama

Lilly can't stay still: she continually travels the breadth of the Glamour Isles and fidgets when sitting or standing. She loves sleeping under the stars, except when it rains—rain brings dreams of Bryn Bresail and these terrify Lilly. She loves water in all other forms and never passes an opportunity to swim. Lilly is polyamorous, but the barkeep Rhoswen, whose father owns the Green Stag Inn, is the only lover that gives her a sense of belonging.

Milo de Villenc

"We have a few viable options for how to proceed, but I would encourage my superiors to consider which one results in the least loss of innocent life. Not that any of our soldiers are ready to desert, but if they were, burying the bodies of children might push them over the edge."

MONTAIGNE • THE EXPLORER'S SOCIETY

Traits

Trait	Rating
Brawn	●●○○○
Finesse	●●●○○
Resolve	●●◐○○
Wits	●●○○○
Panache	●●●●○

Skills

Skill	Rating	Skill	Rating
Aim	●○○○○	Perform	○○◐○○
Athletics	●○○○○	Ride	●○○○○
Brawl	○○○○○	Sailing	●○○○○
Convince	●●●◐○	Scholarship	○○◐○○
Empathy	●●●○○	Tempt	○○○○○
Hide	●●○○○	Theft	○○○○○
Intimidate	●○◐○○	Warfare	●●◐○○
Notice	●●●○○	Weaponry	●●○○◐

Advantages

Able Drinker (148), Camaraderie (151), Quick Reflexes: Notice (152), Riot Breaker (153), Sea Legs (148), Second Story Work (150), Slip Free (150)

Quirks

Soldier. Earn a Hero Point when you stick to the plan regardless of the danger to yourself.
Explorer. Earn a Hero Point when you set your eyes upon a sight few, if any, Théans have ever seen before.

Virtue: The Lovers

Passionate. Activate your Virtue when another Hero takes Wounds to prevent them from suffering those Wounds. You take one Dramatic Wound instead.

Hubris: The Devil

Trusting. You receive a Hero Point when you accept someone's lies or lopsided deal.

Story:

Milo de Villenc

History

Milo was certain war was no place for someone like him. His whole childhood, his family and his teachers lauded his thoughtful and compassionate nature. Only his father, a knight who retired with a knee injury, did not fully appreciate him. Where his father was strong and brash, Milo was sly and subtle.

When l'Empereur's officers came to their village to conscript soldiers, Milo's father practically shoved him into the recruiter's arms. War, he thought, would toughen up his soft son. Milo obeyed, because of course he'd obey his father, but as he did so, he made peace with his own death.

Death almost came for him when he grabbed a Castillian grenade in his trench and threw it back just a second too late. But losing his hand didn't break his spirit. He was still the best-loved man in his squad, physically unassuming, but extremely helpful to the soldiers around him. He developed a reputation as a harmless, stand-up guy who did not want to shoot Castillians, but supported his siblings-in-arms with all his heart and might. The only one who disapproved of his ways was Lord Bodin, Milo's commander. When Milo lost his hand, the commander didn't bat an eye, sending the soldier back into the trenches days after his injury and risking a festering wound.

Yet, the darkness that Bodin casted over Milo's time in the army was lifted by Celeste de Villenc, a woman who captivated him. He had never met anyone like her before. He met the genius tactician by chance one night, helping her cope with a headache. She was his opposite in every way, tough and idealistic. But each one saw completeness in the other's differences. They married secretly, not revealing their liaison until hostilities died down.

Milo and Celeste de Villenc now belong to the Explorer's Society. Their "working honeymoon" brought them to a dozen major ports on the southern Théan coast. Milo assists with excavations while Celeste runs security. Their work continues to take them to far-off lands, but one day, Milo intends to return to the territory that brought them together. He has unfinished business.

Goals

Get the adopted orphan to safety.

Milo and Celeste found Pancho weeping on a battlefield in the aftermath of a major clash. He barely speaks, but he's attached to Milo and Celeste, his *de facto* adoptive parents. Scarred by what he saw in the war, Pancho has made it clear returning to Castille would mean his death. Milo and Celeste need to find someone who's willing to take him in without revealing the treasonous act they've performed by taking a Castillian orphan in themselves.

Get his bloodthirsty former commander, Lord Bodin, discharged.

Jean-Charles Bodin was everything Milo feared a Montaigne officer would be. He was rapacious and bloodthirsty, killing people who had already surrendered and secretly selling captives into slavery with the Atabean Trading Company. During the war, Celeste managed to get Milo transferred to her own unit, and Milo still needs to get proof of Bodin's misdeeds without Bodin finding out he has an enemy.

Secure the Syrneth dig site in Tarago.

The Explorer's Society has had its eye on a mine north of war-torn Tarago where Syrneth artifacts were found decades ago. But that same mine became a factory in the war. Amazingly, the mine hasn't collapsed—but Montaigne and Castille patrols still skirmish in the area.

Playing Milo de Villenc

Milo's retiring, but brightens like the sun emerging from behind a cloud when Celeste is nearby. He possesses an extraordinary character, but does not desire personal glory. When he stands up to a bully, he's not doing so because enjoys conflict. He's doing so because his conscience won't let him go. Celeste says that is what makes him a hero.

Milo has the kindness that makes genius possible. He's the first to ask whether you've had enough water, whether you need another blanket, how that incident made you feel: all the little things that keep you going when you're too focused on a high-minded ideal or lofty goal to take care of yourself.

Reider Ness

"Fear not, but listen to the gods! Sing to lightning! Sing to thunder! Sing to wind and wave alike! This is not weather, but a prayer of the gods! Let us rejoice and join their chorus!"

VESTENMENNAVENJAR

Traits

Trait	Rating
Brawn	●●●○○
Finesse	●●●○○
Resolve	●●●○○
Wits	●●○○○
Panache	●●○○○

Skills

Skill	Rating	Skill	Rating
Aim	○○○○○	Perform	●●●○○
Athletics	●●○○○	Ride	○○○○○
Brawl	●●●○○	Sailing	●●○○○
Convince	●○○○○	Scholarship	●○○○○
Empathy	○○○○○	Tempt	●○○○○
Hide	○○○○○	Theft	○○○○○
Intimidate	●●●○○	Warfare	○○○○○
Notice	●●○○○	Weaponry	●●○○○

Advantages
Bar Fighter (151), Eagle Eyes (149), Reputation: Wild (150), Sea Legs (148), Seidr (153), Signature Item: Skald's Runed Talisman (152)

Quirks
Skald. Earn a Hero Point when you use your knowledge as a Seidr to help another Hero to solve a problem or thwart a Villain.
Sailor. Earn a Hero Point when you put aside your personal desires to ensure the safety and comfort of your allies.

Virtue: The Witch
Intuitive. Activate your Virtue to ask the GM one yes or no question about an NPC. The GM must answer honestly and should be generous—for example, if there is a qualifier, he should tell you and explain more fully.

Hubris: The Hero
Foolhardy. You receive a Hero Point when your brash, cocky, or reckless actions cause trouble for you and another Hero.

Story:

Reider Ness

History

Reider Ness was born in the town of Kinsvarik on the northern coast of Vestenmennavenjar. Always fascinated by tales of the gods, Reider slipped out of the house on stormy nights to commune with the Allfather. Wind and wave, lightning and thunder fired his heart and forged his personality. One fateful evening while Reider was communing with a particularly violent storm, he was struck by lightning. Awakening from a vision of the Allfather, Reider's wyrd bellowed forth from his soul. Staggering to his feet, Reider rejoiced and began his career as a prophet whose chief mode of worship was bardic verse.

Reider's best friend was Gunnar Haftson. Inseparable from their earliest youth, they explored the fjords of Kinsvarik without a care in the world. Young boys became young men, and the call of their wyrd led them to join the Vendel merchant fleet.

Hard working and harder drinking, Reider howled prayers from the rigging during storms, bargaining with the gods for safe passage. He quickly became the good luck charm of many a merchantman and his faith was matched only by his heroism. Whether it was diving into the heart of a tempest to rescue a crewmate or fending off a dozen pirates single-handedly, Reider met every challenge with fearless mirth.

Things changed when Gunnar met Ilse, a wealthy Eisen refugee from the War of the Cross. The change was subtle at first, but Ilse's Objectionist faith began to weaken Gunnar's resolve in the gods. Hard words and harder blows between Reider and his friend saw Gunnar return to Kinsvarik to marry Ilse.

Years passed and Reider met an enigmatic skald who was on his deathbed. The skald sang the song of Aslaug and of the Allfather's great storm. As the skald died, a crack of lightning was seen to the north and Reider knew the skald's words to be true.

Reider returned to Kinsvarik to follow the skald's songs, to sing them to his friend Gunnar and show him the might of the Allfather, only to learn that Gunnar had converted to Objectionism and was planning to build a chapel. Setting his sights on the nearest tavern, Reider resolved to right things with his people before he set off north.

Goals

Embolden the coward, Harlad, through song.

Reider's brother Harlad is everything Reider is not, a generally craven soul who jumps at his own shadow. Reider intends to teach him the song of courage from the crow's nest of a Vendel merchantman during the next great storm. Harlad knows Reider is coming for him and is nothing if not fleet of foot.

Uncover a lost song of the gods.

Aslaug is a shieldmaiden from the time of legend who fell in love with a minor god. The god taught her a song of longing so potent as to render all who hear it senseless. One day, Aslaug's beloved sailed over the horizon, never to return. She sang and sang her lover's song until the snows piled high upon her. Taking pity on Aslaug, the gods froze her in a block of the purest ice. Legend has it that one who lifts Aslaug's grief with a song of hope and joy frees her and claims her song. All who fail are doomed to join her court of frozen skalds. Reider is seeking a stout ship and brave crew to claim his prize.

Witness a miraculous storm of the gods first-hand.

Reider seeks the greatest storm of them all, the storm of the Allfather. This ultimate communion with the gods is said to lie atop the roof of the world itself, setting the sky ablaze with ribbons of fire. Though the site is purportedly guarded by giants made of frost, iron scaled serpents and warrior maidens clad in silvered mail, Reider will not be deterred.

Playing Reider Ness

Reider Ness scorns subtlety and silence with equal vigor. Always boisterous, outspoken and never one to suffer fools lightly, his arrival is like a lightning strike, his presence like thunder. Reider's rapacious hunger for life is reflected in the scale of everything he does. Every voyage his first, every tankard his last, and every song for the Allfather. Reider Ness does not live small, quietly or for tomorrow.

Stanimir Buscov

"Well, you see, that is a funny story. It wasn't one guard, it was three and I didn't punch them, they all fell flat on their faces after I tripped them with a bit of rope. Anyone can fell a clumsy foe with a bit of quick thinking."

USSURA

Traits

Brawn	●●○○○
Finesse	●●●○○
Resolve	●●●○○
Wits	●●○○○
Panache	●●●○○

Skills

Aim	○○○○○	Perform	●●●○○
Athletics	●●●○○	Ride	●○○○○
Brawl	●●●○○	Sailing	○○○○○
Convince	●●○○○	Scholarship	●○○○○
Empathy	●●●○○	Tempt	●○○○○
Hide	○○○○○	Theft	●○○○○
Intimidate	○○○○○	Warfare	○○○○○
Notice	●●○○○	Weaponry	○○○○○

Advantages

Boxer (151), Inspire Generosity (149), Large (148), Staredown (150), Trusted Companion: Mishka (154), Virtuoso: Wrestling (152)

Quirks

Pugilist. Earn a Hero Point when you drop what you're holding to fight with fists regardless of your opponent's weapon.

Performer. Earn a Hero Point when you use your crowd-pleasing skills for something more than making a few coins.

Virtue: The Wheel

Fortunate. Activate your Virtue to delay an Opportunity or a Consequence by 1 Action.

Hubris: The War

Loyal. You receive a Hero Point when your Hero goes back for a fallen comrade or refuses to leave a wounded ally.

Story:

Stanimir Buscov

History

The cold winter of Ussura runs through Stanimir's blood. While it would freeze some people, it spurs him forward, makes him light on his feet and burns his belly that much warmer. Stanimir is a performer *par excellence*, as one Montaigne broadsheet named him. Inheriting his mother Darya's traveling circus, each night Stanimir puts on shows to wow and thrill audiences.

His home and his heart have always been with the circus, a band of people thrown together by circumstance, talent and chance. Having no other blood relative than his mother, the performers became his family. There is only one role not filled in his makeshift family, and that is the role of father.

His mother's stories of Stanimir's father seem more fairy tales than history. Darya met his father when she was traveling Ussura. He applied for a position in her circus, and seeing the man's skill, Darya welcomed him into the circus. The love between the two was instantaneous, electric, the kind of love that grapples hearts and never releases. When Stanimir's father announced he would return to Ifri to ask his family's permission to marry Darya, she was overjoyed. He left one snowy Ussuran night and never returned. The only memento Darya had of her love was a matching heart tattoo and the babe within her belly.

To this day Darya insists her love will return and refuses to speak his name until he does. The love the two felt was real and the only reason he would stay away was if something terrible happened to make him leave her. Stanimir's mother is a wise woman and he was never one to go against the word of a wise woman, so he has molded himself into a man a father would be proud of.

In addition to taking up his father's mantle of wrestling bears, he has also taken to heroics. It all began with him and his bear Mishka preventing bandits from accosting a family on the road. Seeing the father of the family threatened, Stanimir sprung into action, refusing to let two children grow up without a father. A few weeks later, he stopped another robbery.

After these two incidents of heroics, Stanimir was hooked. His circus became a place people visited not only for a good show, but when they needed the Ringleader and his bear's help in situations most dire.

Goals

Find a totem to let him speak to animals.

While Stanimir is now the Ringleader of his circus, every night he still steps into the ring to wrestle his bear Mishka. Sometimes he wins, sometimes Mishka wins, but it is a tradition he has carried on throughout the years. Often, after a fight, in the moments before the crowd roars, Stanimir sees a knowing look in Mishka's eyes, an intelligence. Finding a totem that allows him to speak to animals will not only make his show better, but allow him to speak to his childhood friend.

Wrestle the strongest man in Théah.

While many men use brute strength for wrestling, Stanimir knows it is more about being quick and nimble on your feet. He has heard rumors of a man from Avalon, so strong he has pulled an entire ship out to sea. Stanimir wants to try his hand at fighting this man and see if speed can triumph over strength.

Perform for the Czar.

Stanimir's circus has gained some notoriety, but there is still far for him to go. Performing for the Czar (or Czarina) is one of his biggest dreams and a great honor he would like to accomplish before his mother passes away.

Playing Stanimir Buscov

Stanimir is a large man who is seriously quick on his feet. With lightning-quick reactions and an athletic figure, he cuts quite the dashing figure of an Ussuran man. He is aware of his good looks and isn't afraid to flash his winning smile to get him out of trouble, a trait that would normally chafe on most, if it were not for Stanimir's kind heart. While his ego can get the best of him, Stanimir always has the best of intentions in mind. He has a strong sense of empathy and always makes sure to put the needs of his loved ones before himself.

Tactician Heroes

"War is like a ballroom dance. Troops, politicians, generals, swaying on the dance floor within the lines of decorum. Me, I don't dance, I'm leading the orchestra."
- Celeste de Villenc

A Tactician employs quick wit and intelligence to win the day. She knows the quickest way to win a battle is before the fight even starts and the most triumphant duels are ones of wits rather than swords. This Hero is a natural born leader. She commands her troops with a sharp mind, always thinking five steps ahead to make sure the day is won. She is a lover of debates, and someone who looks into the future seeing thousands of possibilities.

It is easy for a Tactician to get lost in her own thoughts. Whether she is busy solving a Syrneth puzzle in a deep, dark cavern or playing an intense game of chess with a local lord—mental challenges engage and absorb her. She can easily spend hours upon hours unraveling the mysteries of her chosen activity.

What Tacticians relish is a challenge, a test of their wits and resolve. This natural drive toward games and competitions makes them excellent verbal sparring partners. The Tactician is able to quickly pick apart what her opponent has said and teases her own logic, her own understanding, out of another's words.

As natural leaders, they wish to see everyone do their very best and have a keen mind to help make that happen. Because a Tactician is quick on the uptake, she is often able to see when someone is being exploited, and this emotional precognition drives her to help others. Her mental faculties, her abilities, are gifts and should be used for the betterment of all.

To someone who does not know her, the Tactician can come off as snobbish and bossy. She must be wary, because her natural high intelligence and ability to lead others can sometimes get her into trouble. It can be easy for ego to get in the way of this Hero's better judgment and for her to think herself above those with less academic training. This hubris can lead her to underestimating foes and overestimating her own plans. The smartest Tactician sees her own limitations and makes sure she has a strong group of Heroes surrounding her to complement her abilities.

Core Aspect: Intelligence

While Tacticians tend to be highly educated and place themselves in positions of power, intelligence comes in many forms. The high calling of reason drives Tacticians to do what is right, to lead others, using their gut feeling and their aptitudes. What is most important to this Hero is making the smart choice that minimizes the most harm to the ones he cares for.

A wise druid is just as much a Tactician as an old war general. Both may have different approaches to life—the druid leads his people through guerilla tactics, and the war general sticks to what she was taught in the army. Both leaders want the same outcome, protecting those around themselves. They are able to speak with a deeply honed sincerity that makes all listen to their worlds. Weaving their knowledge into social graces with their silver tongues, Tacticians use reason and logic rather than raw charisma to sway minds.

In a fight, Tacticians employ brains rather than brawn. They find it easy to see their opponent's weaknesses and come up with brilliant plans to exploit them. Intelligent creativity is not only a challenge for a Tactician, but something he relishes.

A View of Villainy

Beast

These creatures relish a fight. It should be easy to outwit them, before they get too close.

Chameleon

I must watch my back; the Chameleon dances with the shadows in the back of my mind.

Deranged

I pity these sad souls, so warped and bent in madness.

Juggernaut

To defeat an unstoppable force, you must be an immovable object. Yet the beauty of the world is mutable, ever changing—how can I stop that which is relentless?

Mastermind

A worthy adversary, if it were not for their horrid machinations. I'd best play this game carefully if I am going to outwit such a deadly opponent.

Playing the Tactician

Nothing is impossible, not for Tacticians. There is always a loophole, a weakness, an unseen flaw to exploit. They are emboldened by challenge and the taller the hurdle placed in front of them, the more likely they are to succeed. If they fail, it is only because they did not truly learn from last time and will try a thousand times harder when they are presented with a new obstacle.

Tacticians are seekers of knowledge. They question all that is put in front of them and are not afraid to play devil's advocate. Not known to lose their tempers, Tacticians keep their cool in even the most oppressive scenarios. With a level head, they cultivate their arguments and hone a sharp tongue for any evildoers who cross their path.

Finally, Tacticians are smart enough to know when to back down from a fight. While they may not admit their weakness, their sense of self worth being too healthy for that, they refuse to get themselves (or the ones they care about) hurt. Sometimes, the smartest thing to do is to run away and live and fight another day.

Creating a Tactician Hero

Wits is the most important Trait for a Tactician. This type of Hero is all about quick thinking and pithy comebacks. A close second to Wits can be Panache or Resolve, depending on how the Hero deals with situations.

Aristocrat, Courtier, Doctor, Engineer and Scholar are all Backgrounds that lend themselves to the Tactician Hero type, but it is also common to find them in military professions as well. Convince, Notice, Scholarship and Warfare as Skills are all tools of the trade for a Tactician. A keen observer of her surroundings and a sharp tactical mind are key for this Hero.

Advantages that lend themselves to a Tactician are Friend at Court, Leadership, Linguist, Lyceum, Tenure and We're Not So Different...

Adam Vide

"A moment of your time! I have a mug of beer here if you'll tell me that amusing story you just told your friend..."

MONTAIGNE

Traits

Trait		
Brawn	●●○○○	
Finesse	●●○○○	
Resolve	●●○○○	
Wits	●●●○○	
Panache	●●●●○	

Skills

Skill		Skill	
Aim	○○○○○	Perform	●●●○○
Athletics	○○○○○	Ride	●○○○○
Brawl	○○○○○	Sailing	○○○○○
Convince	●●●○○	Scholarship	●●●○○
Empathy	●●●○○	Tempt	●●○○○
Hide	○○○○○	Theft	○○○○○
Intimidate	○○○○○	Warfare	○○○○○
Notice	●●●○○	Weaponry	●●○○○

Advantages

Able Drinker (148), Connection: Montaigne Nobility (149), Direction Sense (148), Fascinate (149), Friend at Court (149), Linguist (148), Patron: High Society (152), Virtuoso: Storyteller (152)

Quirks

L'Ami Du Roi. Earn a Hero Point when you leverage the King's favor to solve a problem.

Artist. Earn a Hero Point when you make a sacrifice in the hope of making Théah a more beautiful place.

Virtue: The Tower

Humble. Activate your Virtue to gain 2 Hero points instead of 1 when you activate your Hubris or trigger a Quirk.

Hubris: The War

Loyal. You receive a Hero Point when your Hero goes back for a fallen comrade or refuses to leave a wounded ally.

Story:

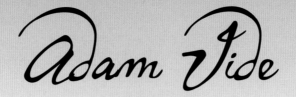

History

The truth about Adam Vide's past sounds more like a story he might write than reality. Adam was born Annabelle de Malencourt, in a beautiful landed estate outside Rogne. He was a bright and curious child. In the strict structure of the Veuvert household, Adam felt pressure to remain the dutiful daughter rather than follow his heart. Yet, he dreamed about the day when a galleon might carry him away to a new life. He would often tell his younger brother Guy that should the opportunity arise, he would hand over the title as heir to the Veuvert lands and leave. Guy never believed it and fought bitterly with him, jealous over the line of succession. Adam planned to escape.

He carefully constructed a new identity, that of a traveling storyteller, and cultivated his talents by performing in local inns under the name Adam Vide. Before long, Adam was invited to a storytelling competition up at the royal court. At the same time, both of his parents were called away on a secret diplomatic mission. Adam said his goodbyes promising to return home soon, knowing he never would, and left for the storytelling competition. His last words to his parents were lies.

Adam arrived at the royal court at the height of fighting between Montaigne and Castille. The storytelling competition was meant to distract l'Empereur and entertain diplomats from across Théah. Adam threw himself into the competition and won acclaim as the top storyteller, receiving countless offers of patronage at court. But the day after Adam won the top prize in the competition, three men were dragged in chains before l'Empereur. It seemed they'd sold secrets to the Castillians, telling them where the nobles would be traveling on the road to make peace. All the Montaigne nobles, including Adam's parents, were murdered. One of the traitors was Guy.

L'Empereur was about to sentence the traitors to death when Adam threw himself on the mercy of the court. He begged His Majesty to exile his brother instead, revealing only to l'Empereur that he was the Veuvert heir. He promised all the Veuvert lands if Guy would be spared. The monarch, in need of war funding, accepted, and Guy was exiled. Adam left the court the same day and hasn't returned.

Now, Adam lives the life of the wandering storyteller. He throws himself into his tales, writing about Théah the way he sees it: as a political powder keg, a continent on the brink of a new age. He believes, through his writing, he can inspire others to stand up and change their lives for the better. Yet deep down he wishes to find his brother and discover why Guy turned against the crown and his blood.

Goals

Reunite with his exiled brother, Guy.

Adam cannot fathom why Guy would betray Montaigne and their family to Castille. Though Guy offered no explanation, Adam wants to ask his brother some tough questions about the past.

Find his stolen book of poems being distributed under the name Férdéric Martin.

Someone took advantage of one wild night too many to pick Adam's satchel. Now, a book of Adam's best work is being passed off as the writings of this Martin person. He needs to discover how this happened and get the original back to prove the fraud.

Perform his work for l'Empereur's courts.

It has been several years since Adam has been at the court of l'Empereur, and he longs for the spotlight. Returning will not be easy, but his new work about the world of Théah outside the court needs to reach the Sun King's ears.

Playing Adam Vide

Adam is the epitome of a deeply passionate and creative Montaigne man, who chose to follow his heart over his duty and gave up everything for his family. Adam loves his drink, his parties and above all a good story. He follows any adventure if he believes it can become a great tale, and loves making new friends if he can ply them for recollections of good adventures gone by. Adam's jovial nature and charm hides the shadows of the intrigues that destroyed his family, mysteries he must one day face for his own sake and for the Veuvert name.

Aoife Ó Raghnaill

"We can do it together. Just keep going and things will get better—they HAVE to. I found a book with information that could help, and..."

INISMORE

Traits

Brawn	●●○○○
Finesse	●●○○○
Resolve	●●○○○
Wits	●●●●○
Panache	●●●○○

Skills

Aim	●○○○○	Perform	●●●○○
Athletics	○○○○○	Ride	●●○○○
Brawl	○○○○○	Sailing	○○○○○
Convince	●●●○○	Scholarship	●●○○○
Empathy	●●●○○	Tempt	●●●○○
Hide	○○○○○	Theft	○○○○○
Intimidate	●●○○○	Warfare	○○○○○
Notice	○○○○○	Weaponry	●●○○○

Advantages

An Honest Misunderstanding (151), Disarming Smile (149), Friend at Court (149), Leadership (149), Rich (152), The Devil's Own Luck (155)

Quirks

Aristocrat. Earn a Hero Point when you prove there is more to nobility than expensive clothes and attending court.

Courtier. Earn a Hero Point whenever you turn the tide of violence with charm and flair.

Virtue: The Emperor

Commanding. Activate your Virtue. The GM gives a Hero Point to all other Heroes in this Scene.

Hubris: The Hero

Foolhardy. You receive a Hero Point when your brash, cocky, or reckless actions cause trouble for you and another Hero.

Story:

Aoife Ó Raghnaill

History

Aoife grew up in a perpetual twilight of ice and mist. Her father's noble estate—small, but well-kept—was brightly lit and perfectly safe, but adventurous Aoife much preferred the mysteries lurking outside. She hid under a fallen tree as a young child, watching with terrified eyes as tall ice-skinned creatures danced and laughed. Later she joined their dance and even took a færie lover on her 18th birthday.

Aoife *knew* the Sidhe were dangerous, but didn't care—life is short, and she'd happily pay the price for living to the fullest. She wasn't the one to pay though, when her younger brother Peadar followed her to the dance. She found him next morning, stumbling around like a child, bereft of his memories. The tragedy changed Aoife's life. Her mother wouldn't stop crying, and her father barely ate—his fine cloak hung off his shoulders like a skeleton's. Servants left the cursed family. Ice crept into the empty halls.

Realizing what she'd done, Aoife set on a quest to repel the Unseelie and heal her brother. She found promising leads, but also stumbled across a greater problem: Elaine's ascendency saw Glamour and the Sidhe return—both the good and the bad. For every fæ that blesses a child, another snatches a babe from its cradle. Aoife set her own worries aside and traveled to the court of Jack O'Bannon, where she now seeks an audience with the King to speak about the Unseelie threat to Inismore.

Aoife has a talent for court intrigue. She knows when someone lies to her, while her own honeyed words always ring true. She can read the mood of a room to quickly identify alliances and rivalries. Her charm and etiquette are flawless. None of that helps with the unpredictable O'Bannon, but it makes her a rising star with the other nobles. Aoife uses her new position to advance twin causes: keeping the Unseelie at bay and protecting Inismore's common folk. She is a proponent of a standing Inish army to protect people from raiders and Sidhe alike, raising taxes on the rich and lowering them on the poor and providing the commoners with free education.

With everything on her plate, Aoife never relaxes. Even dinner parties are *work*: she's building an alliance to protect the people of Avalon. This constant vigilance alerted her to oddities about O'Bannon and his castle. Shadows linger a bit too long, and the King's laughter is too maniacal. Aoife worries that the Unseelie have their hooks in O'Bannon—which means her task just got so much bigger. She reminds herself, though, that the night is always darkest just before the dawn.

Goals

Return her brother's memories stolen by Winter Walker.

Aoife doesn't know that Winter Walker traded those memories to a more powerful Unseelie named Silent Gale. Fortunately, his ancient Seelie enemy, Ice Hollow, works to leak word about the trade to Aoife.

Recover the Dagger of Goia, which cuts through Sidhe enchantments.

Goia was an ancient hero who battled the Unseelie. Her dagger could cut Glamour: a nip on the arm to rebuke a paralyzing spell, or a cut under the eye to pierce illusions. Aoife scours the castle's library for hints of the dagger's location.

Pursue an alliance with the Seelie, by retrieving their "lost crescent."

Aoife heard stories of a "crescent child" tasked with keeping the bargain between Sidhe and Avalon, who was hidden following an Unseelie attack. Aoife plans to return the child to the Seelie as a token of goodwill and is pursuing information about an Inish girl with a crescent birthmark.

Playing Aoife Ó Raghnaill

Aoife is the smartest person in the room, and she owns her brilliance with a sincerity that adds to her charm. She laughs often but briefly—constant worry stifles any true merriment she feels. Her manners are flawless if pointed, even around people she despises. She never dances and becomes gloomy when someone asks. Aoife is ever hungry for knowledge, making her an engaged listener and avid devourer of books. She remains attracted to darkness, and the same passion that fueled her relation with the Unseelie makes her vulnerable to charming ill-doers.

Celeste de Villenc

"Can you really think of only one way out of this? I can think of at least five—and I'm having quite the headache at the moment."

MONTAIGNE • THE EXPLORER'S SOCIETY

Traits

Brawn	●●○○○
Finesse	●●●○○
Resolve	●●○○○
Wits	●●●●○
Panache	●●○○○

Skills

Aim	●●○○○	Perform	○○○○○
Athletics	●○○○○	Ride	●●○○○
Brawl	○○○○○	Sailing	○○○○○
Convince	●●●○○	Scholarship	●●●○○
Empathy	●●○○○	Tempt	○○○○○
Hide	○○○○○	Theft	○○○○○
Intimidate	●○○○○	Warfare	●●●○○
Notice	●●●○○	Weaponry	●●●○○

Advantages

Academy (153), Direction Sense (148), Disarming Smile (149), Linguist (148), Reputation: Brilliant (150), Rich (152), Team Player (150)

Quirks

Army Officer. Earn a Hero Point when you seize command during a moment of intense violence or extreme danger.

Aristocrat. Earn a Hero Point when you prove there is more to nobility than expensive clothes and attending court.

Virtue: The Beggar

Insightful. Activate your Virtue to discover a Brute Squad's type, or to know a Villain's Rank and Advantages.

Hubris: The Hanged Man

Indecisive. You receive a Hero Point when your Hero takes an Action to pause in hesitation, doubt, or uncertainty before she makes a move.

Story:

Celeste de Villenc

History

Celeste did not want to fight in the war. She did not fear the battles, but the war was simply not worth it. It was l'Empereur's war. It was the nobles' war. It was even her father's war, but it was not hers. That is until her mother fell on the battlefield.

According to the death notification, Elodie de Villenc had died gloriously but foolishly, by leading a troop charge into enemy lines. The letter announcing his wife's death slipped from le Duc de Villenc's hands as he wrestled with his grief. Shocked by the news, Celeste picked up the letter, only managing one sentence, "There is no mention of the sword."

The sword was the inheritance of the de Villenc family, passed down from mother to daughter since time immemorial. It was not only a piece of metal; it was Celeste's inheritance, and more importantly, it was her last connection to her mother. She had to go to the front to recover it—or die trying.

After making camp at the front, Celeste suffered her first major headache. The smell, the cold, the noise: *everything* hurt her. That painful, searing moment was the worst thing she ever had to endure.

Little did she know the headaches' frequency and potency would not decrease as time passed, *au contraire*. The sight of blood and the smell of gunpowder became unbearable, forcing Celeste to direct the war from afar, destroying any hopes she had of retrieving her mother's sword personally.

The first night Celeste spent truly pain free was thanks to a fellow noble. "This can help" was all he said as he passed her a fragrant pipe. Celeste considered refusing, but she saw his kind gaze and had not the heart to refuse. So she drew the smoke of the pipe deep within her lungs. The fragrant tobacco made her cough, but she felt the pain subsiding. She returned to the officer's tent and laid out a brilliant yet risky strategy. The rest of the gathering shook their heads and muttered silent protests, but a soft-spoken voice rose above them all.

"It is brilliant! We *have* to do it." That was Milo, the same man that had offered the first relief for her pain in years. The only one that supported her plan when the other officers refused to accept it. Milo, her future husband.

Goals

Retrieve her mother's sword lost in Montaigne.

To her dismay, Celeste found out that her mother's sword is no longer in Castillian hands, but stolen by a Montaigne "noble" at the end of the war. Now she is pulling all the strings she can, political and otherwise, to find out who was stupid enough to steal something from her.

Learn new war tactics in the Crescent Empire.

Celeste's fascination with strategy can never be truly quenched. As such, she is now more than ready to travel the seas to learn from the people of the Crescent Empire, having read stories of their millennia-old traditions in the ways of war.

Ask the "Mother" of Ussura to remove her headaches.

According to the research she and Milo conducted, this is only one way to end Celeste's headaches once and for all. They are ready to dare the wild lands of Ussura in search of the Matushka—overcoming anyone who stands in their way.

Playing Celeste de Villenc

Celeste de Villenc is a brilliant strategist with a fierce attitude towards the world. To those she loves, this is the best insurance against any danger. On the other hand, to those that dare to put those people in danger, it is a sure sign of defeat.

Celeste is not particularly talkative or emotional—except when it comes to tactics. When discussing strategy, she is the most passionate, eloquent speaker you can find. Her plans, however, are not easily accepted by others. This is mainly because she always chooses the *best* plan, even though it may sound strange, far-fetched or even impossible to lesser minds.

Elpis Moraitis

"The only way to ensure the victory is to understand your enemy as much as you understand yourself. Only then can you go beyond mere speculation in battle. But, beware! To understand is to respect—and to respect is to love. Can you defeat someone you love?"

NUMA

Traits

Brawn	●●○○○
Finesse	●●○○○
Resolve	●●●○○
Wits	●●●○○
Panache	●●○○○

Skills

Aim	●●●◐○	Perform	○○◐○○
Athletics	●●○○○	Ride	○○○○○
Brawl	●○○○○	Sailing	○○○○○
Convince	●●◐○○	Scholarship	●●●◐○
Empathy	●●○○○	Tempt	○○○○○
Hide	○○○○○	Theft	○○○○○
Intimidate	●○◐○○	Warfare	●●●◐○
Notice	●●○○○	Weaponry	●○○○○

Advantages

Camaraderie (151), Cast Iron Stomach (148), Duelist Academy: Lakedaimon Agoge (see below), Eagle Eyes (149), Hard to Kill (153), Team Player (150)

Quirks

Docent. Earn a Hero Point when you push another character to live up to her potential, even when it means trouble or when it complicates the situation.

Mercenary. Earn a Hero Point when you choose to ply your trade for a reason that's worth more to you than money.

Virtue: The Sun

Glorious. Activate your Virtue when you are the center of attention. For the next Risk, when you determine Raises, every die counts as a Raise.

Hubris: The Fool

Curious. You receive a Hero Point when you investigate something unusual, especially if it looks dangerous.

Lakedaimon Agoge Duelist Style

You can perform Dueling Maneuvers while wielding a bow. You use your Ranks in Aim to determine the effects of Maneuvers, in place of Weaponry. Your Lunge Maneuver is replaced by the Agoge Thrust. Agoge Thrust deals a number of Wounds equal to your Aim plus the number of Raises you spend, but you must spend your next Action this Round to recover and regroup, spending one Raise to do so (and gaining no additional effect).

Elpis Moraitis

History

"Why is she here? Is she not too young?" Every time men and women in power meet Elpis, the questions are the same. Yet, even after the briefest of encounters, most agree that she is not only charming, but brilliant beyond any expectations—if they only knew what hides beneath that public face.

Elpis was born in Numa. As most children, she attended *agoge* at the early age of five. Despite being the youngest of her class, Elpis demonstrated that a quick mind is a better resource than agile feet or the strongest arms. Her swift thinking made her quicker than anybody else, finishing the five years of excruciating training as the sole graduate of her group. Everybody assumed that the Oracles would have an easy time with her: she was born to become one of the *haimon*, the most disciplined warriors in all of Théah.

Even Elpis believed it so—until Theonoa Dianoia, the Goddess of Craft and Knowledge, came to her in a dream. In the dream, she went to the Oracles and became a great warrior. Yet, her visit heralded a great catastrophe—a great black wave, which overcame the whole world, wiping it clean. Desperate to avoid such a prospect, Elpis humbly asked if there was any way to prevent this terrible outcome.

"There is," said Theonoa, "but it requires that you leave Numa today, never visit the Oracles and find a *haimon* to train worthy of your knowledge."

What the Goddess neglected to say was what not visiting the Oracles implied. Dishonor, not only for her, but for her family for all time. A stain on her *kleos* only an act of amazing courage could erase.

She wanted to ask more, to discuss the situation thoroughly but, as it often happens with the gods, Elpis awoke before she could do so. Left with that terrible decision at the young age of ten, Elpis awaited the dawn meditating on it. When the sun finally appeared with her rosy fingers, she was already on her way out of Numa.

Older and wiser, Elpis has traveled across Théah searching for the *haimon* she must educate. Since then, she has counseled men and women in power—especially those engaged in long and bloody conflicts—as well as politicians, statespersons and everybody who has been willing to listen to a young woman's advice.

Although not many know of her exploits, Elpis was one of the unseen architects of the end of the border war between Montaigne and Castille, and it was her counseling that aided Jarl Hlodversson to become a well-respected and beloved leader of her people. These are only a few of the amazing deeds Elpis has accomplished since she left her native Numa.

Goals

Train a *haimon* in the ways of honor.

Elpis has trained many great people, but has not found the one "worthy" of her wisdom. She is always looking for opportunities to test new prospects, be it by dueling with swords, words or on a board of *poleis* (the traditional Numa strategy game).

Find an idol of the Goddess of Craft and Knowledge to grant her insight.

Since the vision that changed Elpis' life, Theonoa has been painfully silent. Still, Elpis is trying to communicate with the Goddess by all means. She has heard rumors of a statue in Vodacce that could help her to do so—and, as such, she is already on the hunt.

Erase the stain on her *kleos* from fleeing the Oracles.

Although she fled for a good reason—perhaps the best there is—Elpis does not lose hope to one day perform an act worthy of restoring her *kleos*. That is why she is kind and patient, trying to help even the most obnoxious of people.

Playing Elpis Moraitis

Elpis Moraitis is a young woman with the wisdom of a seasoned veteran. She asks only the minimum compensation for her services and refuses to lend her aid to any man or woman whose objectives are dishonorable in her eyes. She may seem boastful or arrogant in public, but she is in reality a humble, caring person.

Acting as a carefree young girl, those that know her understand that that is just a façade, something that can easily be discarded if the situation requires otherwise. Because beneath that loud, almost childish attitude lives a warrior that knows no limits.

Hulda Silje

"I don't need rest. I don't need succor. I need another battle. Glory awaits only those who die sword in hand!"

VESTENMENNAVENJAR

Traits

Brawn	●●●●○
Finesse	●●○○○
Resolve	●●○○○
Wits	●●●○○
Panache	●●○○○

Skills

Aim	●○○○○	Perform	●○○○○
Athletics	●●○○○	Ride	○○○○○
Brawl	●●○○○	Sailing	○○○○○
Convince	●○○○○	Scholarship	○○○○○
Empathy	●●○○○	Tempt	●○○○○
Hide	○○○○○	Theft	○○○○○
Intimidate	●●○○○	Warfare	●●●○○
Notice	●●○○○	Weaponry	●●●○○

Advantages

Able Drinker (148), Duelist Academy: Leegstra (238), Reputation: Dangerous (150), Riot Breaker (153), Signature Item: Kragt (152)

Quirks

Duelist. Earn a Hero Point when you resort to the edge of your blade to defend a noble ideal.
Soldier. Earn a Hero Point when you stick to the plan regardless of the danger to yourself.

Virtue: The War

Victorious. Activate your Virtue the first time you Wound a Villain during a fight to make him take a Dramatic Wound in addition to the Wounds you normally deal.

Hubris: The Emperor

Hot-Headed. You receive a Hero Point when your Hero flies off the handle and loses her temper, causing trouble.

Story:

Hulda Silje

History

Hulda was on her way to be one of the greatest warriors of Vestenmennavenjar, until a bearsarker left her grievously wounded. She worked hard to regain her strength, but the leg wound didn't heal, as if cursed. Hulda pressed on regardless, switching her two-weapon Leegstra style from sword and axe to sword and walking cane. She also added a bit of bluff to make foes believe her leg is fine. Hulda's greatest asset, though, is her keen mind. She instinctively creates a mental map of her surroundings, allowing her to draw on any advantage it offers.

Officially, Hulda is "retired" from combat. Her commander tasked her to train other Valkyries and Hulda obliged. Officially. She *is* genuinely dedicated to the task and would be proud if a student surpassed her, but she still follows the "omens of the gods" from one adventure to another—after all, there's no glory in dying of old age. To dine at the table of the gods, Hulda believes, she must die in combat. Between actual fighting and training, Hulda spends a significant portion of her time with a cup of ale and her lover Ingrid. She doubts dying drunk in bed will see her at the table of the gods, but it's a good way to go if it happens.

Hulda used to be happily married to a man named Brøn. They had two girls and a boy, before he died in battle against a kraken. Their eldest daughter Magda inherited her parents' lands years ago, but Hulda's uncle Gellir has challenged that. Out of her league when it comes to politics, Hulda still recognizes that her uncle has the backing of most carls, so she needs help from the jarls. She plans to call a *thing* to settle the matter once enough jarls back her.

Vestenmennavenjar is a dangerous land, and for all her focus on glory, Hulda fights to keep the people safe. She slays monsters, vanquishes brigands and pirates and fairly arbitrates disputes between landowners and vassals—usually by intimidating everyone involved. Songs tell of Hulda's battle with an ice giant's daughter, who plagued a village for decades and demanded one newborn be left for her every year. Hulda defeated the far stronger and bigger villain by coating Kragt in burning wax and exploiting the ice daughter's weakness.

Goals

Train a woman worthy of wielding her runesword Kragt.

Kragt is an heirloom handed down from the Valkyrie to serve the last Mjötuðr (high king), and Hulda's unhealing leg makes her unfit to wield it. At least that's what tradition states. As Hulda goes through the motions of choosing another Valkyrie to wield the sword though, rebellion rises in her. She's more than just her injury—she is smart, determined and learning to compensate. Doesn't that mean she is still worthy?

Stop the bearsarker woman who bested her.

Hulda learned the identity of the warrior that wounded her: Estrid Lowzow. She also learned that, as a young girl, Estrid alone survived an attack on her city. She questions if the gods want her to slay or redeem the bearsarker.

Appeal her daughter's plight to the jarls.

Gellir claims that, as a Valkyrie, Hulda can't own any land. Her holdings should revert back to Hulda's deceased mother and then to her mother's closest living relative: himself. Hulda believes the land belongs to her daughter. Vesten law allows for both interpretations, making the matter less about legality and more about political backing.

Playing Hulda Silje

Hulda is quick to laugh, quick to anger and quick to forgive. Combat is her life—when she's not on the battlefield, she's training new Valkyries or tending her many arms and beautifully decorated armor. She likes to drink and regale audiences with tales of her battles. If she feels comfortable enough, she might take a lover to her bed for the evening.

On the battlefield, none of Hulda's reckless nature shows. She becomes an implacable, calculating fighting machine. If she sees a weakness, she takes it. If she sees an opening, she presses. Hulda has a thousand counters—and she *always* chooses the right one. She is also highly skilled at recognizing the weaknesses and strengths of a group and quickly takes a leadership position to guide them to victory.

Osterhilde Hummel

"The road to a good life is through good choices, friends. We can discover that road together."

EISEN • THE INVISIBLE COLLEGE

Traits

Trait	Rating
Brawn	●●○○○
Finesse	●●○○○
Resolve	●●●○○
Wits	●●●●○
Panache	●●○○○

Skills

Aim	○○○○○	Perform	●●●○○
Athletics	●○○○○	Ride	●●○○○
Brawl	○○○○○	Sailing	○○○○○
Convince	●●●○○	Scholarship	●●●○○
Empathy	●●○○○	Tempt	●●○○○
Hide	○○○○○	Theft	○○○○○
Intimidate	○○○○○	Warfare	○○○○○
Notice	●●●○○	Weaponry	●○○○○

Advantages

An Honest Misunderstanding (151), Direction Sense (148), Friend at Court (149), Inspire Generosity (149), Ordained (152), University (154)

Quirks

Priest. Earn a Hero Point when you set aside the rhetoric and take action to practice the virtues you preach.

Courtier. Earn a Hero Point when you turn the tide of violence with charm and flair.

Virtue: The Prophet

Illuminating. Activate your Virtue to know whenever any other character lies to you until the end of the Scene.

Hubris: The Devil

Trusting. You receive a Hero Point when you accept someone's lies or lopsided deal.

Story:

Osterhilde Hummel

History

Osterhilde was an inquisitive child. Raised in a rural miller's family, she pestered them with questions about the world and everything in it. Whether it was questions about nature or politics, about village life or gossip she heard, she had a voracious mind that wanted to know everything. Her family was devout. From an early age, Osterhilde believed that the Vaticine Church brought the most good into the world of anything, ever. At age 13, she left home and began studying to become an ordained member of the clergy.

Osterhilde shortly became a rising star in the local church, known for her dedication to good works and supporting those in need. But she became restless with simply helping others. She saw the trouble her beloved Eisen was in and the darkness that lurked around every corner. The War of the Cross had left behind a shattered land struggling to pull itself together again, and so many were in need of inspiration and support.

Osterhilde had started to believe that nothing could save Eisen from self-destructing. She attended a lecture about determinism versus free will and was entranced by how diligently the lecturer fought to present the idea that people have the opportunity to choose their actions. Free will, the teacher said, was people acting out their own will on the world, and that gave meaning to their lives and the actions they chose to take. Osterhilde embraced this idea and took to the road, preaching free will to inspire the people to find hope again.

Unfortunately, these beliefs haven't always been met with open arms. Many within the Church resist giving up the idea of determinism. Osterhilde has kept on the move, traveling the dangerous roads of Eisen to spread her message far and wide. Her latest travels are pulling her to the königreich of Hainzl. This normally sleepy corner of Eisen has been in an upheaval about local mercenaries, deserters of the War of the Cross. Osterhilde cannot help wondering if there's more to the story.

No one has stepped up to defend the mercenaries, thereby condemning them outright. There are too many questions about what happened in the war to let this situation stand unquestioned, and Osterhilde believes she's the perfect woman to discover the truth.

Goals

Convince her fellow priests in the power of free will.

The idea of free will is so misunderstood among the Vaticine Church followers that many malign those who are supporters. Osterhilde must convince her fellows of the power of making one's own choices or risk watching the powerful idea get buried once more by blind devotion to fate and predestination.

Travel to Hainzl's königreich to lecture on her beliefs.

Though Osterhilde has been on the road for some time, the königreich of Hainzl has become a hotbed of discussion regarding personal responsibility and freedom. Osterhilde must brave the long travel across Eisen with all the dangers it presents to find safety and perhaps reception for her ideas in the sleepy section of her beloved country.

Represent accused deserter Hans Eirleicht at trial.

Few things stir up difficult feelings like the War of the Cross, and a recent case before the courts in Hainzl has everyone up in arms. A unit of mercenaries, led by Hans Eirleicht, deserted the fighting during the war, and now they're being tried by the people for their crime. Popular opinion is against them and no one is willing to take up their commanding officer's case. Stepping in won't make Osterhilde very popular, but it is the right thing to do.

Playing Osterhilde Hummel

Osterhilde Hummel is an opinionated Eisen woman. She walks slowly but confidently and always keeps her head up, even when her eyes are downcast. When she speaks, it is with a slow, gentle but firm tone. No matter the conversation, Osterhilde remains calm and collected, arguing passionately for her beliefs without belittling other opinions. She is always ready with a kind smile, though she can be truly cutting and sarcastic in private among those she trusts.

Szymon Naumov

"The heart of the Commonwealth is our freedom, forever and always. Let us not forget this and keep it close to our hearts. Through the darkest nights we will find a way."

THE SARMATIAN COMMONWEALTH

Traits

Brawn	●●●○○
Finesse	●●○○○
Resolve	●●○○○
Wits	●●●○○
Panache	●●●○○

Skills

Aim	●●○○○	Perform	●○○○○
Athletics	●●○○○	Ride	●●○○○
Brawl	○○○○○	Sailing	○○○○○
Convince	●●●○○	Scholarship	○○○○○
Empathy	●●○○○	Tempt	●○○○○
Hide	○○○○○	Theft	○○○○○
Intimidate	●●○○○	Warfare	●●●○○
Notice	○○○○○	Weaponry	●●○○○

Advantages

Academy (153), Direction Sense (148), Leadership (149), Lyceum (153), Team Player (150), Together We Are Strong (155)

Quirks

Poseł. Earn a Hero Point when you insist on democracy when it would be advantageous for you to not take a vote.

Army Officer. Earn a Hero Point when you seize command during a moment of intense violence or extreme danger.

Virtue: The Witch

Intuitive. Activate your Virtue to ask the GM one yes-or-no question about an NPC. The GM must answer honestly and should be generous—for example, if there is a qualifier, he should tell you and explain more fully.

Hubris: The Sun

Proud. You receive a Hero Point when your Hero refuses an offer of aid—for example, if a Hero tries to spend a Hero Point to give you Bonus Dice and you turn her down.

Story:

Szymon Naumov

History

The recent history of the Sarmatian Commonwealth has been rife with relatively unknown heroes, men and women who stood up to support the establishment of the Golden Liberty and uphold its tenets. Few have been so vocal or so dedicated to the cause as Szymon Naumov, general of the people's armies and loyal son of the Commonwealth.

Szymon was born to a small peasant family in the Zupan Mountains during the dark days of the Commonwealth, before the Golden Liberty was established. A hearty boy, Szymon worked with his family herding livestock through the passes and down to the valleys below for market. His early years were full of shearing, caring for animals and traveling barefoot up paths that made skilled climbers queasy.

One day at the market, Szymon saw a message on the town's posting board. It stated that the army was calling for help to defend the country against invaders from Ussura, and they needed any good son of the land to join the fight. Szymon went at once to his father, kissed him farewell and volunteered for the army.

Szymon was immediately singled out as an exceptional recruit and fantastic soldier. Called "the Good Shepherd" because of his background, Szymon distinguished himself as a tactical genius and was awarded the highest medals in the land. The military became his life with few distractions, aside from his passion for reading. He only left for a brief time to journey home and visit his father before his death. It was on that trip that he met Marta, a girl from his childhood. The two were wed, and Marta bore him five children.

Through diligence and dedication, Szymon worked his way up in the ranks until he was awarded the rank of General by the King himself just before the declaration of the Golden Liberty. He was charged with protecting the Commonwealth's new peace. An experienced veteran when Golden Liberty was declared, he retired only years later at age 56.

Happily retired, Szymon watched as his son Pieter went into the military and established himself as a great soldier. Pieter was educated abroad as part of a diplomatic coalition traveling Théah to represent the new Commonwealth, and the boy had brought back many foreign notions that made his father uncomfortable. Still, when the King called Szymon up from retirement to help maintain order, the General took his son under his wing and the two now work together to attend to the needs of the Commonwealth.

Goals

Teach his only son Pieter the true way of Sarmatism.

Szymon's son Pieter is a smart boy and a dutiful son, but his travels abroad have given him many ideas regarding how the government of the Commonwealth should be run. Instruct him in the proper way to be a good son of the Commonwealth.

Rid the Commonwealth of a troublesome *dievas* in the Sejm.

A powerful warrior within the slachta has made a deal with a *dievas* in the hopes of becoming the greatest knight in the Commonwealth. Discover who it is and drive out the spirit before it can consume the warrior, wreak havoc or worse, harm the King.

Weed out the corruption of General Ignacy Roch.

Szymon has discovered evidence that General Ignacy Roch is in league with outside forces who wish to destabilize the harmony of the Golden Liberty and return the Commonwealth to its divided past. Discover who is behind the plot by tracing the bribes Roch is offering and present the evidence in front of the slachta once and for all.

Playing Szymon Naumov

General Szymon Naumov epitomizes everything that is good, fair and upright about the Sarmatian Commonwealth. He sits upright, speaks firmly and looks people in the eye when addressing them. He believes truth, above all other things, gets someone where he needs to be. A fighting general, Szymon can be found eating or drinking with his soldiers, though he never joins in the raucous stories. The only time he can be seen to be openly affectionate is when dealing with his son and constant companion, Pieter. The General is never without a clean uniform, a good shave and a good book.

Titania Paganii

"Society is a dance of give and take—dominance and submission. Balanced they create a beautiful chemistry, unbalanced they cause suffering...and not the good kind either."

VODACCE • SOPHIA'S DAUGHTERS

Traits

Brawn	●●○○○
Finesse	●●●○○
Resolve	●●○○○
Wits	●●●○○
Panache	●●●○○

Skills

Aim	●○○○○	Perform	●●○○○
Athletics	●●○○○	Ride	○○○○○
Brawl	○○○○○	Sailing	○○○○○
Convince	●○○○○	Scholarship	●●○○○
Empathy	●●○○○	Tempt	●●●○○
Hide	●○○○○	Theft	○○○○○
Intimidate	●●○○○	Warfare	○○○○○
Notice	●●○○○	Weaponry	●●○○○

Advantages

Come Hither (149), Connection: Vodacce Court (149), Dynamic Approach (151), Linguist (148), Opportunist (152), University (154)

Quirks

Jenny. Earn a Hero Point when you resolve a conflict with seduction or sexual wiles.
Scholar. Earn a Hero Point when you put yourself in harm's way in pursuit of knowledge.

Virtue: The Moonless Night

Subtle. Activate your Virtue when you act behind the scenes, from the shadows, or through a proxy. For the next Risk, when you determine Raises, every die counts as a Raise.

Hubris: The Beggar

Envious. You receive a Hero Point when your Hero covets something, and does something unwise to get it.

Story:

Titania Paganii

History

Titania was born the child of a courtesan. Her life growing up was woven between heavy skirts, packed ballrooms and smoke filled dens. Within these dreamy places, where men and women whispered secrets to one another too adult for the ears of one so young, Titania colored the world with her imagination. The nature of her mother's profession interested her.

Courtesans were not empty, colorful things, but had deep personal thoughts and dreams. With each whispered secret and promise of good things to come, they politicked through their patrons. As Titania grew older, she yearned for a world where these conversations would happen over a battle map, not a mattress.

Titania's mother grew old; her stream of clients dried up. Men who *visited* her mother for years stopped calling, no longer supporting the woman who had been with them for so long. Before her family became destitute, Titania took up the only trade she knew.

As a courtesan, Titania was not set to fall into the same trap as her mother. While Titania had love for her country, she realized Vodacce was slowly crumbling upon itself, its ruin built on the backs of women who had no say in their own lives—despite what little girls may dream about secret power and control from afar. If Titania was to take up her mother's profession, it would be to break the invisible shackles of servitude, not don them.

Titania is very specific about the clientele she agrees to spend time with. Only men needing a stern guidance need apply. Carefully controlling her clients with a firm hand, she has very strict rules on whom she accepts, and all men who come to see her must adhere to a strict regiment or suffer the consequences.

Titania has begun to shape Vodacce into the country written upon her heart. Having amassed an inordinate number of books, obscure texts and philosophical treatises, she plans on opening a public library. Using the discipline she has over her clients, Titania has pushed forward a number of her texts on the real life of women in Vodacce into print and distribution.

Titania's love for the written word has drawn the eye of the well-known apothecary Agrippa Dell'Aqua. Agrippa has taken to sending the courtesan poetry and other writings. Titania recognizes the adoration the apothecary has written upon the page, but has not brought herself to contact them. When she dreams of love, it is free from the chains that bind and bathed in liberty.

Goals

Learn the Mantovani fighting style from a master.

To assist in her profession and hone her own skills, Titania wishes to find a master of the Mantovani fighting style. She has heard of a Master Nicchi who currently resides in the home of Merchant Prince Lucani. Unfortunately, Titania has fallen out of favor with the Lucani family since they suspect her of smuggling one of their daughters out of the country.

Open a public library for the poor of Vodacce.

Titania has amassed an impressive number of books and texts stored in warehouses throughout Vodacce. Now, she only needs land rights and a Merchant Prince's approval to make her dream a reality.

Get her text on equal rights adopted by schools in Vodacce.

A philosopher at heart, Titania believes she must not only educate women about liberty, but men about equality. In their hearts, people wish to do the right thing, but they must be given the tools to do so. If she can have her text on equality adopted by the schools in Vodacce, the nation can take a giant leap towards the dream in Titania's mind.

Playing Titania Paganii

Titania is the ever-dutiful listener. She can listen to someone talk for hours without saying a word. One part of controlling your surroundings is knowing them. Her voice is calm and authoritative. She is not a woman to repeat herself, and when she speaks, her words carry weight. Each syllable is carefully planned, each word revised and each emotion meaningful or discarded. Privately, Titania has a wickedly dark sense of humor. She isn't above making sly jokes about her profession, and she is utterly truthful to those she holds dear.

Steadfast Heroes

"Why do your threats amuse me? Why do your indignities fall on deaf ears? Why do I persist under torture and fail to bow down when you threaten to set my nation alight? Because no matter what suffering I must endure, some things are simply worth fighting for."
—*Viktor Markovich*

A Steadfast Hero is victory incarnate, an elemental admixture of endurance, willpower and iron resolve that simply does not know when to quit. Not only is he the most unrelenting of foes, he is the source of great inspiration and a beacon of hope to those who follow him. Unlike the Indomitable Hero who moves from one act of heroism to the next, the Steadfast Hero is dedicated and hopeful and sees his promise as a lifelong quest. Less physically minded than the Indomitable Hero, he uses his limitless hope and utter resolve to win the day. If the Indomitable Hero is the unstoppable force—the Steadfast Hero is an immovable object.

Motivated by an unshakable conviction in his chosen cause, a Steadfast Hero is purpose manifest. Some exhibit near supernatural physical stamina, while others possess raw willpower far beyond the norm. Whether driven by a chosen political ideal, the safety of a loved one, the rigors of the wild or simply surviving the next night, he endures.

While he may not be the fastest or strongest opponent, this Hero is certainly the most dedicated. A Steadfast duelist patiently wears down his more aggressive foes until he finds just the right moment to strike, while the Steadfast soldier can suffer the most grievous of wounds and maintain her advance. This same principle applies to his more cerebral counterparts. The Steadfast artist suffers decades of privation to see her perfect work come to fruition, while the Steadfast scholar endures any criticism to prove his chosen theory.

Coming from all walks of life, the Steadfast are as diverse as the nations of Théah. United by iron resolve, the ranks of the Steadfast include noble leaders, grim warriors, flowery poets, enlightened inventors, pious clerics, idealistic merchants and impassioned lovers. All are united by the simple purity of a complete unwillingness to back down in the face of adversity, whatever that adversity may be.

If a Steadfast Hero has a weakness, it lies in his inability to bend before he breaks. Many have a tendency to stay in conflicts far longer than prudence recommends, and this inability to back down can lead a Steadfast and his followers into great peril when faced with equally dedicated opposition. The wise Steadfast attempts to temper this tendency with sage counsel, but when push comes to shove, he always fights to the bitter end before admitting defeat.

Core Aspect: Resolve

The defining characteristic of a Steadfast is her tenacious resolve in the face of adversity. This resolve may flow from her intimidating force of will or near supernatural levels of endurance. Whatever the source, a Steadfast pursues her objectives far beyond the point where others would turn back. This resolve is seldom viewed as a weakness among the Steadfast, and many a villain has spent sleepless nights trying to find a way to halt her relentless march.

A Steadfast Hero is patience manifest, always willing to endure, always willing to soldier on. A Steadfast general patiently wears down his foes, while the Steadfast orator pushes her point home until her audience relents. The Steadfast are masters of the long game and few are moved to rapid action when a patient solution is available. It is this glacial advance that so unnerves their foes—strike her down and she stands, exile her and she returns, flee from her and she waits just over the horizon. A Steadfast Hero takes on all challengers in her pursuit of a right and noble cause, and the only proven way to defeat her is through death itself, and even that is seldom permanent.

A View of Villainy
Beast

Relentless animals and throwbacks to a darker time. We seldom walk away from our conflicts with them unscathed, but we always walk away.

Chameleon

Manipulators accustomed to quick strikes from darkness but are ill equipped to stay in the conflict for the long haul.

Deranged

Madness grants them with great strength and cunning, but seldom the patience needed to achieve their ultimate goal. They deserve our compassion.

Juggernaut

Possessed of a determination as great as our own, they lack the sense of purpose necessary for true victory. Our battles may rage for months or years, but they will make a mistake and we shall be there to exploit it.

Mastermind

A formidable adversary who is the author of much of our misfortune. Lay one trap or a hundred, each will be dealt with in turn until their creator is no more.

Playing the Steadfast

If there is a fundamental truth in the universe, it is that nothing can stop a Steadfast Hero. Patient and resolute, he is the calm in the storm, the rock that breaks the wave, the tireless adversary of the unjust. His steady gaze and calm voice unnerve the most feared of duelists. He has a disturbing tendency to casually walk into the most lethal of circumstances and return.

Bearing a supreme sense of self-composure, the Steadfast seldom lets his opponents fluster him and is an expert at pressing on with grim determination or simple amusement, all in situations that make even the bravest companions wither in fear. This Hero is certain that his chosen objective is correct and he can endure any hardship or suffer any indignity to see things through. This sense of certainty pervades his every action and even his greatest of foes admire the placid demeanor of the Steadfast as he walks resolutely into what should be certain doom. No foe is too formidable, no obstacle too great and no deprivation too hard to endure. The Steadfast Hero stands tall against all comers and even when felled by the most mortal of blows, he never, ever, stays down.

Creating a Steadfast Hero

The most important Trait for a Steadfast Hero is Resolve or Brawn. She never gives up and pushes herself beyond the limits others believed were possible. Therefore she is the epitome of this Trait. These Heroes can come from any Background, but interesting choices could be Crafter, Farmkid and Servant.

Empathy and Convince are important Skills for a Steadfast Hero. As an immovable object, it is important that this Hero understands others and are able to draw them into her cause.

While a wide range of Advantages may be applicable to the Steadfast Hero—Able Drinker, Survivalist, Indomitable Will, Poison Immunity, Hard to Kill and I Won't Die Here all help the Steadfast Hero survive her unrelenting nature.

Agrippa Dell'Aqua

"Don't worry about the baron and his men. They are oafs. They also eat and drink far too readily—an unfortunate weakness that I've put to good use."

VODACCE • MOČIUTÉS SKARA

Traits

Brawn	●●○○○
Finesse	●●○○○
Resolve	●●●○○
Wits	●●●●○
Panache	●●○○○

Skills

Aim	●○○○○	Perform	●○○○○
Athletics	●○○○○	Ride	●○○○○
Brawl	○○○○○	Sailing	○○○○○
Convince	●●○○○	Scholarship	●●●○○
Empathy	●●○○○	Tempt	●○○○○
Hide	●●●○○	Theft	●●○○○
Intimidate	○○○○○	Warfare	○○○○○
Notice	●●●○○	Weaponry	○○○○○

Advantages

Connection: Vodacce Courts (149), Handy (149), Masterpiece Crafter: Medicine (151), Miracle Worker (153), Poison Immunity (150), Streetwise (150), Time Sense (148)

Quirks

Crafter. Earn a Hero Point when you use everyday crafting skills to solve a problem deemed too complex for such a simple solution.

Doctor. Earn a Hero Point when you tend to the injuries of a Villain or the innocents harmed by a Villain.

Virtue: The Devil

Astute. Activate your Virtue after a Villain spends Raises for an Action. That Action fails. The Villain still loses the Raises she spent.

Hubris: The Sun

Proud. You receive a Hero Point when your Hero refuses an offer of aid—for example, if a Hero tries to spend a Hero Point to give you Bonus Dice and you turn her down.

Story:

Agrippa Dell'Aqua

History

Agrippa is the eldest child of Mariza Encantada, one of Vodacce's most famous courtesans. Mariza was an indulgent mother, who provided her children with any luxury they needed—including a string of tutors for math, languages, etiquette and poetry. As Agrippa grew older, their thoughts developed and their studies of Eastern philosophies taught them that all things possessed unseen, interwoven spirits. If all things were spirit, words such as *he* and *she* were insufficient to describe such beings. Thereafter, Agrippa decided to go by *they*.

Growing up, Agrippa requested additional teachers for poison brewing. Soon, they were concocting brews on demand for courtesans, both to aid and to hinder: their most famous brews, a contraceptive tea and a draught that gives chilling nightmares to misbehaving customers. Soon their position was cemented as the "Poison Saint" of the courtesans.

Agrippa loves chess and even learned a smattering of Sabat. They approach the game much like their potion brewing—persisting until they find the right combination of ingredients. Greatly admiring minds more flexible and cunning than their own, Agrippa feels especially drawn to the intellect of Titania Paganii. A philosopher and courtesan, she is the only person Agrippa ever wanted to get to know better. Unsure of how to proceed, they sent her poetry as a token of affection and beauty. Agrippa, anxious not to appear pushy, is now content to let Titania take the next step as she pleases.

Lacking natural charm and leadership, Agrippa cultivated a network of spies and allies. A get-well note to a sick courtesan, a follow-up to a question or a kind touch goes a long way in fostering goodwill amongst the women Vodacce so readily dismisses. Agrippa built an empire from grains of sand, and now, they're ready to act. They prepare to travel Vodacce to help the courtesans rise up against oppression. Time isn't on Agrippa's side though, as they were poisoned by an agent of the Villanova family after inflicting one of Giovanni Villanova's cousins with their nightmare draught. The poison is very slow acting, but Agrippa suspects they have only a year or two to live unless they find the antidote.

Goals

Protect the pregnant courtesan Mizzini from her former client.

Mizzini says the father of her baby is Agrippa's brother Lucius. Yet, the *Strega* sister of one of Mizzini's regulars, Giorgio Salluci, says the child is *his*. Disagreements like this often end badly for a courtesan, so Mizzini turned to Agrippa for protection.

Purchase the popular Lament of Hesta poison.

Lament of Hesta instills sexual impotence and is a popular punishment for those who overstep their boundaries. Agrippa wants to use the poison against Bruno Marzani, a rich merchant who refused to pay his courtesan and threatened to expose her identity if she complained. The poison is untraceable and the effects last until the antidote is taken.

Seek the antidote to Widow's Wail.

A Villanova agent used Widow's Wail against Agrippa. Immune to all other poisons but this, Widow's Wail is very slow acting and Agrippa's death has been years in the making. Unlike mundane poisons, Widow's Wail is infused with magics to strengthen its potency. In order to cure themself of the poison, Agrippa must first unravel the magic behind it.

Playing Agrippa Dell'Aqua

Agrippa is soft-spoken and gentle. They become even more soft-spoken when they get angry: when Agrippa whispers, it is time to stop touching and imbibing *everything*. Disfigured by years of handling poisons, Agrippa wears loose robes. They take them off as a sign of trust around allies who accept them or to intimidate enemies who underestimate them.

Agrippa loves art, and talking to them about books, poetry, paintings or sculptures is a great way to open a friendly conversation. Flirting or romantic overtures, however, greatly put Agrippa off. Underneath the reclusive, art-loving exterior lies a steely determination: Agrippa stops at *nothing* to protect their charges—a trait that might lead them down a dark path if they're not careful.

Cadha Mag Raith

"Sure, I am 'just a lass' m'laird, but that sword o' yers will be cold comfort in the scrap to come. I may as well order me dram now, because this fight won't be long."

THE HIGHLAND MARCHES

Traits

Brawn	●●●●○
Finesse	●●○○○
Resolve	●●●○○
Wits	●●●○○
Panache	●●○○○

Skills

Aim	○○○○○	Perform	●●○○○
Athletics	●●●○◐	Ride	●●○◐○
Brawl	●○○○○	Sailing	○○○○○
Convince	●○○○○	Scholarship	○○○○○
Empathy	●●○◐○	Tempt	○○◐◐○
Hide	○○○○○	Theft	○○○○○
Intimidate	●●○◐○	Warfare	●●○○○
Notice	●●○◐○	Weaponry	●●●◐○

Advantages

Duelist Academy: Drexel (237), Indomitable Will (149), Large (148), Legendary Trait: Brawn (153), Survivalist (148), Valiant Spirit (150)

Quirks

Duelist. Earn a Hero Point when you resort to the edge of your blade to defend a noble ideal.

Farmkid. Earn a Hero Point when you solve a complex problem in a simple, tried and true method from back on the farm.

Virtue: The Thrones

Comforting. Activate your Virtue to cancel the effects of Fear on you and your friends.

Hubris: The War

Loyal. You receive a Hero Point when your Hero goes back for a fallen comrade or refuses to leave a wounded ally.

Story:

Cadha Mag Raith

History

The Highland Marches breed hard people—few as hard as Cadha Mag Raith. Sister of eight brothers with a father hard as iron, she lived with her family near the swamplands that were part of the holdings of Clan MacIver. Cadha tried her hardest to live up to their example. Bereft of her mother who died in childbirth, she failed to learn the ways of a proper highland woman in favor of her brothers' cruder but skilled lessons in blade, buckler and bruises.

Outnumbered by her brothers and never good enough for her father, Cadha tried harder and harder to win their approval. Her days were spent toiling in the fields, at night she explored the MacIver swamplands. There, she befriended a group of kindly refugees. One was a woman named Einhir with one eye and a fiery temper. A veteran of countless wars, she took a liking to Cadha and trained her for hours in the way of the sword, the fist and the dram.

The passage of time and endless toil saw Cadha grow to prodigious height and strength until it was whispered she was kin to ogres. She began winning the fights with her brothers, then with challengers in her village, and then with people from afar, always making her defeated foes buy her a drink.

Word arrived that a new queen lay claim to the throne of Avalon. The Laird MacIver opposed her and conscripted Cadha's father and brothers. All fought bravely for the Laird, but none returned. The only family Cadha had left were the people of the swamp who had grown numerous enough to catch the Laird's notice. The Laird's men came to conscript the people of the swamp. Cadha fought them, none returned.

Declaring herself "Queen of the Swamplands," Cadha defended them against Laird and commoner alike. Once the swamps were safe, she turned her attention south to Queen Elaine. There were plenty more lairds and what better way to challenge them than to be Queen Elaine's personal champion. A defender of the commons and holder of the Graal, Elaine is worthy of Cadha's service. If the High King and commons believe in Elaine, perhaps Cadha can too. To that end, Cadha travels south to "interview" the new sovereign.

Goals

Train a new Queen of the Swamplands.

Cadha knows that Laird MacIver has a long memory and will not leave the people of the swamplands alone forever. She seeks to train a new "Queen of the Swamplands" to protect her people like Einhir trained her all those years ago.

Become Queen Elaine's new champion.

Cadha's desire to defend commoners has far outgrown the inhabitants of her "queendom." As Queen Elaine's champion, Cadha can use her immense fighting prowess to protect the people of the Glamour Isles. Assuming Cadha finds Elaine worthy, she will have an endless parade of foes to challenge, and few foes can be more formidable than those of Queen Elaine.

Challenge every worthy fighter she meets and win.

Cadha's journey south is constantly sidetracked by her incessant need to challenge every mighty fighter she encounters. It recently came to her attention that a cousin of Laird MacIver is an Avalonian lord with a cadre of deadly retainers and a hatred for Queen Elaine. Her trip may be delayed just a while longer.

Playing Cadha Mag Raith

Cadha's laugh erupts from her massive frame with a bellow that sends monsters to flight. The death of her family and failure to oppose the Laird's men when they conscripted them haunts Cadha to this day. Never again will she abandon those in peril. She does not seek out a fight, but takes all comers, anytime, anywhere and the loser always pays for the drinks (and she cannot remember the last time she lost). Always confident, always on the lookout for a good scrap or a commoner in peril, Cadha may well be the next Bonnie McGee...and knows it...

Estandart de Milly

"Can you focus on my eyes for a moment? My name is Estandart, and I've been where you've been. You have a special gift, and you should be proud of it. But you need to listen to me, because certain powerful people don't appreciate your gift, and if we're not careful, they might hurt you or force you to do something you don't want to do."

MONTAIGNE

Traits

Trait	
Brawn	●●○○○
Finesse	●●●○○
Resolve	●●●◐○
Wits	●●○○○
Panache	●●●◐○

Skills

Aim	○○○○○	Perform	◐○○○○
Athletics	○○○○○	Ride	●●○○○
Brawl	○○○○○	Sailing	○○○○○
Convince	●●◐○○	Scholarship	●●◐○○
Empathy	●●●○○	Tempt	●●○○○
Hide	●●●○○	Theft	●●●●○
Intimidate	○○○○○	Warfare	◐○○○○
Notice	●●●○○	Weaponry	○○○○○

Advantages

Foul Weather Jack (151), Got It! (149), Opportunist (152), Sorcery: Porté, Sorcery: Porté (219), Team Player (150), Time Sense (148)

Quirks

Sorcier Porté. Earn a Hero Point when you close a *blessure* that a Villain ripped open.

Servant. Earn a Hero Point when you put yourself in danger to assist another character with a difficult task.

Virtue: The Hero

Courageous. Activate your Virtue to add Bonus Dice to your Risk equal to the Fear rating of your target.

Hubris: The Prophet

Overzealous. You receive a Hero Point when your Hero strongly defends one of his opinions when the time or place is inappropriate.

Sorcery

Estandart has a Minor Mark on a blanket his mother made for him when he was young.

Story:

Estandart de Milly

History

La Magie des Portails is a sorcerous art strictly confined to Montaigne nobility, except when it isn't. Porté has dispersed far and wide with the vagaries of high-society romances and appetites. In spite of purists' cruelest efforts to suppress them, undocumented *sorciers'* numbers grow steadily.

Barnabé de Milly's father, a noble *sorcier*, often pointed out how Barnabé's lack of the talent disappointed him. Barnabé's own legitimate children, who numbered three before his wife passed away, never manifested the talent either. When he realized one of his bastard children, Estandart, was a *sorcier*, he stole him from his mother, legitimized him and put him to work facilitating Barnabé's crooked dealings.

After a long childhood of tirelessly opening portals for Barnabé and his cronies, Estandart woke up one day with the realization Porté would never win his father's love. He packed his things, opened a portal and walked through into his mother's apartment. By the time Barnabé got there, Estandart and his mother were long gone.

Since then, he's stayed one step ahead of the hunters sent by his father. He practices Porté for money when necessary, but spends every free moment helping wayward *sorciers* escape people like his father. While *sorciers de Porté* escape immediate danger easily, few noble bastards have the money and support to flee far from home. Estandart has set up an underground network of safe houses and friendly faces his charges can rely on when they need to escape the nobles' black carriages.

Cycling through a number of different locations just within Charouse, these *sorciers* can hide, rest and train in relative comfort surrounded by friends. When danger comes, lookouts and warnings allow them time to prepare a portal and escape before the nobles' hired hunters show up. The hunters have found a few of these safe houses, but so far Estandart has been able to establish new ones faster. He's the beating heart and brilliant mind of the underground *sorcier* escape network. But if something happens to him, will his network survive?

Goals

Confront the people his father sent to find him.

Barnabé de Milly isn't happy that his son is single-handedly counteracting generations of enforced elitism. He hired three private detectives to go after his son. Estandart saw one of them step into a portal upon being noticed—he is fairly sure he won't be able to run forever.

Secure a new safe house.

Even with Blood Marks, a *sorcier de Porté* needs somewhere to escape to. In addition to apartments in different Charouse neighborhoods, Estandart maintains a personal safe house deep in the Syrneth catacombs. But these days, everyone from the Explorer's Society to misbehaving teenagers is exploring said catacombs. If he wants to stay a step ahead of his pursuers, he needs a fallback plan.

Learn who's leaving *blessures* in Charouse's streets.

A *sorcier* has been leaving terrible *blessures* throughout Charouse, but Estandart believes the person acts with no formal training and ignorance rather than any malicious intent. The Musketeers have closed down and bricked up at least one busy commercial street because of a bloody, screaming hole, however. The nondescript black coaches, which pick up "unanticipated" *sorciers de Porté*, can't be too far behind this poor soul, but Estandart must find the person first.

Playing Estandart de Milly

Estandart is infinitely accepting and forgiving of other people and deeply critical of himself. The weight of his past sin sits on his shoulders like a heavy pack he's carried too long, though he won't let it show unless he thinks no one's watching. For both personal and professional reasons, he's an excellent listener. Whenever someone speaks to him, he has already formulated the next, relevant follow-up question. He switches gracefully between noble refinement and down-to-earth straightforwardness based on his surroundings. He never condescends, but he's firm and compelling when he needs to be.

Gudrun Hass

"A toast! To the bride! To the bride, to the groom and to all here! Try the second pitcher, try them all! Be merry tonight, and pay your tab tomorrow!"

EISEN

Traits

Brawn	●●○○○
Finesse	●●○○○
Resolve	●●●○○
Wits	●●●○○
Panache	●●●○○

Skills

Aim	○○○○○	Perform	●●●○○
Athletics	●○○○○	Ride	●●○○○
Brawl	●●○○○	Sailing	○○○○○
Convince	●●●○○	Scholarship	●●●○○
Empathy	●●○○○	Tempt	●○○○○
Hide	○○○○○	Theft	○○○○○
Intimidate	●○○○○	Warfare	○○○○○
Notice	●●●○○	Weaponry	○○○○○

Advantages

Able Drinker (148), Bar Fighter (151), Cast Iron Stomach (148), Handy (149), Lyceum (153), Masterpiece Crafter: Beermaking (151), Time Sense (148)

Quirks

Crafter. Earn a Hero Point when you use everyday crafting skills to solve a problem deemed too complex for such a simple solution.

Merchant. Earn a Hero Point when you sell an item for far less than it's worth to someone who desperately needs it.

Virtue: The Road

Friendly. Activate your Virtue when you meet a character (even a Villain) for the first time. She treats you as friendly for one scene.

Hubris: The Tower

Arrogant. You receive a Hero Point when your Hero shows disdain, contempt, or otherwise looks down on a Villain or someone who could cause harm to friends.

Story:

History

Gudrun Hass was born during one of the darkest times in Eisen's history in the tiny town of Berlitz, north of Freiburg. Though no longer at war, Eisen had been crippled by conflict and struggled to rebuild. Poverty, inhospitable terrain and horrifying monsters stalking the land made it a hard place to grow up. But the little town of Berlitz had been spared the worst of war, which allowed little Gudrun to focus on the beauty of the world and her life's passion: brewing.

Gudrun grew up in the shadow of Berlitz's namesake, the legendary Braumeister Adel Nachtman Berlitz. She listened to every story about the amazing Berlitz's talent, tall tales almost impossible to believe. Gudrun dreamt of finding his fabled missing book of recipes to help her become the greatest Braumeister who ever lived. Adel's drinks were so good and made so many people happy, they named an entire town after him. Gudrun wanted to be even better.

Many who meet Gudrun believe that she has a one-track mind, speaking of nothing except brewing, recipes and ingredients. Yet, Gudrun has her reasons besides a desperate passion for spirits. She grew up during the long winters and harsh springs of war. She watched as all of Eisen went mad around her and suffered when monsters crawled out of the darkness.

Gudrun was there the day her father's body came back from war, just one of dozens of men who perished in the conflict. Without her father's income, Gudrun's mother and her siblings would have starved had Gudrun not gone to work as an apprentice at the local brewery. Gudrun believes that alcohol uplifts the human condition in the worst of times. To Gudrun, her work is a holy, important thing.

Gudrun learned all she could from the local brewers and became the best the town had seen since Berlitz himself. When she became stifled from lack of new learning choices, the local Braumeister sent Gudrun off to Freiburg where she could learn and try her hand at the annual Braumeister competition. Gudrun has studied for nearly a whole year in preparation for the competition. In her eyes, the competition does not only represent her own pride, but lets her bring a piece of Eisen's innocent beauty back into the world again.

Goals
Collect rare aidelweiz flowers to perfect her Golden Malt Ale.

There are few people who know how to make Golden Malt Ale the way it was meant to be made, and Gudrun is one of them. The aidelweiz flowers only grow on the highest mountaintops during the earliest days of spring and are difficult to preserve. Sounds like a brewing adventure ready to begin.

Win the Braumeister competition in Freiburg.

The festival at Freiburg hosts one of the most prestigious Braumeister competitions in all the world. People come from all across Théah to sample the drinks and compete. It is the perfect place to prove what a master brewer Gudrun has become.

Rediscover the lost recipe book of Adel Nachtman Berlitz.

Long ago, Adel Nachtman Berlitz created some of the most revolutionary brewing recipes known to Théah. There is a rumor of a lost book of recipes, thought destroyed in a fire after the Braumeister's death. So of course, Gudrun will be the one to discover it!

Playing Gudrun Hass

Gudrun Hass is a cocky, arrogant Braumeister, though perhaps it isn't cockiness if she can back it up with talent. Gudrun is aware of her ability and jokes about it with a smile and a hearty laugh more often than not. Still, while some might find her constant drive for perfection and hearty self-congratulation difficult to deal with, Gudrun's good heart and amazing talent earn her more friends than her arrogance loses her. Her parties are incredible, and she can always be found in the middle of a crowd, handing out drinks and soliciting feedback on the brew. Gudrun tackles any mountain, fords any stream, to realize her dream of becoming the best Braumeister in the world.

Keddy Stewart

"Everything in creation has a pattern, from the stones in the earth to the stars in the sky. O'Bannon may be mad, but not even he can defy that."

INISMORE

Traits

Brawn	●●○○○
Finesse	●●○○○
Resolve	●●●○○
Wits	●●●○○
Panache	●●●○○

Skills

Aim	●○○○○	Perform	●●●○○
Athletics	○○○○○	Ride	●●○○○
Brawl	○○○○○	Sailing	○○○○○
Convince	●●●○○	Scholarship	●●○○○
Empathy	●●●○○	Tempt	○○○○○
Hide	●○○○○	Theft	○○○○○
Intimidate	○○○○○	Warfare	○○○○○
Notice	●●●○○	Weaponry	●●○○○

Advantages

Able Drinker (148), Barterer (149), Miracle Worker (153), Signature Item: Druid's Staff (152), Sorcery: Glamour (210), Time Sense (148), Virtuoso: Song (152)

Quirks

Bard. Earn a Hero Point when you solve a problem by following an example set by a Legend.
Doctor. Earn a Hero Point when you tend to the injuries of a Villain or the innocents harmed by a Villain.

Virtue: The Prophet

Illuminating. Activate your Virtue to know whenever any other character lies to you until the end of the Scene.

Hubris: Reunion

Bitterness. You receive a Hero Point when you bring up old grudges or bad feelings when doing so will lead to trouble.

Sorcery

Keddy is the embodiment of Godric, The Pious. His Major Trait is Panache, his Minor Trait is Resolve. He knows the Major Glamour Resist Sorcery (Rank 1), and the Minor Glamours Pain Is Temporary (Rank 1) and No Fear (Rank 1).

Story:

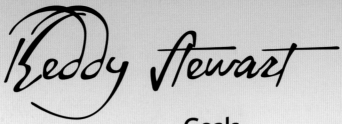

History

Keddy was raised by his father in the small Inish village of Loch Stewart. Ever inquisitive, Keddy would explore the enigmatic loch and drink in his father's tales of his family's mysterious boulder, the Bhollain Stewart. The boulder fascinated Keddy; it was said to contain the entire song of his family, something his father always omitted from his tales. The Bhollain Stewart rested in the center of Loch Stewart deep in the heart of Inismore whose fog-shrouded shores have long protected the Stewarts from conqueror's sword and Vaticine fire.

Keddy tried to row to the loch's mythical island, Olean Roth, to see the boulder. Time and time again he was repulsed by cloying mist. During his last visit, Keddy saw a silver-haired woman staring at him from the watery depths. Turning his boat and rowing ashore, Keddy barely mentioned the woman to his father before the elder Stewart whisked his family away to the Highland Marches. The story of the silver-haired woman terrified Keddy's father, who refused to speak more on the subject.

Keddy's heart ached for home. He begged his father to teach him the ways of the druid, one last tie to home. Yet, each time his father refused, fearful that Keddy's inquisitive nature coupled with ancient teachings would get him in trouble. To prove his father wrong, Keddy molded himself into a responsible, kind young man. Finally, through Keddy's sheer persistence, his father begrudgingly began his training.

It took years of work, but Keddy became an excellent apprentice. On the night of his final rite of initiation, Keddy's father vanished with a bloodcurdling scream under a cloak of shadow. Keddy was left alone, with only his father's staff lying among a set of bare footprints and a strand of silver hair to prove anyone had ever been there.

Keddy vowed to find his father. It was not long before he heard about the return of Mad Jack O'Bannon, Inismore's new ruler, said to bear long locks of silver hair and walk barefoot. Feeling the turn of the great pattern, Keddy quietly watched events in Inismore until convinced O'Bannon had something to do with his father's disappearance. It is time for him to return home.

Goals
Train a bard apprentice.

The pattern of creation has blessed the Stewarts with an unbroken line of druids stretching back to the dawn of Inismore. Even with his father in peril, Keddy cannot resist the pattern's unassailable compulsion to initiate the next Stewart into the puzzle of creation. Keddy has heard tales of a Stewart cousin with a honeyed tongue, a knack for riddles and a head for mischief.

Hear the song of his family at the Stewart Boulder.

Only a Stewart can navigate the tortuous pathways through the forest of Olean Roth without being lost forever in the realms of the Sidhe. Legends state that those who place an ear to the Bhollain Stewart hear a haunting song that grants them all the knowledge of the Stewart family. Keddy hopes this song will equip him with the knowledge he needs to rescue his father.

Discover why his father disappeared when Jack O'Bannon returned.

Jack O'Bannon's return coincided with the disappearance of Keddy's father. Some believe O'Bannon wants the songs of the Bhollain Stewart, and that he cannot acquire them without a Stewart as his guide. Some even say that it was not O'Bannon, but Jack's Sidhe mother come to retrieve her son with the "help" of Keddy's father.

Playing Keddy Stewart

Keddy's knowing eyes drink in his surroundings with gluttonous abandon, yet are girded with iron resolve. None who meet Keddy mistake his sonorous voice or healer's touch as a sign of weakness, but as an extension of an uncompromising determination to fulfill his druidic vocation.

Focused and intent with purpose, Keddy's resolve has increased since his father's disappearance. He glides into a room with the quiet step and quizzical gaze of a druid, but his visage turns hard as marble before any who hinder his investigation. When Keddy is faced with an individual who is truly sympathetic to his plight does his façade crack, and then only rarely.

Rodrigo Félix

"Good luck? Bad luck? Nothing ever happens just because of 'luck'. Everything we experience—especially our suffering—is the will of the Creator. And I, for one, am not going to question His designs; I will accept them and try to make the best I can."

CASTILLE • THE INVISIBLE COLLEGE

Traits

Brawn	●●○○○
Finesse	●●●○○
Resolve	●●●○○
Wits	●●●○○
Panache	●●○○○

Skills

Aim	○○○○○	Perform	●○○○○
Athletics	●●○○○	Ride	●○○○○
Brawl	●○○○○	Sailing	○○○○○
Convince	●●○○○	Scholarship	●●●○○
Empathy	●●○○○	Tempt	●●○○○
Hide	●●●○○	Theft	○○○○○
Intimidate	●○○○○	Warfare	○○○○○
Notice	●●○○○	Weaponry	○○○○○

Advantages

An Honest Misunderstanding (151), Brush Pass (151), Disarming Smile (149), Inspire Generosity (149), Ordained (152), Reckless Takedown (150)

Quirks

Orphan. Earn a Hero Point when you put yourself in danger to ensure someone else doesn't have to be alone.

Priest. Earn a Hero Point when you set aside the rhetoric and take action to practice the virtues you preach.

Virtue: The Hanged Man

Altruistic. Activate your Virtue to suffer a Risk's Consequences in place of another Hero.

Hubris: The Glyph

Superstitious. You receive a Hero Point when you refuse to solve a problem using Sorcery, an artifact, or some other mystical effect that you don't trust.

Story:

Rodrigo Félix

History

Rodrigo Félix has led a difficult life since the day his birth parents abandoned him as a newborn in front of *La Esperanza* chapel. Luckily, Rodrigo has always demonstrated an endurance, a certain tenacity to survive anything life throws at him. It did not matter whether they were difficult subjects to study or bullies trying to prey on him. Rodrigo endured it all.

Meeting Madre Clara, the High Priest of *La Esperanza*, cemented this strength of heart. She took care of him and taught him everything he knows about Theus and His designs. She taught the young boy to thirst for knowledge, bringing him along on her quests to find the Fourth Vigil. To this day, Rodrigo hears the Credo and the verses in her quiet, clear voice.

Growing up, Rodrigo's only friend and confidant was Mario, a fellow orphan. Mario was everything Rodrigo was not. Outspoken, loud and possessing a complete disregard for rules. Despite their differences, the two were inseparable. Then, tragedy ensued.

Madre Clara was charged with sorcery. Although Rodrigo found this accusation unthinkable, what shattered his heart was the witness who brought the charges forth. On the day of the trial, Rodrigo entered the courthouse to find Mario standing as accuser.

Rodrigo testified in Madre Clara's favor, but his words fell on deaf ears. Desperate to free the woman he loved as a mother, he tried forcing his way towards Clara, refusing to back down even when threatened with weapons. It took a club to the head to stop him. Outraged at the boy's actions, the High Inquisitor demanded his confinement, so he could "meditate on his actions, lest they be a result of demonic influence."

Rodrigo awoke to the smell of burnt flesh. Fear spurred him from his bed, to find the whole community of *La Esperanza* standing over their High Priest's scorched body. Without a moment's delay, Rodrigo ran through the chapel looking for Mario.

When Rodrigo found him, he punched Mario with all the fury and strength he could muster. Seeing his former's friend blood on his hands shook him back into reality. Rodrigo's mouth finally opened. "Why?"

At first, Mario was uncooperative, but after a couple more blows, he whispered only a name: "Mother Guineu."

Goals

Find his birth parents who left him with the church.

Rodrigo has only one clue about his origin. Before the trial, Madre Clara mentioned that his parents would have been proud of the man he had become. When he enquired further, she refused to say anything beyond a passing mention to the Sandoval Forest.

Learn the real name of the fiend "Mother Guineu."

After the beating, Mario mysteriously disappeared from *La Esperanza*, and together with him, Rodrigo's hope of finding out more about this monster. From that moment on, he has been frequenting taverns and other less savory places looking for any information about her.

Uncover rumors of the Fourth Vigil hidden in Castille.

Now that he is in command of his life, Rodrigo is determined to help the Church as much as he can. To do that, he is following a trail of clues regarding the Lost Vigil deep into the mountains along the coast of the Vaticine Gulf.

Playing Rodrigo Félix

Rodrigo Félix is a mighty man with a heart of gold. He has an unyielding faith in Theus and His Church. This faith leads him to offer his help to anyone, believer or not. He listens more than he speaks and chooses his words with care so not to offend anyone by accident. He has an easy smile and his laugh is like the rolling of a powerful river.

Rodrigo does everything in his power to correct the injustices he perceives. If they affect the pious and faithful, he goes to any length to expose the truth. He does not believe in violence as a primary solution, but is willing to fight when the need arises.

Viktor Markovich

"... and this, dear children, is Gena, a rare Ussuran leopard! Today, we're going to follow Gena as she hunts for dinner and learn a thing or two about how to prepare an ambush."

USSURA

Traits

Brawn	●●○○○
Finesse	●●●○○
Resolve	●●●○○
Wits	●●●○○
Panache	●●○○○

Skills

Aim	●●○○○	Perform	●●●○○
Athletics	●●●○○	Ride	●○○○○
Brawl	○○○○○	Sailing	○○○○○
Convince	○○○○○	Scholarship	●●○○○
Empathy	●●○○○	Tempt	●○○○○
Hide	●●○○○	Theft	●○○○○
Intimidate	●○○○○	Warfare	○○○○○
Notice	●●○○○	Weaponry	○○○○○

Advantages
Got It! (149), Inspire Generosity (149), Sniper (152), Survivalist (148), Trusted Companion: Forest Animals (154), Virtuoso: Singing (152)

Quirks
Hunter. Earn a Hero Point when you use your hunter's acumen to save someone from danger.
Performer. Earn a Hero Point when you use your crowd-pleasing skills for something more than making a few coins.

Virtue: The Thrones
Comforting. Activate your Virtue to cancel the effects of Fear on you and your friends.

Hubris: The Hanged Man
Indecisive. You receive a Hero Point when your Hero takes an Action to pause in hesitation, doubt, or uncertainty before he makes a move.

Story:

Viktor Markovich

History

Viktor was banished from his lands by his evil twin sister Agafya Markova, but he couldn't stay away and returned to distribute food and medicine to her starving people. Accosted by her patrols, Viktor agreed to face punishment without a fight. Yet, instead of executing him, something broke in Agafya and she banished him once more.

Viktor wandered the wilderness weeping, comforting himself with folk songs he'd learned as a child. Why? Why would his sister damn him to a life of loneliness without his beloved lands or family? In his sorrow, Viktor laid down to rest. During the night, Matushka came to the young man calling out to him. "Viktor Markovich," she said. "I offer you the power to control animals, in exchange for—"

"No thank you, Mother," said Viktor who awoke to find himself surrounded by forest creatures. "I think...I've got it!"

In the night, his sorrowful tune had drawn creatures of the forest to him. Matushka was nonplussed, and with many more tasks to perform that night than dallying with a crying boy in the woods, she let it go. With a grumbling stomach, Viktor cooked some mushrooms sharing them with a wild boar by his side. Realizing he would never truly be alone in nature he stopped crying, and his mood cheered.

Now, Viktor is done running—but he's not done singing. He's become a beacon of hope and resistance against his sister. The animals he loves are his teaching assistants: Viktor's voice calms the creatures and in return his pupils are allowed to safely be in their presence and learn from their movements. Viktor teaches people to fight like tigers, hunt together like wolves, skulk like foxes or run like reindeer. Whenever Agafya's guards come for him, he doesn't even have to hide, as they haven't yet made it past the packs of loyal dogs swarming those who would threaten Viktor.

So far, Viktor has only taught, never fought. He has forged friendships in many villages throughout the Markovich lands. He's trained a robust resistance, joined together by his songs. But the time to string his bow and turn the tide approaches. Must he aim his arrow at his own sister? Or will he find another way?

Goals

Find his lost family's crest.

For more than a generation, Viktor and Agafya's family has had no formal crest. A mysterious incident in their grandparents' time resulted in the destruction of all evidence of their family's arms. If Viktor is to emerge as a true leader in opposition to Agafya, he needs a symbol—which means venturing into Agafya's territory to investigate that incident, or else sending friendly agents to do it for him.

Retake his family's lands from his twin.

Viktor would never suggest violence except as a last resort, but Agafya has no compunction about killing dissenters to her rule. Her guards are brutal and without remorse. Viktor must go among the people and train them to resist Agafya with lessons learned from nature.

Cure his sister of her cruel, frozen heart.

Viktor has never given up hope that the good, caring Agafya has not died. Has some awful curse befallen her? Is someone manipulating her? Or has she just forgotten the love and hope their parents taught them in childhood? Even if he has to do it through prison bars, Viktor will find the sister he lost.

Playing Viktor Markovich

Warm, friendly, hopeful. Viktor might look like a hard-bitten survivalist. But if you approach him, he's bubbly, outgoing and friendly. He loves meeting new people. He gets on particularly well with children and animals. He is able to calm the beasts of the forest and field, singing to them to make them feel safe and at ease. He's a never-ending fountain of Ussuran folk songs, and he spends a lot of his free time improvising little ditties and teaching them to his friends.

Viktor takes no joy in violence, whether hunting for food or leading rebels against his sister. He only hurts other living beings if survival necessitates it. Any time he kills a deer or an enemy with an arrow, he sings a quiet prayer of lament and apology.

Wicus Jachowski

"My darling, I cannot. You are ravishing indeed, but the dievai have cursed me, that my only love might be the Commonwealth herself... that said, I suppose a kiss wouldn't hurt."

THE SARMATIAN COMMONWEALTH

Traits

Brawn	●●○○○
Finesse	●●○○○
Resolve	●●●○○
Wits	●●●○○
Panache	●●●○○

Skills

Aim	●○○○○	Perform	●○○○○
Athletics	○○○○○	Ride	●○○○○
Brawl	○○○○○	Sailing	○○○○○
Convince	●●●○○	Scholarship	●●○○○
Empathy	●●●○○	Tempt	●●○○○
Hide	○○○○○	Theft	○○○○○
Intimidate	●●○○○	Warfare	●●○○○
Notice	●●○○○	Weaponry	●○○○○

Advantages

Come Hither (149), Disarming Smile (149), Leadership (149), Lyceum (153), Rich (152), Together We Are Strong (155)

Quirks

Aristocrat. Earn a Hero Point when you prove there is more to nobility than expensive clothes and attending court.

Poseł. Earn a Hero Point when you insist on democracy when it would be advantageous for you to not take a vote.

Virtue: The Emperor

Commanding. Activate your Virtue. The GM gives a Hero Point to all other Heroes in this Scene.

Hubris: The War

Loyal. You receive a Hero Point when your Hero goes back for a fallen comrade or refuses to leave a wounded ally.

Story:

Wicus Jachowski

History

Wicus Jachowski was the greater Stanisławiec area's most eligible bachelor and protagonist in a new love story every season. Then he met Wawyrzyniec, a mysterious newcomer to his social scene, whose charm finally made Wicus want to settle down. Wicus dedicated his life to making Wawyrzyniec happy, learning something new he loved about the man each day.

When Wawyrzyniec revealed he was not human but a *dievas*, sent to offer a devil's bargain, Wicus' heart shattered. He learned if he ever fathered, or adopted, a child it was destined to contract a fatal disease. Wawyrzyniec could provide a supernatural cure, if Wicus offered up the life of one of the many peasants who worked his fields. Betrayed by the person he loved most in all of Théah, Wicus walked away.

He disappeared from the social scene. He gave up on love and family. Heartbroken, he dedicated himself to the oldest duties of the nobility: caring for the peasant farmers who worked his land and practicing the arts of war to defend his country against invasion. But even in modern Rzeczpospolita, a nobleman's abandonment of an ancient family lineage was a great scandal. Save for their closest friends, the Jachowski family's allies abandoned Wicus. He was on his own.

He's older now, and after his parents passed away, Wicus wrote a new will leaving his lands to the farmers who work them. Wicus disseminates information and training once confined to the nobility to the peasants. Historically, the Sarmatian nobility were a dedicated warrior class, but the Sarmatian people need noble skills to defend their country against invaders who see a nation of peasants as easy prey.

Wicus spends hours each day training Sarmatia's new nobles in arts of fencing, marksmanship, horsemanship, how to wear armor without falling over in the mud and killing yourself. He also teaches chess, wargames, etiquette and negotiation, forging commoners into diplomats as well as soldiers. He spends the rest of the day in the fields. Filling his days with activities, never resting nor abandoning his duties, has kept Wicus going. He has hope for the future of his nation and the people who work his lands, and for this he must persist.

Goals

Convince the incorrigible Lady Leszczyński to stop pursuing him.

Bogumiła Leszczyński reminds Wicus of himself in his younger days, occupying the same niche in Rzeczpospolitan society. The Leszczyńskis are old family friends, so Wicus can't just tell her to stop coming around. Worst of all, she actually tempts him to take a chance on a love affair. She's an unrepentant *losejas*, and Wicus knows it. Her dealings with the *dievai* could spell trouble for him.

Fortify his lands against Ussuran invasion.

Wicus' holdings lie just north of Stanisławiec in Rzeczpospolita, bordering the hills where the blood-thirsty Ussuran Baroness Agafya Markova makes her home. Her family history is steeped in military conquest, and the private army she maintains is formidable. If she attacks Sarmatia, the flatlands Wicus' family has farmed will fall swiftly.

Get the Angel's Hand, a legendary pistol that can kill a *dievas*.

One hundred years ago, a gunsmith who lost everything but his craft to the *dievai* forged a perfect flintlock pistol traced with images of angels in flight. The Vaticine Church stores that weapon in a secret magazine, accessible only to Inquisitorial witch hunters. Perhaps Wawyrzyniec won't retaliate for Wicus' refusal, but the *dievai* who had sent him might not be so gentle or forgiving.

Playing Wicus Jachowski

Wicus Jachowski carries himself like a noble, with the refinement and flair for the dramatic that turned so many heads when he was younger. He's full of romantic passion, but channels it into manual labor and military science. He spent his adult life distracting and convincing himself he cares about high-minded ideals more than his own feelings, but the façade cracks frequently. You see it in the flirtations that slip past his screen of politeness, the care with which he coordinates his outfits and the way he talks about Sarmatia like a lover or spouse rather than a nation.

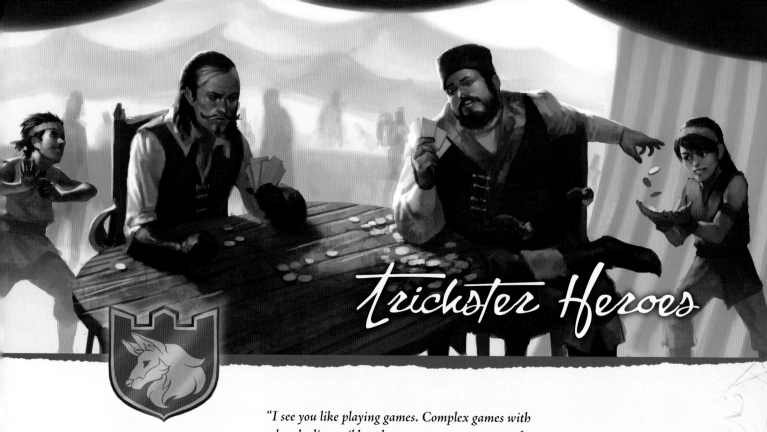

Trickster Heroes

"I see you like playing games. Complex games with barely discernible rules serve to ensnare as much as they reward. Games with people's lives. Perhaps, I can teach you a few games of my own?"
—Samo Sokolof

A Trickster is always a little "different" from those around her. She may not be the smartest, most resilient or even the hardest fighting of Théans, but she is certainly the least predictable. This Hero is a master of panache, and this inherent charisma, coupled with her unpredictable nature, makes it extremely difficult for her enemies to predict her next move. Mad or genius, prankster or wit, a Trickster uses her unorthodox nature and unflagging charm for the benefit of all.

Some mistake Trickster Heroes as insane, but this would be a misnomer. Tricksters have the same goals as other Théans, they simply approach them from a much different perspective. Tricksters love games, whether puzzles, riddles or unraveling great mysteries. A Trickster is inherently fascinated with the human condition and has no problem ensnaring people in playful games or elaborate webs of intrigue in pursuit of the greater good. If she has a little fun along the way, all the better.

A Trickster lives life large and with flair. She is dangerously charismatic and her easy nature allows her to quickly make friends, make fun of enemies and talk her way out of trouble when her pranks are revealed. She is perfectly capable of fighting or complex intellectual endeavors, her silver tongue tends to be mightier than the quill or the sword.

Tricksters are generally difficult to pigeonhole. Non-linear thinking is their strong suit, as is the ability to approach problems from a unique perspective. This, combined with their dangerous allure, is often just enough to tip the scales in their favor.

Weaknesses for these Heroes are as varied as Tricksters themselves and tend to be unique to the individual. She may have an insufferable personality, a penchant for random bouts of absurdity, a complete lack of subtlety or a habit of complex subtlety. Many find the mutable nature of Tricksters difficult to trust and often take affront to their endless pranks. A wise Trickster would do well to note the opinions of others, but her self-centered nature is unlikely to care.

Core Aspect: Mercurial

The key to understanding Tricksters (if such a thing is possible) is that they are fundamentally unique and highly unpredictable. While they tend to be self-centered, prone to pranks, magnetic and more than a little unorthodox, the number and proportion of these attributes in a given Trickster is far from uniform.

Tricksters have a well-developed sense of right and wrong, but tend to eschew naked force and cold intellect in favor of elaborate games, dazzling feats of charisma and complex pranks ranging from the most subtle to the truly grandiose.

Tricksters epitomize the blurry line between delusion and genius and are often near impossible to categorize. Tricksters are as diverse as snowflakes and can be drawn from any social station or walk of life. A wide-eyed crone may have her charge bark at the moon three times before miraculously healing his grievous wounds, a subtle Montaigne courtier may ensnare a corrupt noble in complex games of wit, while an Ussuran peasant may play humiliating pranks on invading Montaigne troops to lead them away from his village. All this eccentricity ultimately leads to a positive outcome and the Trickster gets to amuse himself at the expense of his foes.

A View of Villainy

Beast
Can't take a joke?

Chameleon
Have you been properly introduced to the fine fellow concealed outside your window? Wait! Come back my friend! How unfortunate; it must have taken him weeks to get here from Vodacce.

Deranged
All of our smarts, but none of our good looks. How do they take themselves so seriously?

Juggernaut
These guys are great, always coming back for more.

Mastermind
I'm sorry, could you tell me why you're important again? I love hearing you say it.

Playing the Trickster

A Trickster is mirthful, beautiful and mutable. They are prone to extreme personalities. Wild Tricksters yell at the top of their lungs and imply that secret knowledge is just one quest away. Subtle Tricksters draw the eye of all around with a wink from behind a fan or an enigmatic note. More physically inclined Tricksters grab attention through extremely visible (and satisfying) pranks.

A Trickster's mind is always in motion and filled with endless possibilities. She carefully balances her continually changing nature against her native charisma in an endless cycle. She uses her social grace and dramatic flair to orchestrate her plots and pranks, then uses that same flair to talk her way out of the repercussions. She never stops thinking, never stops planning and never abandons a complex puzzle.

What a Trickster does not do is fade away, for that is a fate worse than death. She always takes the opportunity to be recognized, whether in person or by reputation and never misses an opportunity to express her "unique" nature. After all, life is supposed to be amusing...well, to her at least.

Creating a Trickster Hero

Panache is the most important Trait for this Hero to have. It sees him through all his pranks, quips and poor choices. Fitness and Resolve are good seconds, for when his Panache fails and he either needs to power through a situation or dodge out of the way.

Tricksters do not lend themselves to one Background or another. Because of their unique views on the world, they are not likely to come from military Backgrounds or anything that required them to follow orders strictly.

Convince, Hide, Perform and Tempt are all useful Skills for a Trickster to have. It is important for this Hero to communicate his uniqueness to others, often playing the role of the lovable rogue, no matter how it falls.

Picking Advantages for a Trickster is all about maximizing his survivability. What unique Advantages does this Hero have to keep him going over the long years? Dynamic Approach, Fascinate, Joie de Vivre, Reputation and Time Sense are all great Advantages for Tricksters.

Desideria Colomberia

"No. I am done being a pawn. This time you'll do what I say. And you're gonna like it."

VODACCE

Traits

Brawn	●●○○○
Finesse	●●○○○
Resolve	●●○○○
Wits	●●●●○
Panache	●●●○○

Skills

Aim	●○○○○	Perform	●●○○○
Athletics	○○○○○	Ride	●●○○○
Brawl	○○○○○	Sailing	○○○○○
Convince	●●●○○	Scholarship	●●○○○
Empathy	●●○○○	Tempt	●●○○○
Hide	●●●○○	Theft	○○○○○
Intimidate	●●○○○	Warfare	○○○○○
Notice	○○○○○	Weaponry	○○○○○

Advantages
Disarming Smile (149), Inspire Generosity (149), Opportunist (152), Rich (152), Sorcery: Sorte, Sorcery: Sorte (228), Time Sense (148)

Quirks
Sorte Strega. Earn a Hero Point when you commit to a dangerous course of action that you believe is destiny.

Aristocrat. Earn a Hero Point when you prove there is more to nobility than expensive clothes and attending court.

Virtue: The Glyph
Temperate. Activate your Virtue to prevent any magical effect (Sorcery, Artifacts, Monsters, etc.) from affecting you.

Hubris: The Wheel
Unfortunate. You receive 2 Hero Points when you choose to fail an important Risk before rolling.

Sorcery
Desideria knows the Tesse of Read, Major Blessing, Minor Blessing, Major Arcana, Minor Arcana and Minor Pull.

Story:

Desideria Colomberia

History

Desideria always got exactly what she wanted. New clothes? Her mother ordered a makeover for herself and her daughters. Flowers? A new suitor sent over a massive bouquet. That boy she liked? Boom, he was in love. Except none of it was *really* what she wanted. Desideria remained caged behind black veils no matter how fine their make. Suitors only sought to control the powerful *Strega*. And that boy never genuinely liked her—she just *made* him.

Desideria struggled with herself for years. She hated the submission that came with her sex. She hated that she couldn't consciously direct her Sorte magic. She spent years in a depression, sleeping the days away and barely eating. Until one day, a commoner boy trying to outrun the guards nearly upended Desideria's litter carriage. He looked so small and defenseless. Desideria called upon her magic to aid him, and for the first time in her life, Sorte came to her *bidden*. The boy escaped, and Desideria's first selfless deed broke her ennui.

Her spirit restored, Desideria again clashed with the gilded cage she lived in. Her father demanded she use *her* Sorte to serve *him*. Her mother still admonished her to be modest and shy, to keep her eyes cast down behind the veil she hated. This time, Desideria decided to fight back. In an open act of rebellion, she refused all suitors. They could visit, they could bring gifts, but at the end of the courtship she would firmly reject them. In a *secretive* act of rebellion, she taught herself how to read—slowly and painstakingly—with old letters stolen from her father's desk.

More importantly, Desideria used her Sorte to transform Vodacce. She manipulated one of the Bernoulli sons to reduce taxes for commoners and create trade protections for his family's workers. She has to be careful, lest the Bernoulli's Vaticine allies discover her meddling, but Desideria is confident she can manage.

Desideria makes a natural ally to anyone trying to rise above the restrictions of their birth. She doesn't actively look for these causes, but her empathy lets her relate—she *knows* what it feels like to be held back. Her focus wanders, however: right now she has her sight on the Bernoullis, but it could easily be another family. Vodacce has *so much* inequality, and Desideria hasn't fully defined her own greater goal yet. For now, she goes from fight to fight as they cross her path—making her both an asset and potential liability.

Goals

Expose Facio Contarini's exploitation of workers.

Desideria planned to use her Sorte against Facio, but he found out and threatened her: if she makes a move, he'll expose her efforts to learn to read. She pretends to be cowed while seeking a new way forward, but will accept mutual destruction if that's what it takes.

Discover what happened to her childhood friend Julianna Onesta.

Julianna and Desideria grew up best friends, until Julianna became withdrawn and finally stopped visiting after a family tragedy. Desideria believes she wasn't supportive enough when her friend was grieving. She wants to find her, apologize and pick up the friendship.

Track down a Sorte teacher.

Desideria's teacher is paid and controlled by her father. She wants a teacher to teach her what *she* needs to become independent.

Playing Desideria Colomberia

Desideria paints the picture of a polite and shy noblewoman who has no thoughts or ambitions of her own. She drops this pretense only around close allies and then rails against the boundaries of her gender. She loves talking to foreign women about gender norms in *their* land. Highly empathic but young, Desideria fights against any form of oppression even if she unconsciously prioritizes her own inequality and that of other noblewomen. She immediately pushes back if she thinks an ally is trying to control her.

Desideria's raw power in Sorte is nearly unmatched, but she struggles to control the magic. This is especially true when she feels frightened or angry. Whenever she benefits from a lucky coincidence, or an unlikely ally, Desideria wonders if maybe she made it happen.

Kassidy Minihan

"Everyone has a chance to be a hero, especially in Avalon!"

INISMORE

Traits

Brawn	●●○○○
Finesse	●●●○○
Resolve	●●○○○
Wits	●●○○○
Panache	●●●●○

Skills

Aim	●○○○○	Perform	●●○○○
Athletics	●●○○○	Ride	●●○○○
Brawl	○○○○○	Sailing	○○○○○
Convince	●●●○○	Scholarship	○○○○○
Empathy	●●●○○	Tempt	○○○○○
Hide	●●○○○	Theft	●●○○○
Intimidate	○○○○○	Warfare	○○○○○
Notice	●●●○○	Weaponry	○○○○○

Advantages

Barterer (149), Virtuoso: Pan Pipes (152), Able Drinker (148), Quick Reflexes: (152), Second Story Work (150), Sorcery: Glamour (210), Camaraderie (151)

Quirks

Bard. Earn a Hero Point when you solve a problem by following an example set by a Legend.

Explorer. Earn a Hero Point when you set your eyes upon a sight few, if any, Théans have ever seen before.

Virtue: The Road

Friendly. Activate your Virtue when you meet a character (even a Villain) for the first time. She treats you as friendly for one scene.

Hubris: The Devil

Trusting. You receive a Hero Point when you accept someone's lies or lopsided deal.

Sorcery

Kassidy is the embodiment of Sæwine, The Sailor. His Major Trait is Panache, and his Minor Trait is Finesse. He knows the Major Glamour Resist Sorcery (Rank 1), and the Minor Glamour Vanish (Rank 2).

Story:

Kassidy Minihan

History

For as long as he could remember, Kassidy Minihan was not allowed to leave home for fear he would wander away, talking to someone who wasn't there. His mother, a simple seamstress in the little Inismore town of Colleen, was deathly afraid that her son was mad and that he would harm himself or others.

He wasn't mad. He was simply speaking to his færie friends. Kassidy was touched since birth by the powerful creatures that lived alongside people in Avalon. He tried to quell his mother's fears and explain that he and his friends meant no one any harm. Still, his mother kept him locked away, from any friends or outside contact. Kassidy's days were spent with his "invisible" friends, listening to their stories about heroes and fantastical creatures. He wished more than anything that he could be the hero of one of those stories.

When Kassidy turned 16, his mother fell ill. She brought Kassidy to her deathbed and apologized for keeping him locked away. She made him promise that once she died, he would go into the world and seek out happiness. Kassidy agreed and stayed to care for her until she passed. Only then did he pack up his belongings and take to the road, an innocent soul ready to explore the glorious world outside.

Of course once on the road, Kassidy discovered that not everything about life in Avalon was beauty and majesty. In many places, the once-venerated færies have been overturned, maligned or otherwise abused. There were people in need of help and those that would take advantage of those without power. Wide-eyed and innocent, Kassidy took to wandering, going where people needed his help the most.

Kassidy encountered the northern Inish town of Hallibury, under siege by Eisen mercenaries. Trapped in Avalon after their gold ran out, these mercenaries needed coin to return home and decided that the færies of the area could provide it. In response, the local færies threatened to take out their vengeance on everyone in Hallibury. Kassidy has stepped in to mediate a truce between humans and the local færies. During their dealings, the færies have let slip a secret: they know of the lost crown of Inismore. To Kassidy, it's time to become the hero he always dreamed.

Goals
Calm the færies after the incident with the Eisen mercenaries.

Kassidy arrived at Hallibury just in time to keep an all-out war from breaking out between færies and humans. With Eisen mercenaries raiding the area and harassing færie-folk for treasure to repair their boats, it's only a matter of time before the færies strike back. It's up to Kassidy to keep that from happening.

Find out where his father went before his birth.

Kassidy never knew his father and always wondered what happened to him. His mother's only clue was a silver ring with a blue stone she passed down to Kassidy upon her death. Now Kassidy wishes to seek out his father, in the hopes the man may know more about his mysterious connection to the færies.

Follow the færies to the lost crown of Inismore.

His good deeds helping the færies at Hallibury have given Kassidy the first clue to the secret location of the lost crown of Inismore. A trail of blue butterflies will lead him to someone who knows more about the crown. Kassidy knows that Inismore's lost crown is far more than a simple treasure and won't stop until he's recovered it for the sake of the kingdom.

Playing Kassidy Minihan

Kassidy Minihan is a true innocent, a wide-eyed, fresh-faced young man with an easy grin and no pretensions. He loves everything new and revels in every experience, tackling everything from long walks to hard work with gusto. Every emotion is amplified for Kassidy, and he expresses feelings like sorrow, fear, happiness and jealousy openly without masking anything. Kassidy loves to talk and does so animatedly, waving his hands and grinning from ear to ear. When he is dealing with færies, Kassidy is nearly transcendent, faraway and a little inhuman, but easily switches back into his happy self. He appears confused by how fearful people are of færies, and during confrontations, he is selfless, brave and a little too cocky to be completely safe.

Ludwig Schlammmann

"I promised to pull fifteen carts by my teeth while fighting off a horde of kobolds, shear thirty sheep and give your granny a foot rub all in one day? Well, let's get started then, it seems it is going to be a long day."

EISEN

Traits

Brawn	●●●○○
Finesse	●●○○○
Resolve	●●●○○
Wits	●●○○○
Panache	●●●○○

Skills

Aim	●○○○○	Perform	●●○○○
Athletics	●●●○○	Ride	○○○○○
Brawl	●●○○○	Sailing	○○○○○
Convince	●○○○○	Scholarship	○○○○○
Empathy	●●○○○	Tempt	○○○○○
Hide	●●○○○	Theft	○○○○○
Intimidate	●○○○○	Warfare	○○○○○
Notice	●●●○○	Weaponry	●●●○○

Advantages

Direction Sense (148), Duelist Academy: Eisenfaust (238), Indomitable Will (149), I Won't Die Here (154), Reputation: Brave (150), Streetwise (150)

Quirks

Ungetümjäger. Earn a Hero Point when you choose to hunt down an inhuman creature so it will never hurt anyone ever again.

Duelist. Earn a Hero Point when you resort to the edge of your blade to defend a noble ideal.

Virtue: The Glyph

Temperate. Activate your Virtue to prevent any magical effect (Sorcery, Artifacts, Monsters, etc.) from affecting you.

Hubris: The Fool

Curious. You receive a Hero Point when you investigate something.

Story:

Ludwig Schlammmann

History

It is said the Schlammmann was birthed from the very mud of Eisen. Just a babe, he crawled through the forests dark until he came upon an imp. The imp set upon the boy, but the schlammkind (mud child) was smart and as the imp dove down, he jumped onto its back. Using the imp's wings to steer, the babe flew high into the sky over Eisen.

He traveled for many days until he came to the home of a blacksmith. There, the child landed to rest. When the blacksmith's husband went out to the well to fetch water, he found the child sleeping in the shade. Overjoyed, the man picked up the child and brought him inside. The childless couple saw this babe as a gift from Eisen. They named the boy Ludwig.

The child grew up strong like his mother, wise like his father. By the time he was ten he had fought his first Horror and by the time he was 20, the Schlammmann was set to defeat his greatest foe—a Horror that rose in the east. Like Ludwig, it was birthed from the very earth of Eisen. Where the Schlammmann was born in a forest dark, this creature was bred in the blood soaked mud of battle and hungered for the flesh of the living.

Then, the Schlammmann vanished. The menace in the east faded from memory. Many say the Schlammmann defeated this creature or that a hero as great as the Schlammmann was enough to sate the creature's hunger. No one knew.

Ludwig awoke from slumber, a year later, in a haze. He remembered his name and could recite the name of every town he passed, yet he could not remember who he was. Looking for answers, Ludwig set upon a new journey—to find himself.

Traveling from town to town, Ludwig gathered hints as to who the Schlammmann truly is. Everywhere he went he heard tales of the folk hero of Eisen, and while many strike this kind-hearted man as tall tales, he does his best to live up to people's expectations.

When arriving in a town, if he is lucky, a permanent memory comes back to him, a puzzle piece he is able to keep from one night to the next. As he sleeps he dreams of bloody violence and a woman all in white, screaming in rage. He believes this woman must hold the key to unlock his memories and he must find her.

Goals

Hear a tale of the Schlammmann.

Ludwig yearns to hear more of who he was and what caused him to lose his memories. Each day he seeks out bards, travelers and folk who know his tales, so that he may get some sense of what he was put on this earth to do.

Find a woman with skin and hair as white as snow.

As he sleeps, the Schlammmann dreams of a woman pale as snow. He has heard rumors of a great lady in Hirschblut as pale as the moon and they have stuck with him. Perhaps, he will pay her a visit.

Regain his memories.

While relying on stories is fine and good, at the end of each day Ludwig's eyes close and he forgets most of what he has learned. Each time Ludwig travels to a place related to his old life, if the memories are strong enough, they come flooding back to him. He hopes by traveling and accomplishing heroic deeds, as the tales say the Schlammmann should, one day he will learn who he truly is.

Playing Ludwig Schlammmann

Ludwig can't remember anything from one day to the next, but this doesn't stop him from being a kind, trusting man. He loves to hear stories of the deeds he has done. Deep down a part of him knows some may be tall tales, but hearing that he has done good in the world brings him peace. The Schlammmann is not afraid to laugh at himself, as only a person who lives his life covered in mud can, and he is rarely seen without a smile on his face and a roaring laugh in his belly.

Quinn Leroy

"The gap between rich and poor in Montaigne is a serious problem. I believe there is no use letting ourselves be brought down by even the gravest of issues so why not try and have a good time while we attempt to fill the hole."

MONTAIGNE

Traits

Brawn	●●○○○
Finesse	●●●○○
Resolve	●●○○○
Wits	●●●○○
Panache	●●●○○

Skills

Aim	●○○○○	Perform	○○○○○
Athletics	●●○○○	Ride	○○○○○
Brawl	●●○○○	Sailing	○○○○○
Convince	●●●○○	Scholarship	○○○○○
Empathy	●●○○○	Tempt	●●○○○
Hide	●●○○○	Theft	●●●○○
Intimidate	●○○○○	Warfare	○○○○○
Notice	●●○○○	Weaponry	○○○○○

Advantages

Brush Pass (151), Camaraderie (151), Dynamic Approach (151), Reckless Takedown (150), Second Story Work (150), Streetwise (150)

Quirks

Criminal. Earn a Hero Point when you break the law in the pursuit of a noble endeavor.

Orphan. Earn a Hero Point when you put yourself in danger to ensure someone else doesn't have to be alone.

Virtue: Coins

Adaptable. Activate your Virtue to take your first Action before anyone else in a Round.

Hubris: The Hero

Foolhardy. You receive a Hero Point when your brash, cocky, or reckless actions cause trouble for you and another Hero.

Story:

Quinn Leroy

History

Like many terrible ideas, this one was born at a wine-stained table in the infamous bar *Auge À Cochon*. The night was nearing its end, and two people sat arguing, their speech slurred. "You are full of shit, Quinn! Crash the Duke's banquet! I'll bet you'll never even *smell* a banquet before meeting Theus." Quinn had never been good at backing down from a challenge, and so on a dare by her friend Antoine, Quinn began her long career as the most admired party crasher of Montaigne.

Antoine had good reason to be skeptical about her boasting. The Duke was not in the habit of inviting paupers to his table and Quinn Leroy raised herself on the streets. Left on the doorstep of the Vaticine orphanage as a babe, she ran away as fast as her legs could carry her when she was old enough to escape.

No more lessons, no more curfews and no more whips with the cane. She learned how to live with very little, where to find shelter when she ran out of rent and where to go for scraps when her stomach was growling. Odd jobs at the docks got her enough money to scrape by most of the time and while life was tough, she was completely free to follow her own path.

Quinn's first con started with a servant's stolen livery and a chicken and ended with her walking into the *Auge À Cochon* wearing one of the Duchess´ silk dresses, make-up and most expensive jewelry. The story is still told by the patrons who witnessed it. Getting into the Duke's estate was easy and the feeling she might get caught made the experience exhilarating. So, Quinn didn't leave it at that one dare, but kept trying again and again, heightening the stakes every time.

As stolen goods from her forays piled up in her moldy room in the docks, Quinn realized that she needed to do something with all her ill-gotten gains. She didn't feel bad about taking things from the lords and ladies. For every item she took they had a hundred more, but she did feel bad about keeping everything to herself. That made her no better than the greedy dukes, and possessions only tied a person down. She started selling things little by little and leaving purses of Guilders on the doorsteps of the poor and unfortunate. Quinn started with the servant and the chicken farmer from her first heist, richly recompensing them for their losses. After that she began leaving donations at orphanages, struggling farmers and city folk earning meager salaries from opulent masters.

Goals

Play a prank on Sir Leo Aurele Gilbert.

Sometimes Quinn doesn't wait for a festive occasion to show up at a noble's estate, some nobles require immediate attention. Sir Leo Aurele Gilbert, nicknamed the Serf's Scourge, is one such noble. Crushing taxation in his provinces and cruel punishment of those unable to pay causes suffering and despair among the peasantry. Time to teach the pompous buffoon a lesson.

Crash a party hosted by l'Empereur.

Since her first heist, Quinn has managed to con some of the highest and most well-respected nobles in Montaigne. If she could crash a party hosted by l'Empereur, it would be her *pièce de résistance*.

Steal the Crown Jewels of Avalon from Sir Gerald Maximilien.

The name Quinn Leroy may be known in high society, but her past as well as the details of her life on the streets are less well known. Someone has found out though, and they are threatening to harm her oldest friend Antoine if Quinn doesn't use her unique skills to steal the Crown Jewels of Avalon guarded by Sir Gerald Maximilien.

Playing Quinn Leroy

Quinn Leroy is a thrill-seeker. She loves the excitement of her heists, and you might even say she needs it. She never backs down from a challenge and even when she suspects it may be a trap, she is more likely to accept the danger than to decline. Although she may be a troublemaker and a thief, she does have her heart in the right place and would never take something from a person who would miss it.

Samo Sokolof

"I know it's tempting, but you cannot say yes to that thing. It's not only my experience I draw on. I've spoken to dozens of people who all suffered the same way, and I've spoken to none who have no regrets. Let me buy you a beer and explain what I've seen...but let's find a pub that's not so close to the university, first. I think that's my face on a wanted poster."

THE SARMATIAN COMMONWEALTH

Traits

Brawn	●●○○○
Finesse	●●○○○
Resolve	●●●○○
Wits	●●●○○
Panache	●●●○○

Skills

Aim	○○○○○	Perform	●●○○○
Athletics	○○○○○	Ride	●●○○○
Brawl	●●◐○○	Sailing	○○◐○○
Convince	●●●○○	Scholarship	●●●○○
Empathy	●●●○○	Tempt	●○○○○
Hide	●●◐○○	Theft	○○○○○
Intimidate	○○○○○	Warfare	○○○○○
Notice	●●○○○	Weaponry	○○○○○

Advantages

An Honest Misunderstanding (151), Indomitable Will (149), Miracle Worker (153), Team Player (150), Tenure (152), Time Sense (148)

Quirks

Professor. Earn a Hero Point when you use knowledge from an obscure text to solve a complicated problem.

Doctor. Earn a Hero Point when you tend to the injuries of a Villain or the innocents harmed by a Villain.

Virtue: The Witch

Intuitive. Activate your Virtue to ask the GM one yes-or-no question about an NPC. The GM must answer honestly and should be generous—for example, if there is a qualifier, he should tell you and explain more fully.

Hubris: The Glyph

Superstitious. You receive a Hero Point when you refuse to solve a problem using Sorcery, an artifact, or some other mystical effect that you don't trust.

Story:

Samo Sokolof

History

The fight took all night. Dr. Samo Sokolof stayed a few steps ahead of the monster, going back and forth between violent instinct and crushing doubt. The woman whom the *dievas* resurrected was once his wife, but now her hungry, soulless corpse wanted to devour him. Once he watched her die of a disease he couldn't cure. Now he killed her once more.

A despondent Samo closed the physician's office where he practiced and stopped eating, stopped sleeping. His friends convinced him life was worth living, but the scars of that night never healed.

Samo fell in with other ex-*losejai* who met secretly in a Szablewo tavern basement. Each had had a different experience with *dievai*, a different cluster of behaviors in their wake. Some behaviors, moodiness especially, appeared in almost all cases. Perhaps, he thought, humans who underwent trauma fell into mental states like diseases, but for the soul. He'd heard of melancholia, but there was more, much more.

When Samo presented his hypotheses to his university's medical society, the audience laughed him off the stage. Disease of the soul, not the body? Absurd. Unscientific. An embarrassment to medical theory! But when he started receiving death threats from the *Ratas*—and noticing shadowy figures stalking him—he wondered whether the *Ratas* might know something mainstream medicine didn't.

Now, he travels Théah giving secret lectures to interested university students. The mainstream medical establishment has all but stripped him of his license, forbidding doctors and students from listening—and yet they do, because even those who aren't sick have begun to realize he's right. Everywhere he goes, he reaches out to *losejai* burned by their *dievai* or by the *Ratas*. These people are lost, alone and afraid, unable to take their problems to anyone else. Samo is there to talk to them, to coach them through recovery and teach them techniques that helped him rejoin society.

Théan medicine thinks Dr. Sokolof a disingenuous, dangerous crackpot. But one day in the future, they'll hail him as the founder of modern psychology.

Goals

Hunt the Wailing Wight plaguing the roads.

Samo's not sure why only folk with conditions like his ever actually see the Wailing Wight. Have they some quality that makes them more sensitive to monsters? He has to strike a balance between researching a fascinating side effect and keeping more innocents out of the Wight's clutches.

Pass a law in the Sejm guaranteeing amnesty for remorseful losejai.

Various Sarmatian regions, especially in Vaticine Rzeczpospolita, make dealings with *dievai* illegal. Since city watches are uncommon here, angry mobs often attack suspected *losejai*. Legal protection for *losejai* who recant their deals won't stop those mobs, but it's still an important first step.

Identify the witch hunter murdering losejai.

Whoever's been murdering *losejai* can't be an Inquisitor. The Inquisition publicizes their kills, but this mystery witch hunter kills silently and hides the bodies. Also the witch hunter is probably not a Purifier, since some of the victims have been Purifiers themselves—unless this is an internecine quarrel he doesn't understand. But Samo's just one man, and this witch hunter, or hunters, could be anywhere.

Playing Samo Sokolof

Samo has gone through heartbreak, betrayal and trauma out of love for his wife. He lives with a melancholia, which he's only just beginning to understand. He's an excellent listener and is always willing to hear someone's side of the story, even if no one else believes or cares.

Dr. Sokolof has an excellent sense of humor. In the unpopular-medical-theories line of work, he needs one to survive, and it livens up otherwise dry psychological lectures. In spite of its disdain for him, he's never railed against the mainstream medical establishment or accused them of conspiring against him. He has faith in the system that trained him, even if his jokes about their inflexibility might not sound like it.

Tove Byströrm

"Stealin' the magic sword of Ur? Boring. But the cup of Hymin the Giant—it brews MAGICAL BEER. It lies in the hands of a tyrant, but..."

VESTENMENNAVENJAR

Traits

Brawn	●●●○○
Finesse	●●○○○
Resolve	●●●○○
Wits	●●●○○
Panache	●●○○○

Skills

Aim	○○○○○	Perform	●●●○○
Athletics	●●○○○	Ride	○○○○○
Brawl	●●○○○	Sailing	●●○○○
Convince	●○○○○	Scholarship	●○○○○
Empathy	●○○○○	Tempt	●○○○○
Hide	○○○○○	Theft	●○○○○
Intimidate	●●○○○	Warfare	○○○○○
Notice	●●○○○	Weaponry	●●●○○

Advantages

Camaraderie (151), Handy (149), Masterpiece Crafter: Weaving (151), Sea Legs (148), Seidr (153), Team Player (150)

Quirks

Crafter. Earn a Hero Point when you use everyday crafting skills to solve a problem deemed too complex for such a simple solution.

Skald. Earn a Hero Point when you use your knowledge as a Seidr to help another Hero to solve a problem or thwart a Villain.

Virtue: The Tower

Humble. Activate your Virtue to gain 2 Hero Points instead of 1 when you activate your Hubris or trigger a Quirk.

Hubris: The Sun

Proud. You receive a Hero Point when your Hero refuses an offer of aid—for example, if a Hero tries to spend a Hero Point to give you Bonus Dice and you turn her down.

Story:

Tove Byström

History

Tove was born during the worst storm, when the sea drowned the land. The ocean took Tove's father that night, but left the newborn in her mother's arms—a trade-off Tove's mother deemed harsh but fair. Feeling, perhaps, that it still owed the babe a debt, the sea has been exceptionally good to Tove. The first ship she boarded came across an Avalonian monastery and returned to Vestenmennavenjar laden with gold. The second was captained by Ketil Ulfsson, who gave Tove her first child. The third vessel—well, it sank, but Tove alone made it back to shore.

After a decade of sailing, Tove commissioned her own ship: the *Sultry Dog*. Tove and her crew were famous on the oceans, until a Castillian ship sank the *Sultry Dog*, and Tove was once again the sole survivor. She hasn't been to sea since, unable to bear the thought of being left alone once more—suddenly the sea's blessing seemed more like a curse.

Tove abandoned seafaring and tried an assortment of trades. She's a poor wood-carver and a fine weaver. She took up and quickly abandoned skald training and retains some skill in Seidr from that time. Finally settling down in a small village near the coast, she now makes a living as a fisher—the sea practically drives its bounty into her nets, as if still caring for its long-lost lover. At night, Tove painstakingly weaves her magic in kerchiefs and nets. These she trades with heroes for services and information, though she never accepts payment in coin.

Tove is as fertile as the ocean, and she has seven children by various fathers. She doesn't make a good mother, and mostly lets her own mother and neighbors raise the children. She loves them though, and has taught each the Grumfather Cycle—the only thing of her skald training, other than Seidr, that stuck—and how to wield a weapon. Tove firmly believes a sharp blade and good story will get you anywhere, so these she passed to her children.

Following her restless feet, Tove frequently joins heroes on their journey. She lends them her magic and advice, and once they triumph she suggests another journey—and another and just *one* more for old times' sake. She has an unending thirst for adventure, but more importantly she has a profound sense of equality and justice—Tove always finds one more tyrant to bring down and one more downtrodden to liberate.

Goals

Save her small-time pirate son from Einar Ibsen.

Ibsen doesn't know his captive is Tove's son Ulf, so she has to move carefully lest the villain use the boy against her. She has discreetly put out word to Ibsen's rivals that she can pay for information about the boy's location and security.

Train a student in rune magic.

Fearing that Seidr will die out as Vestenmennavenjar becomes increasingly civilized under the carls, Tove seeks a student to pass her knowledge on to. She wants someone wild and stubborn, with an abiding love for Vestenmennavenjar.

Catch the ancient Nix fish that escaped her nets.

Nix never stop growing, and Tove caught one bigger than three people, but it escaped her enchanted nets. Tove doesn't know if the fish was a herald of the gods, or simply that her magic was too weak, but she intends to find out.

Playing Tove Byström

Whatever the plan is, Tove is too old for it. Her magic isn't as strong as it once was, her back hurts and she just wants to stay home and drink tea. Then, *just* as the adventure is about to pass her by, Tove gets a twinkle in her eye and with an exclamation of "Gotcha!", grabs her ever-waiting travel bag. Her magic *has* weakened, but that does not diminish her sense of adventure.

Tove loves to meet people and listen to their stories. She tells her own, too, but only half of them are true. Despite her outgoing demeanor, she's fiercely independent—two shipwrecks have taught her not to get attached to people. Always willing to help and meddle in other people's lives, she resists any efforts to return the favor: Tove doesn't need any help, and her business is her own!

Vasilii

"Are you hungry? I've got some bread you can share and a fire. No, I don't need anything in return. And maybe, after you've eaten, we can try to find your parents."

USSURA

Traits

Brawn	●●○○○
Finesse	●●○○○
Resolve	●●○○○
Wits	●●●●○
Panache	●●○○○

Skills

Aim	○○○○○	Perform	●○○○○
Athletics	●●●○○	Ride	○○○○○
Brawl	●●○○○	Sailing	○○○○○
Convince	●●○○○	Scholarship	○○○○○
Empathy	●●○○○	Tempt	●●○○○
Hide	●●●○○	Theft	●●●○○
Intimidate	●●○○○	Warfare	○○○○○
Notice	○○○○○	Weaponry	○○○○○

Advantages

Brush Pass (151), Quick Reflexes: Hide (152), Reckless Takedown (150), Second Story Work (150), Sorcery: Mother's Touch, Sorcery: Mother's Touch (217), Survivalist (148)

Quirks

Touched by Matushka. Earn a Hero Point when you teach someone a lesson in a way that would make Matushka proud.

Orphan. Earn a Hero Point when you put yourself in danger to ensure someone else doesn't have to be alone.

Virtue: The Tower

Humble. Activate your Virtue to gain 2 Hero Points instead of 1 when you activate your Hubris or trigger a Quirk.

Hubris: The Glyph

Superstitious. You receive a Hero Point when you refuse to solve a problem using Sorcery, an artifact, or some other mystical effect that you don't trust.

Sorcery

Vasilii has the Gifts Command (Raven), See (Bear), See (Raven) and Sew. Her Restrictions are Kindness and Moderation.

Story:

Vasilii

History

Matushka takes care of orphaned children. Or so legend has it. She didn't come for Vasilii and her two younger brothers though—when Vasilii went to look for her and found Grandmother's chicken hut, she wasn't even home. But Vasilii showed her: if Matushka wouldn't *give* any help, Vasilii would *take* it. She stole a magical sewing needle and a glass eye that night. The sewing needle lets Vasilii repair anything it can pierce, from clothes to bookbindings. The glass eye allows her to see through the eyes of any raven. Between these two boons, Vasilii provides for her brothers and keeps them safe as they travel.

The greatest thing Vasilii took from Matushka's hut was herself. Her entire life, Vasilii had to contend with people insisting she was a boy. When she looked in Matushka's silver mirror, she saw her true self—and from that point so did everyone else. Leaving the hut that day, Vasilii had a new body and a sense of gratitude she could never forget. Now, in the body written upon her soul, Vasilii is proud. Strong. Woman.

Matushka was impressed by the young woman's spirit, but also scorned by her thefts. She allowed Vasilii to keep the items and magic she stole, but placed a curse on the woman. For her digressions she may never take that which is not freely given.

Vasilii aids anyone who needs it. She complains loudly while she does so, but the truth is she likes helping people. She goes the extra mile to see people home safely and presses enough coin in their hand to see them through the winter. She especially cares about children and extends her protection to any abandoned child she comes across. She has collected quite a motley. Vasilii teaches the older kids to fight, hunt, cook and take care of the younglings. When Vasilii touches down in a city, the group fans out to entertain, steal and trade their way across the area, to pack up again when Vasilii does.

Vasilii would dearly like to learn Mireli, but has yet to find a teacher. Still, she's watched enough duels to fake the fighting style. While this bluff doesn't con an actual dueling master, it cows the less informed. Despite being genuinely handy with a sword, Vasilii uses this trick to bluff her way out of a confrontation if need be.

Goals

Lift Matushka's curse, which prevents her from stealing.

Since her foray into Matushka's hut, Vasilii cannot manage to take anything that isn't freely given. This stifles her efforts to provide for her extended family and redistribute wealth. Does a merchant really *need* all that gold? Exactly, it would be much better off with the peasants. Now if only she could persuade Matushka.

Return to Matushka's hut to steal a magical raven's heart.

In addition to redistributing wealth and uplifting the poor, Vasilii also has her eye on a raven's heart she saw in Matushka's hut. The heart allows her to transform into a raven and fly, but Vasilii doesn't know that—she just wants it because everything else she *redistributed* from Grandmother's hut has come in very handy.

Investigate rumors that her family descends from Matushka.

Vasilii *stole* from Grandmother Winter. Yet she's alive and well, apart from one little curse. The answer might lie in a peasant's story—the old man told Vasilii that he knew her parents, and that her mother is a granddaughter of Matushka. Vasilii seeks to debunk or corroborate this tall tale.

Playing Vasilii

Vasilii worked hard for everything she has, and she never apologizes to anyone. She is wary of Matushka though, finding the one curse quite enough, and carefully follows Grandmother Winter's rules while complaining loudly about them. Vasilii is always munching on something. Hard cheeses and fresh bread are her favorite foods, but she has an unending appetite and tries just about anything.

Vasilii is gruff in her dealings with others, even when she's helping them, but she has a soft spot for abandoned children. This comes from a caring heart, but it also taps into a deep and abiding anger at her own lonely youth. Confronting parents who abandon their children leaves Vasilii vulnerable, as she struggles with her anger towards such cruel folk.

Zaltko Karyevskov

"I'm a revolutionist in a land of traditionalists, but I have seen that change is possible, and I will not rest until I can bring justice for my people."

USSURA • THE RILASCIARE

Traits

Brawn	●●○○○
Finesse	●●○○○
Resolve	●●●○○
Wits	●●●○○
Panache	●●●○○

Skills

Aim	○○○○○	Perform	●●●○○
Athletics	●●○○○	Ride	●○○○○
Brawl	●○○○○	Sailing	○○○○○
Convince	●●●○○	Scholarship	○○○○○
Empathy	●●●○○	Tempt	●●○○○
Hide	○○○○○	Theft	●○○○○
Intimidate	●●○○○	Warfare	○○○○○
Notice	●●○○○	Weaponry	○○○○○

Advantages

Connection: Ussuran Revolutionaries (149), Extended Family (149), Handy (149), Inspire Generosity (149), Large (148), Specialist: Convince (154), Virtuoso: Public Speaking (152)

Quirks

Progressivist. Earn a Hero Point when you risk life and limb to secure a piece of advanced technology.
Performer. Earn a Hero Point when you use your crowd-pleasing skills for something more than making a few coins.

Virtue: The Sun

Glorious. Activate your Virtue when you are the center of attention. For the next Risk, when you determine Raises, every die counts as a Raise.

Hubris: The Thrones

Stubborn. You receive a Hero Point when your Hero is stubborn and refuses to change his mind in the face of evidence.

Story:

Zaltko Karyevskov

History

Whenever Zaltko Karyevskov makes a big decision, he always asks himself, what would his Zoya have said about it? The question invokes an image of her with that scrutinizing smile she'd have when he just told her one of his world changing ideas. The memories of Zoya warm his heart and the question helps him steer away from rash decisions. He wants to change the world, or at least Ussura, but if his beautiful wife taught him anything, it's that all his passion is nothing without a well-constructed plan.

Zaltko saw it numerous times: *muzhiks* work their hands bloody to stock up for the long winter, then the *boyars* sweep in collecting a tithe while the *muzhik* barely scrape by. As a boy, Zaltko questioned his father, how could landowners reap so many rewards for so little work? His father replied, "It has always been that way."

Baron Feodor working his beautiful Zoya to death was the final straw. Zaltko refused to stand by any longer as the rich reaped profit from the backs of the poor. A man of impressive stature, Zaltko pulled the Baron from his bed one night and forced him into the fields to work. The grieving widower had no purpose, but having no heart to murder, he believed at least he would have the satisfaction of seeing the Baron humiliated.

The Baron lived with his servants, ate their meals, performed their chores and saw the abhorrent conditions he placed upon them. Zaltko never dared hope that after a month of hard toil Baron Feodor would repent and realize the folly of his actions. When it actually happened, Zaltko realized maybe some good could come from his own misery, and the pain in his aching heart could be lessened.

Now, Zaltko travels from town to town and speaks to the peasants about his vision of a better Ussura. His ardent speeches no longer draw a hesitant crowd looking for amusement but growing groups of excited *muzhiks* walking miles through rough weather to hear him. Doing more than just speaking, when he sees injustice on his way, Zaltko takes up arms against it.

It seems to Zaltko that Ussura is certainly ready for change. With the Czar and Czarina fighting it should be easier for a new leader to step in, but that leader is not going to be one person, it can be every person. the Commonwealth has just shown the Ussuran people what the future can look like. If only those people weren't so set in their ways. A mountain range changes more in 80 years than the Ussurans. But Zaltko isn't giving up; if a man like Feodor can change, so can the rest of Ussura.

Goals

Muster a peasant-led army to defend Ussura.

Zaltko knows he needs the support of the Ussuran people to have any hope of changing the nation. A revolution cannot be fought alone, nor does Zaltko wish to. He hopes to open the eyes of the *muzhiks* so they see the injustice of the system that tradition has forced on them and take up arms against it.

Smuggle a Sarmatian democratic agitator into Ussura.

Zaltko is traveling Ussura and rallying the *muzhiks* in the villages. If a Sarmatian can tell the Ussuran people about the success of the Golden Liberty, they will know democracy is not just a fantasy but a realistic possibility.

Secure the aid of a banker to help him conceal his stolen wealth.

The money Zaltko took from Feodor is useful if it can fuel his cause, but he needs to make sure it is concealed well or else it will just land him in a jail cell. It might also put him in a precarious position with his poor *muzhik* supporters if he turns out to be rich.

Playing Zaltko Karyevskov

Zaltko is a man with fire in his eyes. He was not born to work the fields although he would do that with the same passion and dedication he seems to bring to all his endeavors. He has the kind of voice you want to listen to and the keen intelligence to word his ideas. He may seem like a dangerous fanatic to his enemies, but even though he fights to win, he understands that the ends don't always justify the means.

Chapter 3

Villains

VILLAINS

Villains of Théah

7th Sea is not a game about shades of gray. In other games or types of fiction, a Villain might simply be misguided. The "dark hero" is a common character archetype, and many compelling stories surround issues and subjects where the "bad guys" are not necessarily wrong, or evil. **7th Sea** is not that type of game.

A Villain sees the world as a thing that should serve him. This might mean he wishes to reshape the world into his own image, or sees it as nothing more than a coffer waiting to be plundered. A Villain is willing to do whatever it takes, to kill whoever stands before him, to burn any city that stands up against him, in order to accomplish his goals.

This does not mean that the two teams are set in stone, but it does mean that they are distinct. Heroes can fall, and Villains can find redemption, but there is never any question as to which team a character belongs to, especially once all the facts are known.

Villains and Conflict

In storytelling, one of the biggest questions authors face is, "How do you build up excitement for conflict between protagonists and antagonists?" **7th Sea** GMs might ask, "How do you build up excitement for conflict between Heroes and Villains?" What is going to make this conflict interesting and exciting? What will hook the players and make them want to explore the plot you have laid out?

In most fiction, you do this by providing something the Hero wants to protect, which the Villain then puts in danger. Your Hero has a son she loves—so the Villain abducts the Hero's son. Your Hero is a devoted patriot—so the Villain betrays the Hero's nation. Your Hero holds a particular virtue or ideal in high esteem—so the Villain spits on your Hero's values.

In **7th Sea**, this process has been simplified: Half of the work is already done for you, the GM, because the Heroes have already been created. All you need to do is discover what your Heroes care about.

Then your Villain threatens it, takes it away, or destroys it. In short—make it *personal*. Believe us when we say you have never seen a player go after his adversary so relentlessly as the thief who stole his mother's sword, the assassin who murdered his father in cold blood, or the soldier who burned down his childhood home.

The Right Target

If you are looking for something beautiful for your Villain to destroy, there are three easy ways to pick the right target.

First, look at your Heroes' Stories. If a Story mentions an important place or person, put your Villain in direct conflict with that place or person. Does your Hero want to win the heart of a Vodacce nobleman? The Villain showers the nobleman with gifts and attention—and perhaps even uses her influence to arrange her own marriage to the object of the Hero's desire. Is there an important event in your Hero's past, or a mystery they wish to solve? Put your Villain in the center of that event or mystery, perhaps even as the ultimate cause. Does your Hero seek some specific treasure or artifact? Perhaps the Villain killed the Hero's mentor to get a secret map of its location, and she has already set sail for the uncharted island.

Second, give the Heroes someone or something to love. Does your Hero have a dockside tavern that she always visits? Give the tavern keeper a name and a personality quirk. Every time the Heroes return here, make sure that he remembers their names and favorite drinks. Encourage the Heroes to get to know him and look forward to talking to him, even if it is only for a few seconds at a time. Then put him in peril—maybe he is being hassled by a local loan shark because of his father's debts—and that loan shark works for the local crime boss.

Third, have the Villain target the Hero directly. This is especially effective if the Hero has encountered and thwarted the Villain's underlings before. A Villain tends to take that kind of thing personally, and while she can ignore a few annoyances here and there, eventually she will get tired of all these diversions and go on the attack. RPG players are notoriously territorial—they like to feel that the only action taking place is on their terms. Have the Villain remind them that this is not true. As the Heroes celebrate a victory, have a Villain crash the party. Maybe she steals something, or leaves a calling card (literally or figuratively). Have the Villain mock the Hero and his efforts to stop her. If you want the Hero to take a personal interest in fighting the Villain, have the Villain take a personal interest in the Hero.

All of these efforts, however, should be aimed at the final confrontation. Your ultimate goal as the GM is to put the Hero to the test and see if he has what it takes to succeed. You should want him to succeed, of course, but you should also make him bleed and sweat and suffer for it. An easy victory is bland—but a hard-fought one, unbelievably sweet.

Beware Your Favorite Villain

What you should absolutely avoid as the GM is placing your Villains on a pedestal. This is dangerous because it's tempting to want the Villain to win and so, to stack the odds in her favor. "Well, the Hero doesn't have to win here; he can win later," you might think.

The cardinal sin is when later never comes.

Balancing the build-up of a conflict with its payoff is one of the hardest things to do in any fiction. The build has to last long enough to ratchet up the tension and drama, but not so long that the audience starts to cool down and lose interest.

A good general guideline is the *rule of three*. The first encounter sets the stage, and the Villain should escape; the Hero wins, but at a cost. The second encounter ratchets up the stakes, and the Villain triumphs while the Hero escapes. The third encounter is the climax, resulting in an extremely hard-fought and final victory for the Hero.

This is a simple and straightforward blueprint for how to structure a Villainous conflict. You can have more conflicts if you want, but every single confrontation should escalate the overarching conflict and result in a change in the relationship between the two.

Remember—you *want* your Hero to win—you just want to make him sweat as much as you can, first. You want him to feel like he *earned* it.

Villains and Schemes

When a Villain sets her sights on something she wants, she creates a Scheme to get it. In this case, "it" can be anything tangible or intangible—such as obtaining a Dracheneisen sword; forcing a swordmaster to teach her a new dueling style; or stealing a boatload of guilders. These Schemes enhance her power and prestige, but also give Heroes a chance to thwart her before she grows stronger.

In this section we provide a system for Villains' Schemes that adds to the mechanics presented in the Core Rulebook (page 194), structuring them more like Heroic Stories, with discrete steps that Villains can follow to advance their Schemes. This system is designed to replace the core rules, offering the GM a chance to create more nuanced and detailed Schemes for Villains.

Schemes as Stories

Instead of simply building a bank of Influence, a Villain can use his Schemes to gain specific benefits. He can create a Scheme to gain an Advantage, increase his Strength, or corrupt an NPC Hero. These kinds of Schemes have variable costs based on the effect that the Villain wishes to achieve.

You can think of Schemes as the Villain's version of a Story. At the beginning of each session, a Villain can spend Influence to create one (and only one) Scheme. When a Villain creates a Scheme, the GM decides what the Villain wants to gain once the Scheme is achieved. The Villain then pays the Scheme's cost and can assign any Lesser Villains or Brutes in her employ to the completion of the Scheme. Heroes that wish to stop a Villain's Scheme must face any such Lesser Villains or Brutes in order to stop the Scheme from coming to fruition.

Each Scheme has a number of steps equal to the amount of Influence invested in them. If a Villain wants to increase her Strength from 6 to 7, for example, she would need to create a seven-step Scheme that would make her a more formidable opponent. She might send a Brute Squad to steal a magic sword or try to complete a ritual that would give her incredible strength.

At the end of every game session, any unresolved Schemes advance by one step. In other words, any villainous plot the Heroes have not yet thwarted gets one step closer to coming to fruition. Maybe the Brute Squad figures out where the sword is hidden, or the Villain manages to secure a few crucial ritual components.

Any unspent Danger Points can also go toward resolving Schemes. One Danger Point causes a single Scheme to advance one additional step. Multiple steps can be completed in this way, but each subsequent step costs an additional Danger Point (i.e., advancing a Scheme by one step costs 1 Danger Point, but advancing it by a second step costs 2 additional points, for a total of 3). The GM decides how to allocate these Danger Points.

Once a Scheme has gone through the number of steps equal to its cost, the Scheme is completed and the Villain gains the Scheme's benefit. Successfully completing any Scheme results in the Influence invested being returned to the Villain, in addition to the Scheme benefit listed. For example, if your Villain successfully completes a Scheme with three steps to increase their Influence, she regains the 3 Influence she spent to create the Scheme and 3 Influence for the Scheme benefit.

Revealing Schemes

Remember that the effects of Schemes are not instantaneous or spontaneous. Part of your job as GM is to show these effects occurring over time, or to make certain that you portray your Villain as pursuing these Schemes. For example, if the Villain has a Scheme to turn a Hero to Villainy, you should make sure that you have a general plan for how he intends to do that and that you reflect this plan in the Villain's actions.

In short, your objective when creating Schemes is to push your Villain toward conflict with the Heroes, with the intent that your Heroes will stop some (but probably not all) of the Villain's Schemes. *You want your villain, eventually, to fall.* And when he does fall, it is in an appropriately dramatic and epic fashion, maybe taking somebody else down with him.

To achieve this, your Heroes must find out about the Villain's Schemes. After all, it is difficult for a Hero to stop a Villainous ritual when he does not know the ritual is happening until it is already over. The best way to go about this is to show your Villain taking action in accordance with one of his Schemes.

Does your Villain have a Scheme to gain possession of one of the masks of El Vagabundo? Your Heroes should get word that the Villain's head spy is asking a lot of questions regarding the Society's agents.

Your Villain is planning to learn a new Dueling Style? Rumor has it that the Villain has put out a bounty on a swordmaster of the Aldana style, explicitly stating that the master is to be brought in alive.

Do not simply tell the Heroes that your Villain is up to something fishy. Reveal an action the Villain takes in order to achieve his objective, and let the players start pulling at the threads. A player is a lot more committed to thwarting a plot that she feels like she's done the work to uncover.

Lesser Villains

Not every Villain has her own kingdom, guild or army. Many work under the thumb of a greater Villain for any number of motivations (loyalty, promise of rewards, intimidation, etc.). A Villain has the option to "Hire or recruit another Villain" (CORE RULEBOOK, page 195), but this person does not necessarily need to be on the same power level as herself. Instead, this can be a Lesser Villain.

These lieutenants function identically to other Villains in most ways except one—Lesser Villains do not have Influence. Any Influence needed to accomplish a Lesser Villain's tasks is spent by the boss, and any Influence gained from actions goes to the boss. This puts a Lesser Villain somewhere between a regular Villain and a Brute Squad: capable of causing real trouble for the Heroes, but lacking the real power to be trouble without someone backing him up.

A Lesser Villain might also be on the lookout for how to break free and establish her own Influence. This might happen when a Lesser Villain manages to escape or avoid conflict with Heroes, while her boss is not so fortunate. Often this means a power vacuum develops as the boss is rendered unable to manage his affairs. Lesser Villains are usually in a unique position to take control of such a situation, due to their knowledge of the organization's workings and prominent players.

If a Lesser Villain's actions directly result in her boss gaining more Influence than his Strength in a single game session, the Lesser Villain's Strength increases by 1. If a Lesser Villain's Strength would surpass her boss', she can choose to break free and establish her own Influence, starting at 1. This sort of betrayal is rarely taken well by bosses. After all, there is no rule that says a Villain cannot target another Villain.

Brutes and Influence

The often nameless and faceless guards, goons, thieves, bandits and ne'er-do-wells in the employ of Villains are called Brutes. Brutes can neither gain nor spend Influence, but any actions taken by Brutes that would result in the gain of Influence are gained by the Villain who employed them.

If a Brute Squad's actions result in the gain of at least 5 Influence in a single game session, one of the Brutes gains a promotion—they become a Lesser Villain, complete with a name and brief biography. A Lesser Villain created in this way is Strength 5. The Brute Squad does not lose any Strength, and remains in the employ of their boss under the command of the Lesser Villain.

INFLUENCE COSTS

SCHEME BENEFIT	INFLUENCE COST
Gain a new Advantage	Advantage cost x3
Increase Strength	New Strength Rank
Increase Influence	Current Influence Rank
Gain the effect from spending Favor with a Secret Society	Favor cost
Corrupt a Heroic NPC to Villainy	Hero's Strength Rank x2, or Hero's highest Trait x2

Villains and Duels

Once a Hero has broken through all of a Villain's defenses, his final confrontation may very well result in a duel. Here we have provided an expanded example of one of these duels, so you can see exactly how this would happen.

Dominique's rival is Renard, a Villainous spy from Montaigne. Dominique has spent months eroding Renard's Influence, defeating his allies and foiling his Schemes. The two have had multiple encounters in the past, and the GM believes it is now time for a dramatic end.

While the Heroes are infiltrating one of l'Empereur's palaces in a Dramatic Sequence, the GM lays a trail of breadcrumbs for Dominique. He knows how to interest her—she finds a letter bearing Renard's seal, she overhears a guard griping about having to make special accommodations for l'Empereur's "esteemed guest," and she catches a glance of a figure wearing a black cloak and an outlandish red hat slipping around a corner (Renard leads a group of spies called *La Chapeaux Rouges*, "The Red Hats").

The Hero group's other objectives are time-sensitive, so Dominique urges her friends to go on without her while she faces Renard. She corners him in a trophy room in the palace.

Due to the relationship between the two characters, as well as the circumstances involved, the GM believes the two should have a duel. While he is not entirely certain how it will turn out, he believes this might be a good time for the conflict to end, if Dominique can best Renard. The two have come face-to-face in the past, but Renard has always managed to escape or defeat her. If Dominique is clever, and maybe a little lucky, this time things will be different.

> GM: Renard draws his rapier and holds the blade up before him in a sarcastic salute. "I see the scar I gave you on Sandoval Island has healed nicely," he says. "It surprises me that you are so eager for another one—the first seemed quite painful at the time."
>
> Dominique: I reach up and pull the two stilettos out of my hair. I say, "I have had enough of your lies, Renard! I will not let you destroy any more innocent lives! This is your end!"
>
> GM: "Bold words. Let's see if your blades can back them up." Renard drops into a dueling stance. Get your dice!
>
> Dominique: I have 4 Finesse and 4 Weaponry. I've also got the Fencer Advantage, so that's 1 more die. I have a total of 9 dice. I'm going to use Boucher style, with my two stilettos.
>
> GM: Remember, you get bonus dice for Flair as well, since you haven't used Weaponry yet in this scene and you've described your action. That means you have 11 dice. Renard has 13 dice. He's using the Torres style.
>
> Dominique: "Torres? I see you have been studying, Renard! Still stinging after our last duel? To be fair, your Valroux did leave something to be desired..."
>
> GM: Renard struggles to keep himself from snarling in anger. "Take care of your tongue, mouse. If you don't, I will carve it out!" Let's roll!
>
> Dominique: I'm going to spend a Hero Point for a bonus die, so that will give me 12. (Rolls dice.) I have 6 Raises.
>
> GM: All right. Renard does not spend anything yet. (Rolls dice.) He has 7 Raises.
>
> Dominique: Close!
>
> GM: So on 7, Renard will take his first Action. He steps toward you and lets the tip of his sword dip down and to the side, taking a quick swipe at your arm. He performs Feint. That deals 1 Wound, and the next time you take a Wound this Round, you'll take an extra Wound.
>
> Dominique: Ouch! All right, 1 Wound.
>
> GM: Next is 6.
>
> Dominique: I have 6!
>
> GM: So does Renard, and Villains get to go first. As your guard dips to the side to defend against his feint, he attacks high and across your shoulder. He performs Slash. That will deal 5 Wounds to you, since Renard is Strength 10 and his Weaponry is considered half of his Strength for Maneuvers.
>
> Dominique: Okay. So 5 Wounds. Wait, is that counting the extra one that he has from Feint?
>
> GM: No, you're right. So 5 Wounds, plus the extra one from Feint. His Slash deals a total of 6 Wounds.

Dominique: That stings! I'm going to spend my Action to Parry that, and reduce that by 3. So I'll take 3 Wounds. Added to my 1 from before, that's a total of 4 Wounds. No Dramatic Wound yet!

GM: Sounds good. Next is 5. Renard takes a small step back after your little exchange, then stutter-steps forward again and makes a quick thrust at your face. He will perform Feint again, so that's 1 Wound, and the next time you take Wounds you take one more.

Dominique: There's my first Dramatic Wound.

GM: Renard laughs. "I do not know if that one is deep enough to scar, ma chère, but give me another chance. I can do better."

Dominique: All right, it's time to stop playing around. I'm going to step in close and draw his guard to one side. My turn to Feint!

GM: Renard takes 1 Wound. Next is 4. Renard will Slash again, for 6 more Wounds—5 for his Slash, and 1 for his previous Feint.

Dominique: Perfect! Okay, my turn. I'm going to use Riposte. That will prevent 3 Wounds, and deal 3 back to him—plus one extra Wound, since I just used Feint. So I have 1 Dramatic Wound, and 3 Wounds on my next tier.

GM: Renard has taken 5 Wounds! On his turn—

Dominique: Wait, I'm not done. I'm going to use my Dueling Style ability, Boucher Step. That lets me perform two Maneuvers back to back. So, next I'm going to perform Bash. That deals 1 Wound to him, and reduces the damage he deals with his next Maneuver that deals Wounds.

GM: That adds one more Wound for a total of 6. You step in close to avoid his Slash. He still gets a bit of your upper arm and a splash of blood, but now you find yourself inside his guard and cut a deep gash along the inside of his forearm. Before he can recover, you slap the pommel of your stiletto across his jaw for the Bash. His head whips to the side and a spray of blood flies from his mouth.

Dominique: I smile and step back again, spinning my stilettos between my fingers. "Want another kiss, Renard? Come and get it."

GM: Renard grits his teeth and growls angrily. "You WILL pay for that, rat!" Next is 3. Renard stalks forward, clearly abandoning all pretense of Finesse, intent on just inflicting pain. He screams in frustration and rage, and spends all 3 of his remaining Raises to Lunge. That's going to be a total of 8 Wounds—3 from his Raises, and 5 from his effective Weaponry.

Dominique: Does my Bash reduce that?

GM: Yes, it will be reduced by your Weaponry—so by 3. However, this is a Lunge, so you can't avoid or prevent the Wounds. So the remaining 5 Wounds are unavoidable.

Dominique: Oof! 5 Wounds! The first one fills up that tier, the second one gives me my second Dramatic Wound. So that's 2 Dramatic Wounds total, and three on my next tier.

GM: Next up is 2. Renard has no Raises left, so you get to do whatever you want for the rest of the Round and he has nothing to say about it.

Dominique: Time to make him bleed! First I'm going to Slash for 3 Wounds.

GM: Okay, 3 Wounds. And your final Raise?

Dominique: I'm going to do my own Lunge, for a total of 4 more Wounds.

GM: Cool! The first 3 Wounds take him to 9. The first Wound from your Lunge will bring him to 10 Wounds, and the second will give him his first Dramatic Wound. The remaining 2 Wounds will go to his next tier. So, Renard has taken 1 Dramatic Wound and 2 Wounds.

Dominique: Sounds like Renard won't go down without a fight.

GM: Nope! So Renard lets out an enraged roar and rushes toward you, just barreling forward with all of his body weight, and drives the point of his rapier into you. You see him coming and rather than moving aside to try to evade him, you step in deep and drive both of your blades to the hilt into his shoulders. The two of you struggle there for a few seconds, face to face. Then, as one, you both shove away from each other. You're both bleeding heavily, and your weapons are dripping. The room is completely silent aside from the two of you panting for breath and the quiet patter of blood drops landing on the stone floor.

Dominique: "Hah! Is that all you have, Renard? The famed leader of the Red Hats can't last for more than a minute with a real woman?"

GM: Renard coughs through blood-spattered lips and wipes the back of one leather-gloved hand across his mouth. "I'm going to enjoy watching you bleed to death, cur!"

Dominique: (Laughs) "Oh, it sounds like I struck a nerve! Come on then! Enough foreplay!"

GM: All right, time to roll dice again. Unless you want to surrender?

Dominique: To him? Never!

GM: I didn't think so. Renard is still at 13 dice, but you have 2 Dramatic Wounds, so he gets two bonus dice. That puts him at 15. He is also going to spend a Danger Point, and go to 17 dice. As the two of you circle one another for a moment, he reaches down to his belt and draws a dagger into his left hand. He's going to change to Valroux style.

Dominique: Pulling out all the stops, huh? Let's do it! I have the same die pool as before—9 dice—plus a Dramatic Wound, so that's a bonus die. I'm going to spend 2 Hero Points this time, so that brings my total to 12. I'm still using Boucher style. I am also going to spend a Hero Point to activate Joie de Vivre—any die that rolls a three or less counts as a 10.

GM: Remember to add one bonus die for Flair from your banter with Renard. That gives you 13 dice. Sounds like the spymaster is in trouble. Anything else?

Dominique: Not yet. I have a few tricks up my sleeve, still.

GM: All right then. (Rolls dice.) Renard has 8 Raises.

Dominique: (Rolls dice.) I have 11 Raises.

GM: Nice! It looks like you're up first at 11!

Dominique: Slash! I step in close and swipe a stiletto toward his eyes! That's 3 Wounds.

GM: Renard now has 5 Wounds on his second tier. It's still your turn, on 10.

Dominique: Bash! While I'm in close I'm going to drive the point of my elbow into his stomach and get him winded. That's 1 Wound, and the next time he deals Wounds he does 3 less.

GM: Okay, 6 Wounds on Renard's second tier. On 9, it's still your turn!

Dominique: Slash! I'm going to reverse the grip on my stiletto and drive it into his thigh, as deep as I can! That's 3 more Wounds!

GM: That brings Renard to 9 Wounds on his second tier. On 8, Renard acts. He tries to avoid your slash at his face but you cut a deep gash across his forehead, and blood starts to drip into his eyes. He doubles over from your strike to the stomach, then howls in pain as your knife plunges into his thigh. He drives his shoulder into you to push you back, then goes in for a Slash of his own! That's 5 Wounds, but you used Bash before, so it's reduced to 2.

Dominique: That's a third Dramatic Wound.

GM: Renard leers at Dominique. "You seem to be losing your spirit, mouse!" Your turn on 8.

Dominique: I don't dignify that with a response. I try to stay in close, so I can keep inside his guard. I'll spend my Raise to perform Feint. That's 1 Wound, and 1 additional Wound the next time I hurt him.

GM: That fills up Renard's second tier of Wounds. On 7, Renard will use Valroux Cross. He catches your knife with his sword and dagger. That reduces the Wounds he takes by 5—but it can't go lower than 0, so it just negates the Wound. He also chooses a Maneuver that he knows you can perform on your next Action. If you do any Maneuver other than the one he chooses, you have to spend 2 Raises instead of 1. He chooses Bash. "I can read you like a book, little mouse! You are mine!" Your turn.

Dominique: I smile. "I belong to no one, least of all you." I'll perform Bash. That's 1 Wound to him, plus 1 Wound since I used Feint before, and the next time he deals Wounds it's reduced by 3.

GM: Yep. That makes it 2 Wounds on Renard's third tier. On 6, Renard will act. He laughs. "You dance to the tune I play, Dominique. You can't hope to win!" Renard will Slash, for 5 Wounds. It is reduced by 3 since you used Bash, so it's 2 Wounds. Your turn, Dominique.

Dominique: I will use Riposte. So I take no Wounds—I reduce the number of Wounds he deals by my Weaponry Skill—and deal 3 back to him.

GM: Okay. That means 5 Wounds on Renard's third tier. On 5, Renard will Feint. That's 1 Wound, and 1 extra Wound the next time he deals Wounds to you.

Dominique: That's 1 Wound on my fourth tier.

GM: "I have you now, Ruisseau!" Your turn, on 5.

Dominique: I'm going to put all my weight into swiping at his sword with both of my knives, to try to knock him off balance. I'll use Bash. That's one Wound, and he deals 3 less Wounds the next time he deals damage.

GM: 6 Wounds onto Renard's third tier! On 4, Renard will Slash for 6—5 from his Weaponry, and 1 extra from his Feint. But you used Bash, so that reduces it by 3. So, that's 3 Wounds to you.

Dominique: I'll Parry. That reduces the Wounds by my Weaponry—which is 3—so he deals no Wounds to me. Ha ha!

GM: Renard recovers from your Bash and steps in close, sweeping his sword. You bat it aside, but he only smiles and keeps up the aggression. "What will you do now, mouse? You lose!" On 3, Renard will go for the throat. He spends all 3 Raises to Lunge. That is a total of 8 Wounds.

Dominique: I am going to activate my Virtue, "Astute." It says that I can activate it when a Villain spends Raises for an Action. That Action fails, and the Villain still loses the Raises.

GM: Uh...oops. Yeah, that completely works. He spends all of his Raises, but his Lunge fails.

Dominique: "So predictable, Renard!" As he Lunges, I effortlessly step to the side. I'll spend my first Raise to Slash for 3 Wounds.

GM: That takes Renard to 9 Wounds on his third tier.

Dominique: Next, I'll use Feint. I step heavy to one side. Since he's still probably trying to catch his balance from his missed Lunge, I want to make him over-correct, and I lay a small cut across his side as I do.

GM: That takes him to 10 Wounds on his third tier, filling it completely. You have 1 Raise left.

Dominique: "Who dances to whose tune now?" I'll spend my last Raise to Lunge, burying both of my knives in his stomach. That's 4 Wounds, plus 1 more for the Feint, for a total of 5.

GM: That gives Renard his third Dramatic Wound, and 3 Wounds on his fourth tier. You plunge your twin stilettos into his gut and he howls in pain, then with his last bit of strength he shoves you away. You both collapse onto the floor, winded and on the verge of death. You're both covered in blood—some of it is yours, some of it his. Renard draws a ragged breath and starts to crawl away from you, dragging his sword across the floor behind him.

Dominique: I'll stand up slowly, dropping one of my stilettos—I don't have the strength to hold both of them anymore—and take a shaky step toward him. "Where are you going, Renard? Do you think we are finished? I thought I was clear—this is over, here, today."

GM: Renard struggles to his feet as well. He's lost his dagger in the struggle, and only has his rapier left. He waves the tip of the sword in your direction with one hand, using the other to try to keep the blood from pouring out of his stomach. "You're a madwoman. You would rather certainly die here than let us both escape? Why?"

Dominique: I swipe at his sword with my knife. "Because you have hurt too many, and I will not let it happen again. Even if it costs me my life, you will never hurt anyone else. I swear it! Surrender now, and I will see that you stand trial before those you have wronged. Refuse... and we'll throw the dice, and see whose luck is better today."

GM: Wow. Normally, I'd ask you for an Intimidate Risk, but I'm convinced. Renard locks eyes with you. "Give me your word."

Dominique: "Ha! A man whose word is worth less than nothing, and he asks for a promise? I swear, if you surrender, you won't die by my hand, and I'll risk my life to see you arrive safely to your trial. After that, your fate is in the hands of the people. Now—drop your blade."

GM: Renard's sword hits the ground with a clatter. "I surrender."

Beast Villains

"I'll cut you ear to ear and feed you to the ocean.
Cannibal you call me? No, m'dear—I'm a survivor."
—Mary Galloway

Stoking a cruel fire in his heart, a Beast relishes the dirt under his nails, the sound of breaking bones and the taste of blood on his lips. He lives every day spoiling for a fight, and if someone does not pick one with him, he will surely take offense to something, if it means he can crack a few skulls together.

A Beast secures power for himself by carving it from the cold dead corpses of his enemies. Words, schemes and plans are all fine and good, but true victory comes at the sharp end of a sword. A Beast is a terrifying animal to behold on the battlefield—whether because of his skill with a sword or his sheer ferocity with his bare hands. Only the mightiest Heroes would face a Beast alone. This savage might say he holds himself to a higher power, honor, or even the law, but deep within the heart of every Beast is a stone cold killer.

This drive for destruction can take many forms. A Beast might seek out others like himself, or those with weaker wills, to bend and shape into a pack to prowl the countryside and dark alleyways looking for trouble and causing havoc wherever it goes. Another Beast might be a solitary creature who prefers to hunt alone, relishing the chase and flirting with the light only to plunge his prey into darkness.

What a Beast has in mind, what he wants and what makes him fight, varies from person to person. One man may nurse a grudge against a Nation in which his family died, whereas another may wage a personal vendetta to murder the doctor who misdiagnosed her now-deceased son. The commonality behind each Beast's driving goal is a singular ability to destroy everything in his path until he reaches it. Often this lust for a fight, for blood, does not abate when he accomplishes what he set out to do, but instead becomes the bloody reality of the Beast's past, present and future.

While many might see this deep-seated need for aggression as a weakness, for a Beast it is the source of his strength. Rooting out and bullying a victim is not a compulsion that causes stress, but a sincere joy for a Beast. This callous creature's true weakness comes from the fever with which he fights. When a Beast finally has his victim at hand, a blood haze comes over him and his need for destruction is irresistible. A clever Hero will use this to his advantage to win the day.

Core Aspect: Rage

Rage drives each and every Beast. This fury manifests in the Beast's need for confrontation, but is not always born with the person. Often a Beast experiences a moment which broke something within her, a moment where she learned the world was not a safe place, and her fight-or-flight instinct was set permanently to fight. While a harrowing experience would shape and mold most people into wiser versions of themselves, the Beast uses these traumas as further excuse to plunge headlong into darkness.

A few Beasts have had no harrowing experiences at all. This type of Beast grew up with a happy childhood, without trauma and as normal as one can get, but always possessed a spark of anger within her heart. With each passing year the ember grew brighter, until her passion and anger ignited and the flames grew to consume her. For this Beast, there is no return from the edge of darkness, because she was born into it.

A View of Heroism

Deft

Lurking around in the shadows, dodging out of danger, this just proves how weak they really are. If they could fight, why do they hide?

Indomitable

At least they will provide short-lived challenges!

Steadfast

Every man can be broken, every woman has a weakness. Chip away at hope and all that is left is a shell of a person.

Tactician

Only a fool thinks they are smarter than everyone else. Get them down in the streets, in the mud, dirt and filth—I'll show them!

Trickster

I have no use for a wry smile and mysterious ravings. Let us see how their witty words stand against my axe.

Playing the Beast

A Beast is often gruff and to the point. He sees very little use in small talk and does not suffer fools. What infuriates him the most is not getting what he wants, and the smartest Beast uses this aura of violence to bully others into giving up easily.

Beasts are rarely described as likeable people. It is possible for a Beast to show a softer side, but it is often difficult for him to maintain this façade and hide the more disagreeable side of his personality. He wears the fury within him as a deep gaping wound on his shoulder and is not afraid to show others the brunt of his anger. A Beast's mind is always swimming with his next Scheme, and suspicions about the person sitting across the table from him. This does not make it easy for him to get to know people, or them him, and he likes it this way.

A Beast often stalks the streets with a furrowed brow or a clenched fist. Each move he makes is deliberate, violent, purposefully propelling him towards his next objective. If a Beast is truly enraged, above and beyond the normal agitation he lives with, he makes his victim's blood run cold with fear. Seething at the mouth, enraged like a rabid animal, there is little anyone can do to subdue him.

Beast Schemes

Below is a list of example Schemes you could use for your Beast Villain. Do not take them literally! They are jumping off points for you to write Schemes unique to the Villain you are creating.

- Intimidate a local power into permitting your crimes.
- Murder an old enemy, rival or loved one.
- Take hostages to gain a temporary advantage.
- Make a public example of someone to cow resistance.
- Discover a magical means to increase your power.
- Destroy a public monument so the people lose hope.
- Torture someone vulnerable for information.
- Crush an opponent who slighted you.

Austyn Engelhart

History

Austyn was a monster hunter from a family of monster hunters, each more dedicated to the craft than their predecessor. His own grandmother, the hardest woman he had ever known, trained him from early childhood to fight monsters of all kinds. He could wind an arbalest faster than anyone and he handled a giant axe as easily as an ordinary warrior used a fork and spoon.

Austyn was a natural recruit for die Kreuzritter. He had an impressive monster-hunting pedigree, but battle gave him no satisfaction. After his training was finished, his grandmother died before his eyes in their first major engagement with an army of ghouls. He survived the battle, but was never the same afterwards, becoming taciturn and withdrawn. A brief affair with another Kreuzritter agent left him with a daughter, Susanne, who remained with him after the Inquisition captured Suse's mother. Austyn fought because it was his job, but Suse was his only real joy.

Tired of hunting and wanting to spend more time with his daughter, Austyn retired early. One night after a terrible storm, Austyn found the young girl standing in front of a broken window, staring out into the darkness. When he asked her what happened, Suse turned her head and said, "Nothing is wrong, Father." Then she walked to her bed, tucked herself in, and went to sleep. Austyn woke her up to question her, and checked the entire house, but—as his daughter kept saying—there seemed to be nothing wrong.

When Suse began to suggest twisted ways he might pass his time, he never even thought to doubt her. The little girl's voice turned dark, her thoughts warped, her movements disjointed, but when Austyn looked in her eyes all he saw was his beautiful daughter.

A week later, Austyn murdered all his neighbors, ending everyone who lived near his woodland cabin. He dragged their bodies into his yard, and by the time the sun rose each was a smoldering pile of ash. Suse, who had become sickly, said it made her feel better: She hoped desperately her father would kill again. The deaths brought a smile to her face.

It only became worse after that. Austyn drifted swiftly away from all his old Kreuzritter connections except for Wilhelmina Rapp, his former partner, a gunslinger who specialized in tracking and gathering information. They still had dinner together once a month, but they didn't talk about work, at Austyn's request. Every now and then, hearing rumors of deaths and marauding monsters in his area, a Kreuzritter agent would call on Austyn to seek his insight. These agents never returned alive.

As Suse's body slowly withered, the devil in her mind grew stronger. It reached out to other monsters in the area, providing Austyn with ghouls, wights and sirens to command. Lurching mobs of Horrors began to wander out from the parish where Austyn was based, gaining it a reputation as a place to be avoided.

Schemes

(1) Kill the Kreuzritter agent trailing him.

Austyn's old Kreuzritter compatriots are not on to him yet, but his partner, Mina Rapp, definitely is. She stayed in touch with Austyn after his retirement and watched every hint of his slow decline. Austyn has to make sure no one else finds out, but will killing Mina really reduce the trouble on his tail? Can she be corrupted?

(3) Find a strong new body to host the Horror.

Like a roach beset by a parasitic wasp, Austyn follows the Horror's orders instinctively, his intellect never quite realizing who is guiding his hand. The Horror controlling Suse is eating her body away from the inside and soon the little girl will be too weak to hold it. Austyn is tasked with finding a new body for the Horror, although this most likely means the death of his daughter.

(5) Establish a principality in Eisen with the Horror as Eisenfurst.

Unspeakable monsters are Eisen's largest minority. Isn't it about time they had a state of their own? When Austyn's master takes and holds a state in Eisen populated by Horrors, humans finally will have to treat monsters as equals. As a last, cruel twist, the Horror plans to reveal itself and rescind its psychic dominance at its moment of triumph.

Austyn Engelhart

"Eisen is lost, dead, done! Only by consigning ourselves to death can we bring her back to life. My master shall be the first of our new gods, a ruler from beyond the grave!"

EISEN

STRENGTH	INFLUENCE	RANK
8	2	10

Advantages
I Won't Die Here (154), Quick Reflexes: Weaponry (152), Riot Breaker (153)

Virtue: The Magician
Willful. Activate your Virtue and target a Hero. Until the end of this Scene, you cannot spend Danger Points and the Hero cannot spend Hero Points.

Hubris: The Thrones
Stubborn. You receive a Danger Point when you are stubborn and refuse to change your mind in the face of evidence.

Monster Qualities
Although Austyn is still human, the Horror has invested some of its power in the man. When Austyn is within sight of the Horror, he has the Monster Qualities of Regenerating and Powerful.

Servants and Underlings
Austyn's underlings are exclusively monsters. He has no small amount of Unliving Brutes that serve him. In addition, the woods are patrolled by a pack of feral, rabid dogs led by a massive alpha. The dogs are mostly unremarkable, but the alpha is a Strength 6 Monster with the Qualities of Relentless, Fearsome and Swift. Finally, Austyn's daughter Suse is possessed by "the Horror," the capabilities of which are unknown.

Redemption
Any attempt to return Austyn to sanity must begin with the salvation of his daughter. While she is under the control of the Horror, Austyn is both unwilling and unable to turn away from his dark path.

Roleplaying Tips

Austyn is of two minds, but the one that kills people to sate an eldritch horror is the one in charge. The scraps of Austyn's former personality struggle to reach the surface, splinters of subvocalized doubt that his path is the correct one...but these are rare exceptions.

When Austyn is near his daughter—who is sick nearly to death, barely able to speak, almost always unconscious—his old personality emerges. He is gentle, kind and caring for a few minutes before he becomes the monster again. The original Austyn, hidden in there somewhere, has quietly catalogued information about the Horror, its strengths, weaknesses and plans.

Drieu Riquesse

History

Drieu Riquesse wakes up every day with the sun. He makes himself tea and breakfast, works in his garden, goes into town and has lunch at the café. He returns home for a siesta, spends the afternoon running errands, makes himself dinner and goes to bed early. He is polite to his neighbors, but rarely has anything interesting to discuss. They assume he must be independently wealthy or engaged in international trade, because he never seems to work—although he will disappear for weeks at a time, explaining that he is visiting family or conducting business.

Drieu Riquesse is a professional assassin.

In his youth, Drieu was full of fire and passion. Everyone in his family was—especially his younger brother, Danilo. Danilo wanted nothing more than to join the Duelist's Guild, and took every opportunity to practice…even if that meant dueling illegally. Danilo accepted a challenge by an amateur duelist Bertaut, thinking Bertaut would honor the agreement to duel to first blood. Bertaut stabbed him, fatally, in the neck.

Drieu's heart crumbled to pieces when he heard of this. Fencing was about challenge and family for him, a pastime he shared with his beloved brother. Losing Danilo showed him the opposite: that swordplay was about blood, pride—and death.

Bertaut mercilessly used his connections and clout to grind out any hope Drieu ever had of legal restitution for his brother's deat. Drieu could find only one source of solace: more death. He employed his skill with a blade to kill for money. This was not the honorable and epic duel of a Swordsman. This was a knife in the dark, a murder so gruesome and grisly it left no evidence the city watch could trace.

Each person who dies for no reason, justified only by money or ambition, confirms to Drieu that human life has no meaning. The only moment he truly feels anything is in his victim's last gasp, light fading from dead eyes, and in that intense moment Drieu feels it—anger. He hungers after this feeling, this awakening fury deep within himself.

Drieu has a manager, a distant cousin of his, Barbara Riquesse. She collects job offers from a number of what amount to postal office boxes scattered throughout Montaigne. Drieu has been able to amass a small fortune, stored in banks scattered throughout Théah, by fulfilling these murder contracts. An expert in languages and disguise, he is preternaturally skilled at turning himself into the most boring person on the street, no matter where on the continent he goes.

Schemes

(1) Fulfill the murder contract on Salvador de Barros.

Drieu Riquesse will kill anyone for money, but his favorite contracts are on Duelists. Loriega, a fencing master whose school in San Cristobal keeps losing students to Barros' school, wants Barros dead. Now, all Drieu needs to do is to isolate Barros and kill him.

(3) Kill Bertaut and everyone he knows.

Once Barros is dead, Drieu wishes to make Bertaut suffer as he did. Hunting down Bertaut's friends and family will isolate him. Bertaut has made a lot of enemies along the way, and Riquesse plans to talk Loriega and his students into going after other Duelists like Bertaut who might compete with Loriega.

(5) Burn down the courthouse of San Cristobal, and let none escape.

What is justice? A lie held up by other lies. Drieu believed in justice once, and mercy, and noblesse oblige—until Danilo's death disabused him of those notions. Drieu needs to see the courthouse, the place where justice was denied for his beloved brother's death, go up in flames. Let all who would believe in justice, burn, just as Drieu's heart once burned.

Drieu Riquesse

"You have unsettled me. I commend you for it. That is rare, and it displeases me. But rest assured, this is not the fair fight you are hoping for. For instance, I have a musket."

CASTILLE

STRENGTH	INFLUENCE	RANK
9	6	15

Advantages

Fencer (151), Indomitable Will (149), Linguist (148), Perfect Balance (150), Poison Immunity (150), Second Story Work (150), Slip Free (150)

Virtue: The Moonless Night

Subtle. Activate your Virtue when you act behind the scenes, from the shadows or through a proxy. For the next Risk, when you determine Raises, every die counts as a Raise.

Hubris: Reunion

Bitterness. You receive a Danger Point when you bring up old grudges or bad feelings when doing so will lead to trouble.

Servants and Underlings

Drieu is a solo operative, and as such any underlings or servants he employs are likely to be temporary and disposable. Local Thieves, Brutes or Pirates might be hired to harass the Heroes—anonymously, of course.

Redemption

Drieu is completely amoral, consumed by a thirst for vengeance. Redemption is extremely unlikely. Any efforts would have to begin with bringing Bertaut to some form of retribution, and then assuaging Drieu's view of the failures of the justice system.

Roleplaying Tips

Polite, proper and utterly nihilistic, Drieu can stab a man and then sit quietly by while he bleeds out. The most unsettling thing about Drieu is the seemingly perfect equanimity with which he commits atrocities, almost always some variation of murder.

He is unlikely to display any emotion whatsoever, unless unexpectedly blocked from his goal—and even then, it will only be an errant eye twitch or clenched muscle. His voice is even, calm and disarming. Spend a few minutes with him on the job and you will be praying to return to the usual bloodthirsty pirate captains and Vesten bearsarkers.

Julianna Onesta

History

Julianna Onesta's father murdered her mother when Julianna was six. Julianna does not actually remember what happened, but in the years since that night, the story has developed details in her memory the way a fallen log grows fungi. However, the role of Julianna's sister, Giachetta, has remained constant. It was Giachetta who drove her father mad. Giachetta guided his hands, forcing him to murder his wife for reasons Julianna has never investigated, nor cared to investigate for the sake of the truth she might find. This memory—half-real, half-fictional—is the burning engine driving Julianna forward, as a Vaticine and an Inquisitor.

The Inquisition was a phantom terror for the other little girls Julianna's age, something that would get them if they did not say their prayers or go to bed on time. To Julianna, the Inquisition was a goalpost. It was the reason she studied hard enough that a Vaticine academy recruited her; the reason she woke up before any of her classmates and exercised and drilled her marksmanship until she could outshoot any of her instructors. By age 16 she was an Inquisitorial cadet. By age 18 she was a full-fledged Inquisitor—but once she reached her goal, she found her compatriots wanting.

The Inquisition's own bloodthirst hamstrung its effectiveness. Juliana knew from her studies that the Inquisition had not always been a militant bogeyman. Orginally, Inquisitors were sharp and subtle, stepping softly, not revealing their true purpose until their quarry was all but captured. The modern Inquisition did not work that way—but Inquisitor Onesta realized they did not have to.

Juliana used her position to network with Vodacce's Merchant Princes, promising to turn a blind eye to their indiscretions if they allowed her access to their business networks and territories. She entered Inquisitorial prisons and released carefully vetted criminals to act as informants. The treachery and crime might have increased for the cities into which she released these criminals, but the information she received allowed Inquisitor Onesta to catch and kill many more witches and heretics than could her pistols alone.

Now, she travels across Vodacce, following up on her information networks, in the hopes of preventing incidents like the one that happened to her. The one weakness in her armor is her habit of granting tacit amnesty to people close to her. Giachetta, for example, still lives. Disguised as a servant in Inquisitor Onesta's home, Giachetta never uses her Sorte powers; yet Julianna channels her rage outward, unable to bring justice to one so close to her.

Inquisitor Onesta would be horrified to find that what she explains away as mere selfishness might be growing into something she could never tolerate: compassion.

Schemes

(1) Steal a Malleus Maleficarum from Hierophant Sixtus's tomb.

The famous "Hierophant General" created blessed hammers for himself and his officers to use against enemies of the Faith, naming each after the famous witch hunter's manual. Juliana can think of no one better than herself to wield such an artifact. Unfortunately, the Office of the Hierophant controls access to the holy tombs, and is not letting the Inquisition anywhere near them.

(3) Expose Sophia's Daughters within House Villanova.

Inquisitor Onesta's network of informants has found evidence that Sophia's Daughters are active under Giovanni Villanova's nose. Finding witch-coddlers meddling in the most powerful reaches of Vodacce society will exalt Julianna above her fellow Inquisitors, and set her up for even greater success. Perhaps, one day, she may even lead the Inquisition.

(5) Locate and attack the Daughters' headquarters.

It is bad enough that the Fate Witches run rampant in Vodacce, but at least they are under control. Witches operating outside of Vodacce, where their heresy can spread unchecked, is even more unthinkable. It is time that Inquisitor Onesta made an example of Sophia's Daughters.

Julianna Onesta

"You have two choices. One is to die here,
messily, shamefully. The other is to do exactly
what I say for the rest of your miserable life.
I actually hope you choose the first."

VODACCE

STRENGTH	INFLUENCE	RANK
7	8	15

Advantages
Connection: Vaticine Inquisition (149), Deadeye (151),
Lyceum (153), Sniper (152)

Virtue: The Devil
Astute. Activate your Virtue after a Hero spends Raises
for an Action. That Action fails. The Hero still loses the
Raises she spent.

Hubris: The Tower
Arrogant. You receive a Danger Point when you show
disdain, contempt, or otherwise look down on a Hero
or someone who could cause harm to friends.

Servants and Underlings
Julianna's underlings are almost always Inquisitors.

Inquisitors. Spend a Danger Point when the Squad's
Strength would be reduced using Convince, Intimidate,
Tempt or any similar effect of coercion. Their faith is
unshakeable, and the Inquisitors ignore the effect.

Redemption
There is a burning coal of growing compassion in
Julianna's heart that causes her to doubt her cause.
This is not a case where tough love will win out—to
turn Julianna away from Villainy one must display
compassion, kindness and mercy.

Roleplaying Tips

Julianna is excellent at her job. Her back is always
perfectly straight, her hand never far from her
pistols, her eyes always watchful for the merest
hint of heresy or weakness. She never smiles unless
she is causing someone pain. When Julianna's more
caring nature is exposed to someone she cares
about personally, she becomes anxious. Her work
has consumed so much of her identity that she does
not know what to do with herself when her gentler
nature emerges, the nature that might have friends
and family. Her feelings of guilt and self-doubt are
ever present, and often turn to rage.

History

Liphilt was orphaned during the War of the Cross by a mother who feared her child so greatly, she took her own life. Abandoned in darkness, Liphilt was rescued from an ore cart deep in the Baaken iron mine at the base of the Drachenberg Mountains. The kindly miner who discovered the child shuddered and crossed himself at her feral gaze, then took her to the nearby town of Atemlos. There, he left the cold little girl in the loving care of the Vaticine-administered Strauss Academy for War Orphans.

Touched by Legion, Liphilt was always a malevolent child. Nothing the sisters did could stymie the hard-hearted child's hatred for all she surveyed, and they often had to lock Liphilt away to protect the other children. From her window perch high in a tower cell, Liphilt stared hatefully over Atemlos and its people. She hated the town for its wealth, she hated the cathedral that wealth built and she especially hated mining magnate Baaken for financing them both. There was very little Liphilt did not hate.

As she grew older, hatred turned into a brutality that resulted in the death of the kindly sisters who fought so hard to save Liphilt from herself. Fleeing into the night, Liphilt joined the Objectionist cause in name, but not in heart. The fools gave her an opportunity to burn, pillage and murder her way across the countryside in a mad quest to raze Atemlos to the ground. Reveling in destruction, Liphilt participated in no less than three full-scale attacks on the town. Each failure saw Liphilt's rage soar to new heights and her actions sink to new depths of depravity.

At every turn, the Baaken family and the people of Atemlos thwarted her. When Liphilt tried to burn their crops, they replanted. When she tortured them, they endured. When she fought them savagely, they fought back ever harder. Captured during a final suicidal charge, Liphilt found herself tried before Atemlos' august judge, The Honorable Gerhard Stein. Stein sentenced her to live out her days on a chain gang in the Baaken mines.

Years of toil in the place of her birth inflamed the feral hatred in Liphilt's soul to a fever pitch with each scarring stroke of the lash. It was not long before Liphilt's sinister intellect devised a plan of escape.

Strangling a guard with her chains, Liphilt took his keys and escaped into the Drachenberg Mountains.

Through fear and intimidation, Liphilt assembled a gang of criminals and refugees and set about raiding the mines up and down the Drachenberg Mountains. With each raid, she offers the mine workers the choice of killing a guard to buy their freedom, or certain death at her hand. Each recruit is forced to leave a signed confession on their victim's body to bind their loyalty. The time for patience has come to an end as Liphilt returns to Atemlos once more. Nothing will stop her from drowning it in darkness.

Schemes

(1) Kidnap and work to death the judge who sentenced her.

The first stop in Liphilt's quest for vengeance is to settle the score with the judge who sentenced her. Gerhard Stein has a passion for hunting near the base of the Drachenbergs. Little does he know Liphilt has every intention of kidnapping him, chaining him to his hunting companion and working them to death.

(3) Kill mining magnate Tomas Baaken and his family.

The second phase in Liphilt's campaign of vengeance is to kill the Baaken family. Wary of the recent attacks, Tomas hired outsiders to protect his family, sequestered in Atemlos. What Tomas does not know is that his youngest daughter Elsa and her brother Conrad like to slip away to play soldiers in the mines.

(5) Undermine and collapse the Cathedral in Atemlos during the Prophet's Mass.

Liphilt has extensive knowledge of the mines and tunnels beneath Atemlos. As the day of the cathedral's consecration draws near, the entire town is expected to turn out for its inaugural Prophet's Mass and Liphilt and her gang are working tirelessly to undermine the cathedral to the point of collapse. Rapidly constructed wooden beams will support the cathedral's weight until the mass begins. Then the gang will set the wood ablaze and watch from afar as the cathedral—and Atemlos—burns.

Liphilt

"Freedom is one life away. Yours or theirs? Your choice."

EISEN

STRENGTH	INFLUENCE	RANK
10	3	13

Advantages
Boxer (151); Indomitable Will (149); Psst, Over Here (150); Quick Reflexes: Brawl (152), Slip Free (150), Staredown (150), Survivalist (148)

Virtue: The Fool
Wily. Activate your Virtue to escape danger from the current Scene. You cannot rescue anyone but yourself.

Hubris: Coins
Relentless. You receive a Danger Point when you refuse to leave well enough alone or quit while you are ahead, and it gets you into trouble.

Monster Qualities
Liphilt is technically human, but her life of wanton savagery has granted her the Fearsome Quality.

Servants and Underlings
Liphilt's gang follows her out of terror of what she will do to them if they refuse. Many are Thieves or Pirates, but the majority are simply Brutes. There are no charismatic or influential members in her gang—Liphilt views any such individual as a threat.

Redemption
There has always been a shadow in Liphilt's heart. She cannot be redeemed.

Roleplaying Tips
Lithe, brutal, dark eyed and constantly in motion, Liphilt's hatred for all that is good, honest and pure drives her to ever increasing acts of savagery. Her perpetual sneer quickly becomes a rictus grin when faced with the seductive allure of wanton mayhem. She does not walk, she lopes. She does not smile, she bares her teeth. She does not look, she glares hungrily. Liphilt knows her hatred will consume her one day...she means for it to consume everyone else first.

Luysio Barozzi

History

Luysio was a strong boy who lived among tall mountains in a distant land he can no longer remember. One day, barbarians dressed in strange clothing came from afar and killed his family. They would have killed Luysio too, but his strength overwhelmed them. Bathed in blood and surrounded by enemies, confusion overtook the boy. Just as he was about to be run through by a henchman, the leader of the invaders intervened. Instead, the henchman clubbed him and Luysio fell unconscious. When he woke up, he was in a place with no mountains, and he had no memories. The boy decided to survive by any means necessary. And he has done so ever since.

Christiano Barozzi, the man who saved him, became his father. He quickly realized that Luysio's strength could be useful. He set out to prove the boy's mettle by assigning him the most despicable tasks, those that even grown men and women were reluctant to execute. Break an old woman's fingers for an overdue debt? No problem. Killing innocents whose only sin was to have witnessed what they should not have? They were dead before *Signore* Barozzi had finished giving the order.

Luysio was *too* good at the tasks set before him and his father grew suspicious. Christiano offered Luysio, now a young man, all the temptations he could, directly and through others. Courtesans? Luysio declined them gracefully. Riches? He accepted only the barest minimum. The finest food? He excused himself, saying that he followed a frugal diet. Finally, Christiano was left with only one choice: to confront his son with the ultimate test. And so he ordered Luysio to kill Piero, his little brother—and only rival for the family's inheritance.

Luysio, believing Piero's blood was the same as his own, refused to do so, and offered his own life in payment for his failure. Instead of accepting, Christiano embraced Luysio with tears in his eyes. "You are my son, and you will be the head of *la famiglia* when I die," he said, "even though you were not born of me." That is how Luysio found out he had been adopted and Piero's inheritance was stolen.

Luysio never sounded a word of protest, nor demanded any explanation about his origins. As usual, he honored his father by kissing his hands, maintaining his usual immutable expression. In time, everyone in the family respected and feared Luysio. He was the ever-present figure at his father's side in all meetings, whispering softly in *Signore* Barozzi's ears from time to time.

When Christiano Barozzi died, poisoned by Piero, Luysio was named *signore*. Before Luysio could punish him, Piero fled and a few weeks after his father's death, the household woke up to the terrified screams of Luysio. No one had ever heard Luysio scream— and no one ever wanted to again. The bodyguards who stormed his room reported that he was alone, drenched in sweat and speaking of a far off land and a life he must reclaim. *Signore* Barozzi has said little on the matter since.

Schemes

(1) Find and kill the person who abducted him from Aztlan.

Luysio has one recurring nightmare. In this vision, he is in a distant land surrounded by mountains he has never seen, his family's blood drenching his clothing. He is picked up and thrown on a ship, never to see his home again. Now, Luysio will move heaven and earth searching for the person who did this to him.

(3) Kill his younger brother Piero, who turned from the family.

After what he has done, Piero has to die. The problem is that most of the family henchmen are hesitant to harm a member of the Barozzi family. In his current state, Luysio cannot put his mind to it, so he is actively looking for anyone willing to find and capture Piero alive. His death will be Luysio's duty—and pleasure.

(5) Destroy the rival Antonini family's empire.

As soon as rumors about Luysio's condition spread, one family immediately tried to benefit from the situation—the Antonini. Now that they have been foolish enough to reveal their ambitions, Luysio is ready to annihilate them. After he is done with them, there will no sign, nor trace, not even a memory that there once was an Antonini family.

Luysio Barozzi

"If you know his reputation, you will know that begging will not make a difference. That time is long past. Now, you will pay your debt in blood."
—Roberto Donati, middleman of the Barozzi family

VODACCE

STRENGTH	INFLUENCE	RANK
7	9	16

Advantages
Connection: Vodacce Underworld (149),
Reputation: Ruthless (150), Time Sense (148),
Trusted Companion: Enzo Calabrese (154),
We're Not So Different... (155)

Virtue: The Sun
Glorious. Activate your Virtue when you are the center of attention. For the next Risk, when you determine Raises, every die counts as a Raise.

Hubris: The Emperor
Hot-Headed. You receive a Danger Point when you fly off the handle and lose your temper, causing trouble.

Servants and Underlings
As the head of an influential criminal enterprise, Luysio has no small number of individuals willing to do his bidding. Luysio's most formidable asset is his personal enforcer and adviser Enzo Calabrese. Luysio trusts Enzo completely, and that trust is well placed. Enzo's loyalty lies with Luysio personally.

Redemption
To turn Luysio away from Villainy is to solve the problem of his nightmares. It is unknown whether the nightmares are a sign of his own fractured psyche, or some sort of sorcerous effect from his homelands.

Roleplaying Tips

Luysio Barozzi is a monster whose guilt has caught up with him. For the first time he is displaying weakness, caught off guard by bursts of rage and awakening screaming from the nightmares he experiences each night. However, Luysio is still able to maintain some kind of composure. He always talks through a middleman, keeping a characteristic blank expression.

When speaking of his nightmares, Luysio's stony façade breaks. He demands to talk in private with anyone that approaches with information on the matter and, astonishingly, no one that has brought news about the topic has died—unthinkable to all who know him.

Mary Galloway

History

Them that know of Mary Galloway—"The Butcher"—know that her husband, Teague, sold her off to coastal raiders one autumn evening to save his own skin. What few know is Teague also sold his daughter.

Johanna Galloway was a beautiful girl, lithe and graceful, fair of face. It was she who helped her mother bear the first hard months of slavery, she who befriended the other captives on the ship and built an informal society of abductees.

Then the boat went North and sailed into the ice. At the top of the world, when the year is ending, falling snow eats the sound around you. Cold frost paints the deck glittering white and ice crystallizes on the rigging and sails. Days fade in a matter of hours, nights last forever, and nothing echoes. All is a shivering whisper.

The crew took to half rations, then less than that. Starvation thinned fingernails, sent hands trembling; the pirates hid in their bunks and ordered the slaves to maintain the icy ship. Is it any wonder the old rope maker died?

The ship's captain was practical. "Carve him up and we'll eat him," he said, and so Mary butchered the man. After weeks of half-frozen hardtack, the meat tasted delicious. But the pirates were still hungry and Johanna had developed a cough, and a few days later, the captain came back on deck.

"Johanna," he said. He called the sick girl to his side and snapped her neck. When Mary saw Johanna's body laid out and ready for butchery, her eyes grew dull. She gave the captain a peculiar look.

"There's better meat on this ship than my Johanna," she said, and slit the captain's throat.

What followed was a mutiny, as the slaves slaughtered their masters, for Johanna's death had broken something in them. When the massacre was done, the slaves carved up the meat and ate their fill. Johanna's body was given to the water, spared the grisly fate of those who murdered her. They feasted for nights, weeks, the pirates bodies preserved in the snow and ice. When the former slaves were down to half rations again, they were spotted by a pirate-hunting ship.

Starvation is a harsh mistress and human meat is sweet. Winter was still blowing and the ice had not yet cracked to free the captive ship. The pirate-hunters themselves were almost out of rations. Some members of the cannibal crew told themselves they had no choice. Some of them knew better.

It was a little funny and also a little sad how, even when spring came, Mary's crew kept eating people. It is what defines them now, their founding myth; it's what brought them together, what separates them from everyone else. They joke about picking through brain meat and fight over favored cuts during feasts. The crew is wrapped in a state of hysteria, and Mary is the furthest gone among them. They are monstrous, invincible. Bound together by taboo, desperation and bloody hands.

Schemes

(1) Attack Mary's old village and kill her husband.

Teague, the butcher, sold his daughter and wife to coastal raiders—his village was complicit. Mary wants revenge. She and her crew will raid the town, round up Teague and the villagers, kill and eat all they can and leave the rest for the horrified authorities to find. It's that simple.

(3) Send King MacDuff the best cuts of his pirate-hunter fleet.

Mary and her crew have met pirate-hunters and they do not think much of them. One of King MacDuff's lieutenants discovered the cannibalized hunter ship and news is spreading. MacDuff has sent out several ships specifically to identify and end the cannibals. Mary hopes to up the ante by catching those ships, butchering the crew and sending the best cuts back to King MacDuff.

(5) Blockade the Marches with a fleet of merciless cutthroats.

In the dark, when the food runs out, any man might eat his brother. Mary and her crew want to blockade the Highland Marches in winter and watch as the country is forced to turn cannibal. During the long winters, the Marches receives most of its food from imports, so real starvation could happen. But first, Mary must expand her cannibal clan into a cutthroat fleet.

Mary Galloway

"Think you can defeat us? We've eaten our own just to keep breathin'! When your ship's splintered and your crew's trussed and tied, then we'll feast!"

THE HIGHLAND MARCHES

STRENGTH	INFLUENCE	RANK
10	4	14

Advantages
Cast Iron Stomach (148), Duelist Academy: Boucher (237), Fencer (151), Leadership (149), Married to the Sea (150), Team Player (150)

Virtue: The War
Victorious. Activate your Virtue the first time you Wound a Hero or Villain during a fight to make her take a Dramatic Wound in addition to the Wounds you normally deal.

Hubris: The Hero
Foolhardy. You receive a Danger Point when your brash, cocky or reckless actions cause trouble for you and another Villain.

Servants and Underlings
Mary commands *The Sweetbread*, a Ship with the Origin of Avalon and the Background of Pirate Hunter. The Ship's Crew of 10 functions as normal for a Crew of any other Ship, in addition to any Brutes that Mary creates with her Influence. Most of those under Mary's Influence are Pirates.

Redemption
Mary is a stone cold killer without remorse.

Roleplaying Tips

Mary speaks like a salty sailor, roaring and cursing, and exhorting violence. Her voice is deep and coarse, and she waves a cleaver to threaten people. Her humor is low and she is fond of kitchen puns—she's the one who renamed the icy ship *The Sweetbread*.

When she wants to rally the crew, she speaks of their sufferings as though she is chanting a religious mantra. They survived slavery, they survived hunters, they survived winter by the blood on their teeth—they are monstrous now, invincible, no longer like the common man.

Mikhaila "Misha" Oksanova

History

Now, knowing that Mikhaila "Misha" Oksanova grew up to make dogs and humans murder one another for sport, you might expect that she had a traumatic childhood: Perhaps she or a relative was attacked by a dog. That is not the case. Misha's parents made sails for Ussuran fishing boats, before they retired. They had planned to train Misha in their trade, but Misha wanted to leave home and make her own way.

Originally, Misha wanted to be a wrestler, but disdained the rules and regulations on "acceptable behavior," preventing her from being a true champion. Then she wanted to be a promoter, but there was too much competition for that job. So Misha got started working for a dog breeder. These sad creatures grew up in cramped, unhealthy conditions and sold for low prices as guard dogs, poacher's aides or food.

A year or two after she began working there, Misha's boss fell into a pen at the wrong time and his own dogs tore him to shreds. That was all right with Misha—he was a terrible employer, and she rather enjoyed watching his death, especially because then she got to take over the operation. It occurred to her at that point that she might not be the only one willing to pay good money to see this kind of gore.

She brought her dogs into Ekatnava and arranged fights. This business was not as lucrative or as popular as humans wrestling humans, but it had some advantages. The combatants did not have to be paid. The fights were bloody, to the death, and she could easily control them. She brought a bookie on staff and began to take a cut of each bet, while sending low budget leg-breakers around to crack down on anyone who tried to gamble on the fights without her getting in on the deal.

The fights at this point were between dogs and other dogs; but then one day a wrestler who was down-on-her-luck came to Misha with a crazy idea—what if the wrestler fought a dog? Or maybe a few dogs? Misha's mind drifted back to the excitement she felt when seeing her previous employer torn apart and quickly agreed to the challenge.

The fight drew a gigantic crowd to a fairground just outside the Ekatnava city limits. The event included dogfights and boxing and wrestling matches, and finally, the battle between the wrestler and the dogs. The wrestler did not survive the fight, but she killed three of the dogs before she went down, the crowd went wild.

Money changed hands, and feeling the release and joy of such a display of violence, Misha realized there was a future here for her. Now, human and dog fights are commonplace for Misha. When she cannot find a volunteer, she sends her henchmen to find someone who owes her too much money and offers them a deal—fight in the ring and clear your debts, or die. It is amazing how many people agree to fight with the proper motivation.

Schemes

(1) Steal Miron the Giant, the strongest hunting dog in Théah.

Misha offered a renowned breeder a king's ransom for Miron the Giant, a legendary hunting dog who has accompanied die Kreuzritter on monster hunts. The breeder refused, because she had heard rumors of Misha's unsavory fights. Yet, this rejection means little to Misha. Time for drugs and kidnapping.

(3) Secure the Ussuran throne's patronage.

If Misha can convince whoever becomes Czar of Ussura that fights between dogs and humans are a fine and noble pastime, she will get seriously rich. After all, humans fight bulls in Castille, do they not? And in those fights, there are more humans than bulls, so this is, if anything, more fair and humane. Besides, a national sport would be good for Ussura.

(5) Legalize dogfighting as an international spectator sport.

International sporting competitions have not really taken off yet in Théah the way they have in the New World and the Atabean region, but Misha could change that. Dogfighting has yet to be widely outlawed, although in the places where the authorities have taken notice of it, they have cracked down pretty hard (out of classism as much as altruism). But if Misha has the Czar on board, surely Ussura and Eisen will at least entertain the idea.

Mikhaila "Misha" Oksanova

"It's looking bad for Vitya right now! He's got two on his left and one on his right and he's still. It looks like he's left himself open! He's struggling... he's flailing...he's down! What an upset!"

USSURA

STRENGTH	INFLUENCE	RANK
3	7	10

Advantages
Barterer (149), Connection: Ekatnava Underworld (149), Virtuoso: Oratory (152)

Virtue: The Road
Friendly. Activate your Virtue when you meet a character (even a Hero) for the first time. She treats you as friendly for one scene.

Hubris: The Beggar
Envious. You receive a Danger Point when your Villain covets something, and does something unwise to get it.

Servants and Underlings
Misha has no shortage of leg-breakers and thugs willing to do almost anything it takes to earn her favor, and thus earn more of her coin. Most are Pirates and Thieves, although she tends to keep a handful of Guards close when she is in public, just in case.

Redemption
Misha loves blood, gristle and agony. She treats her dogs as terribly as she treats humans, feeding the weak to the strong for sport. She needs to be locked up—or put down.

Roleplaying Tips

Excited, enthusiastic, totally comfortable with bloodshed and murder. Misha is fan of sport and an event promoter first and foremost. She has a big smile and an even bigger voice. She is happiest when she is in her box seat overlooking the ring, stoking the crowd's excitement and bloodlust and commenting on the action so even the people in the cheap seats know what is going on. She is also completely committed to her business, to the point where it really does not bother her when people or dogs suffer or die. To her, it is all about the show.

Ondro Róg

History

If you knew Ondro Róg as a child, you are probably dead. The shame of his early years was too great to leave witnesses. What if someone would tell his enemies about the time his parents locked him into the space under the bedstead for three days without any food or drink?

It took Ondro ten years of abuse before he escaped his miserable life. Having just stolen an apple to silence his grumbling stomach, he ran into the impressively rotund frame of a man named Cezary Górski. Cezary helped him up and with a wink complimented the boy on being fast on his feet. That is how Ondro became a messenger boy for Rokosz's most infamous criminal.

Cezary Górski became the caring father Ondro never had. For the first time, Ondro had a taste of what it felt like to be powerful and wealthy. On his 21st birthday, Cezary gave Ondro a very special gift. He took him to a warehouse, gave him the key and told him to do as he pleased with what he found inside. Within, Ondro discovered his parents. He strangled both of them with his bare hands and a smile on his face. A year passed, while Ondro explored and refined his homicidal tendencies in the employ of his benefactor.

When the first snow fell, Cezary invited Ondro and a few trusted friends for a formal dinner. Cezary explained that the next day a warrant would be issued for his arrest, and Cezary would go into hiding or they would send someone to take him, dead or alive. Nobody was to know the location of his safe house and Ondro would supervise his ventures while Cezary was gone.

Ondro held his new position for only one week. He reconsidered things the moment he found out he could more easily satisfy his appetite for murder working on the right side of the law. The hanging of a Castillian merchant brought this realization to him. The man was convicted and sentenced to death for smuggling, but Ondro knew this merchant was a honest man.

Out of curiosity, he looked into the matter only to find that the Castillian had foolishly demolished the home of an officer's elderly mother, casting her out onto the street. Clearly far more power and recognition were waiting for Ondro among the lawmen.

Ondro went to the authorities and told them a crow flew from Cezary's former residence every evening at six sharp. To find Cezary, they only needed to follow the crow. That evening Ondro sent the bird to Cezary carrying two words: "Death comes." As Cezary read them and cursed Ondro, the officers were already banging on his door.

For his help catching the town's most influential criminal, Ondro received a minor honorary title and a job with local law enforcement. But just when Ondro Róg gained his new position, the King took it away by making all Sarmatians equal. Ondro hates the Golden Liberty. He will have his revenge; nobody takes something from him without paying the price.

Schemes

(1) Build an informant network to report on the townsfolk.

Knowledge is power. Information is essential for blackmailing, and of course it is good to know which people support King Stanislaw I and his son. Ondro might want to get rid of them if they start getting in his way. Who better to groom as his spies than the truly destitute? Luckily the orphanage is not too far away from the constabulary.

(3) Beat the standing record of 37 executions in one day.

What is life without a little sport? Measuring your own accomplishments with those of others keeps a man on his toes. It also gains the recognition and respect of those in power and could lead to bigger and better opportunities.

(5) Blackmail Kapitan Zurek into granting him membership in the Slachta.

King Stanislaw I created the Golden Liberty, so to get rid of it the King must be dealt with. What better position to strike from than his own honor guard? Kapitan Zurek is one of the few that can grant membership to the Slachta and like any good citizen there must be something he would rather keep in the dark.

Ondro Róg

"The ignorant and gullible are the cobblestones on the road to success; flatten them under- foot, and a smooth journey lies ahead."

THE SARMATIAN COMMONWEALTH

STRENGTH	INFLUENCE	RANK
7	1	8

Advantages
Boxer (151), Brush Pass (151),
Connection: Law Enforcement (149),
Reputation: Incorruptible (150), Streetwise (150)

Virtue: The Wheel
Fortunate. Activate your Virtue to delay an Opportunity or a Consequence by 1 Action.

Hubris: The Beggar
Envious. You receive a Danger Point when your Villain covets something, and does something unwise to get it.

Servants and Underlings
Ondro has no underlings to speak of, and only a small amount of wealth with which to hire them; he plans to recruit truly desperate individuals to aid him.

Redemption
Ondro loves killing. There is little to no hope left for him.

Roleplaying Tips

Ondro enjoys killing and even more so if it gets him what he wants. He does not care about morality or idealism. He only opposes King Stanisłav I because he sees the Golden Liberty as a personal affront. Ondro can pretend to care about other people, but he really only cares about one person—himself. If others can be taken advantage of, it just means they are weak and deserve to be misled or used.

Chameleon Villains

"My life is unbearable, only when I set foot on my beloved Commonwealth again... Ugh, the look of the corpse is really ruining my mood. Will someone please remove it from the deck?"
—Dana Gwozdek

A Chameleon is a pain in the ass. She likes tricking people, lying to them, getting that little masturbatory thrill when she manages to successfully dupe someone. But unlike Heroic Tricksters, there's no fun in it. Nothing funny. Her 'jokes' have no end in sight—what is more bitter than a laugh that never comes? And when the joke becomes deadly, Theus help us all.

Most people have a truth bias: Say something and they want to believe it. Shifty eyes and shifting feet may cue them otherwise, but keep an honest face and most people will go straight from "that sounds within the bounds of normalcy" to "that sounds so unbelievable you cannot be making it up." The Chameleon is a master at making her lies either totally banal or so impossible that everyone who hears her wants to believe.

Chameleons are the saboteurs of Théah.

As Villains, Chameleons are rarely on the side of law and order. If the law was with a Chameleon, she wouldn't have to deceive so much, now would she? No, she likes throwing the world into chaos with her own cleverness. She'll say, sometimes, that she tricks the world for the sake of some good or noble cause but this, too, is a lie. A Chameleon tricks the world to show herself how smart she is, and sometimes, to show others as well.

Hence, ego is the means to a Chameleon's defeat. A Chameleon will rarely turn away from an opportunity to outwit an opponent, even when that opportunity distracts from her ostensible goal. Ironically, the Chameleon's specialty proves key to her defeat: She expects her opponents to approach straightforwardly. Relishing in the destruction of predictable Heroes, Chameleons are easily tricked more often than one might expect.

Of course, outwitting a Chameleon requires first that a Hero realize her existence—and this is where Chameleons truly excel. No Chameleon worth her salt appears a Villain at all. And in the case of the elusive Chameleon who survives a Heroic encounter, her best trick is convincing the world she never existed.

Core Aspect: Deception

Every Chameleon's career starts with a moment of enlightenment, when he realizes just how powerful a lie can be. Sometimes that moment comes in bitter desperation; many Chameleons only realize the power of tricks when pursuing seemingly impossible tasks. Others are trained in intrigue from childhood—the effects of family ambition have taught more than one clever scion the value of strategic falsehood. And some learn to play on others' truth-biases in the course of less-than-scrupulous careers grifting, thieving, politics and the like.

To a Chameleon, lies are tools, and powerful tools they are: A properly applied lie can bear fruit entirely disproportionate to the original deception. Honeyed words can start a war, a good disguise can steal a life, and sleight of hand can seem to be sorcery. Chameleons love the beauty in that, lies become the art. A Chameleon is tremendously good at lying to himself as much or more than he lies to everyone else. Ask a Chameleon of his quest and, likely as not, he will say that when he gets it, he will be satisfied. That, too, is a lie. He will never be satisfied.

A View of Heroism
Deft

They're like me, and I like that. But those they are "helping"? They're really just holding them back.

Indomitable

I hear they're good at hitting things. Why would I let myself get hit?

Steadfast

Running against a wall a hundred times will not break the wall before it breaks their heads.

Tactician

They build lovely houses of cards. Shame if someone were to, say, *breathe* near them.

Trickster

They're less predictable than most. Outwitting them should be a ball—assuming they're not simply insane.

Playing the Chameleon

The first question a person playing a Chameleon should ask is: How does the Chameleon trick the world into thinking she doesn't exist or is not what she seems? The second is: How will she then give herself away?

Often Chameleons do not seem like bad guys or tricksters. She may be complicated, seemingly deep, but she never appears as her true self. So how is the Chameleon hiding herself from the world? Is she merely being overlooked? Or maybe she is pretending at Heroics, or a different type of Villainy? Skulking in the shadows—or simply anonymous?

As a Chameleon accomplishes (or fails to accomplish) her aims, what tricks does she fall in love with? What lies give her a particular thrill? Does she have a favorite type of victim? How does she congratulate herself for a job well done?

Chameleons, as a rule, are amoral, calculating, selfish and self-satisfied. This can cue up a fair bit of taunting, creative torture and monologuing, but in fact a Chameleon's malice is rarely central to her identity. Speak to a Chameleon of redemption and you will often get a laugh—but it is not unheard of for a Chameleon to see her talents redirected productively.

Chameleon Schemes

Below is a list of example Schemes you could use for your Chameleon Villain. Do not take them literally! They are jumping off points for you to write Schemes unique to the Villain you are creating.

+ Manipulate the authorities into pursuing the wrong person.
+ Use subterfuge to gain entry to a secure area.
+ Blackmail someone with his own secrets.
+ Kill someone who knows you too well.
+ Lead someone searching for you into a deadly trap.
+ Spread misinformation about your whereabouts and activities.
+ Create an alternate identity for yourself or an ally.
+ Join an organization to shield you from your crimes.

Bogdan Snegovik

History

Bogdan's earliest memory isn't the screaming, or the stench of alcohol, or his mother bleeding on the floor. It's his father's three short knuckle raps before he would open the till and drop in the coins—Bogdan hated that sound. His father, the great barber, so pristine and polite. Bogdan hated the lie, the smile that faded after dark when his father drank. One night—when Bogdan had grown tall, lanky and oh-so quick—his father tried to hit his mother again. This time Bogdan stopped him. He grabbed one of the barber knives and slit his father's throat, until the perfect clothes were as bloody as Bogdan's own hands.

Bogdan's mother, not ready to lose her son in the same night as her husband, bade him run—run far, do not stop, and steer clear of the law. Two decades later, Bogdan still runs across Ussura. Having discovered the country is no place for travelers without coin, he has taken up the only profession he knows: that of barber. He is good at it too, earning invitations to the homes of the rich and powerful, under an assumed name (normally a clever anagram of his true name—Bogdan Snegovik.)

That could be the end of it, if Bogdan were not broken inside. Perhaps, it is the horror of having been beaten by his father, and watching his mother be beaten, all his life. Or maybe it is the power he felt when he finally turned the tables and slit his father's throat. Either way, Bogdan has an unquenchable appetite for power and blood.

Bogdan announces his presence with three short knuckle raps on the window and, after being let inside his customer's home, sets up his barber's table. He is impeccable at his craft: He keeps warm, scented towels at the ready, his shaving creams are soft and luxurious, and his blade is preternaturally sharp. He takes great pride in what he does. Until he is provoked.

A customer who disdains to speak with a "lowly tradesman." Bogdan's knife scrapes and scrapes and then—a quick, neat slit from ear to ear. Afterwards he makes off with their valuables, feeling that he earned them simply by right of being Bogdan the Barber.

Bogdan pretends to be a necessary evil. He collects his customers' secrets—and weeds out the "devils." He insists that he only kills the greedy and the prideful. In reality, he selects his victims on the flimsiest of provocations. He follows them home from the market place or the brothel, and sets himself up as their barber.

Bogdan does not care about the grieving families he leaves behind. The woman he killed for treating him haughtily was a loving and doting mother. That man Bogdan cut down as boastful—an accusation he levels against everyone more successful than himself—spent his life providing for his aging parents. All that matters to Bogdan is how they treat him—if they fawned enough over his skill and intellect. Nothing else makes it past his deranged ego.

Schemes

(1) Hire a streetwise thug to bring him customers who need to be cut down.

Bogdan only kills those he feels deserve it—but there are so many of them. He plans to expand his empire of death by hiring Brutes to bring more victims to him. Despite being rich from all the money he stole, Bogdan pays his helpers as little as possible. The only good money is that in Bogdan's pocket.

(3) Train an apprentice suited to his business, perhaps a Hero.

The world is full of people who dismiss Bogdan's brilliance, and he needs help to kill them all. Corrupting a Hero would bring him pleasure, as it would reaffirm how great he really is. In the end though, Bogdan will settle for any thug, as he always gives in to his baser desire to kill.

(5) Build a reputation so that he will be invited to court.

Serving as barber to the Czar would be Bogdan's greatest ascension of all—and give him a chance to leave his mark on history, as he slices down one of the two contenders for the throne. He is already on his way with a barbing request from a minor noble named Bort Ivanovich.

Bogdan Snegovik

"Three taps is all you hear, three taps and he is near.
He's come to drag you from your bed, come to make
your clothes run red. Three taps and it's time to run,
your neck be open when he is done."
—Ussura Children's Rhyme

USSURA

STRENGTH	INFLUENCE	RANK
8	1	9

Advantages
Disarming Smile (149), Fencer (151),
Quick Reflexes: Weaponry (152),
Signature Item: barber's razor (152), Staredown (150)

Virtue: The Road
Friendly. Activate your Virtue when you meet a character (even a Hero) for the first time. She treats you as friendly for one scene.

Hubris: The Hero
Foolhardy. You receive a Danger Point when your brash, cocky or reckless actions cause trouble for you and another Villain.

Servants and Underlings
Bogdan works alone, but is looking for an apprentice.

Redemption
Bogdan's father was a terrible man who left him permanently scarred, physically and mentally. A true reformation of Bogdan will never be possible. However, convincing or forcing him into some sort of treatment might go a long way to making him less dangerous.

Roleplaying Tips

Bogdan is unfailingly pleasant and polite, right until he slits his victim's throat. He even adheres to Ussuran rules of hospitality. He has a refined palette, especially for meat pie delicacies, and rarely passes an opportunity for a good meal. Despite his tortured childhood, Bogdan has no empathy for others—he kills those that offended him because it makes him feel elevated. Seeking recognition for his greatness, Bogdan brags about his murderous pursuit in the seediest of taverns. He relies on his frightful mien to scare his audience into silence. Ussuran children sing about Bogdan and he is quite proud of that.

Dana Gwozdek

History

The three dievai who happened upon Dana Gwozdek wondered at first whether they were the victims of some kind of elaborate practical joke. There lay a Commonwealth nobleman in a drunken stupor after a night out with his friends, lamenting the death of the Sarmatian caste system, beside a crossroads on the outskirts of town. When they kicked him awake, he mumbled something about porcelain cats and told them to leave him alone.

"We will leave you alone if you promise never to return to your homeland until you have sacrificed one hundred truly noble souls to my dark appetite," said one dievas, prompting a snicker from her companions. The three were quite surprised to hear Gwozdek slur, "Yes, whatever you say."

The fact that this agreement nonetheless was mystically binding should serve as a cautionary tale about the dangers posed by dievai, crossroads and Curonian honey liqueur.

This is not to say that the dievai left Dana Gwozdek completely high and dry. He awoke the next day fully rested and on a pier in Memel Harbor. He picked himself up, brushed off his clothes, started towards the landward side of the dock—and bounced off an invisible wall before he could set foot on Curonian soil.

A few minutes of panic later, Dana was approached by a street urchin who announced that a creepy lady had paid him a zloty to pass on a letter. The letter reiterated the terms of Dana's agreement with the dievai and announced that the dievai had provided transportation and a crew to help him complete his task. A furious Dana, now a losejas, named his new frigate the *Fatal Mistake*.

The *Fatal Mistake* is an impressive craft, largely because it is invisible. The ship also has a crew of damned souls, and Dana suspects that the dievai are using him as an opportunity to get rid of unwanted items that have passed into their clutches.

Especially when its cargo hold is empty, the *Fatal Mistake* excels at sneaking up on other ships. Dana and his unholy crew wrap up in wine-dark outfits and are at their victim's gunwale before anyone realizes

what is going on. Often the defenders stare slack-jawed at the strange floating figures for so long that their ship is boarded before they even have weapons in hand.

As it stands, Dana has taken to spending days on board the ships he has conquered, dressing in the finery of the captains, drinking their ale and sending letters to their loved ones. No petty game seems to quell the banality he feels about his task, but toying with the emotions of people does lighten his mood. Seeing families ripped apart when they find out their loved ones are dead makes him feel a little better about losing his. Dana cares very little for any life that is not his own; he wants nothing more than to be done with his onerous burden.

Schemes

(1) Send the best riches back to his love, Róża.

Poor, sweet Róża. If Dana had only stayed home with his wife that night to organize her porcelain cat collection, he would not be in this mess. She was not happy, to put it mildly, to discover he had become a losejas. But maybe a few boatloads of treasure will keep her true to him while he hunts the seas.

(3) Take leadership of the pirate flagship in Stróż Bay.

Dana is accustomed to having his orders followed—his soulbound crew, who are little more than animated corpses, do what he tells them, but it is not particularly satisfying to see them lurch to the task. Lording over a pirate fleet, though, would make him feel more powerful.

(5) Kill his dievas with the Bone Knife of Seven Saints.

The absurd demon thought she was so smart, tricking a drunk man into giving up his freedom forever. Well, Dana has heard of a few weapons which could do something about that. The Bone Knife of Seven Saints, wrought by martyrs, should do nicely—if he can win it from the Vaticine Church's relic stockpile.

Dana Gwozdek

"I love my country, more than anyone or anything else in the world. the Commonwealth's lush fields, her bustling cities, her mountains, her rivers—you know what, I am not getting through to you. Walk the plank!"

THE SARMATIAN COMMONWEALTH

STRENGTH	INFLUENCE	RANK
6	3	9

Advantages
Fencer (151), Leadership (149), Legendary Trait: Wits (153), Married to the Sea (150), Sorcery: Sanderis (222)

Virtue: The Fool
Wily. Activate your Virtue to escape danger from the current Scene. You cannot rescue anyone but yourself.

Hubris: The Devil
Trusting. You receive a Danger Point when you accept someone's lies or lopsided deal.

Servants and Underlings
Dana's crew is made up of Monsters. They all have the Unliving and Nocturnal Qualities, and obey his orders without thought or question.

Redemption
Dana was essentially tricked into Villainy. While he certainly has played his part since then, he did not choose this path—he made a mistake, and has been overpaying for it ever since. Breaking the curse on Dana is the first step to turning him away from his dark fate.

Roleplaying Tips

Dana is always fidgeting: tapping his foot, pacing, sharpening his blade. During any interaction, he will become annoyed and angry as he thinks of how much time it is taking away from his busy schedule of blood sacrifice and murder.

At Dana's core, lies a deep and abiding love of the land of Sarmatia (albeit *not* The Commonwealth). You can see it in the look in his eyes or the straightening of his back when the subject comes up. He was born and raised thinking his identity was the same as the land his family ruled.

Einar Ibsen

History

In Vestenmennavenjar, where the coin supports the sword's rule, whoever controls the coins has the real power. At least that is what Einar Ibsen keeps telling himself. Born to a long line of jarls, Einar was destined to become one as soon as he came into his inheritance. The problem was that this inheritance was meager when his father inherited it and by the time Einar received it? It was almost nonexistent.

Friends and family alike tried to console Einar. They reminded him that it was his wyrd, the will of the nornir, and the immutable vision of the Allfather that had determined his destiny from before the dawn of time. He had been born into a line of rulers—that was his wyrd—but this also entailed that he had to uphold a now poor, powerless office. Einar, to put it succinctly, was inconsolable.

He abjured his title and his bloodline, denying his wyrd, and chose a new name for his new life: Ibsen. All those who knew and loved him warned of the dangers of such an enterprise, but Einar's refused to listen. Riches were what Einar's heart desired. And power, real power. Absolute power. What is the name people give those with absolute power? God.

The gods who denied Einar's birthright saw fit to chastise him for his sacrilege by taking away his beard. After a fevered dream he awoke to find his beard gone, not a hair left on his chin, which was now as soft as a newborn babe's. To a man as vain as Einar, that was the worst punishment possible. When those closest to him saw this, they reminded him of the warnings. There was still time for atonement. However, he was focused on the power awaiting him if he walked the path he chose for himself.

He forswore the sword for the coin, and the honor of a fair fight for that of hired daggers in the dark. After all, what are rules and regulations to a man who is forging his own destiny? He lied, cheated and stole, quickly becoming a principal shareholder in the Atabean Trading Company. Anyone who tried to stop him was removed by any means necessary.

Then a miracle occurred. One night, a spirit appeared, complimenting him on his will and determination. She said she had never seen a man so unstoppable—nor one more worthy of a fine appearance. She lamented his once-majestic beard. After all, who else was more deserving of that symbol of greatness than Einar?

Einar was seduced beyond his ken, and begged the spirit to help him regain his beard. Laughing, Blodskjeg the Vain—as she revealed her name to be—offered him the hint of a chance to remove the curse and grant him the one desire all his riches could not buy. The cost? Nothing excessive: only the life and soul of Jarl Hlodversson.

Schemes

(1) Trick a Hero into indentured servitude.

Einar needs a good slave, one that can die in his place if need be. He is particularly interested in testing and measuring a Hero's strength, through apparently random attacks that he closely monitors. If he finds a Hero that catches his eye, he will investigate her price. If he discovers that price, he will leave no stone unturned until the Hero becomes his.

(3) Sacrifice Jarl Hlodversson to the spirit Blodskjeg the Vain for a majestic beard.

To achieve this nefarious goal, Einar is considering any and all avenues. His main problem is that the spirit requires him to perform a *real* sacrifice, so Einar cannot simply send hired muscle to remove Hlodversson. This has made Einar resort to all the political and social maneuvering necessary to dishonor the man, then buy his body and soul.

(5) Find the fabled Sapphire City in the New World.

Since he first heard about this marvel, Einar is no longer satisfied with any other wealth he obtains. He has invested the vast resources of the Atabean Trading Company at his disposal—and then some—to discover reliable information on the city's location. Einar is determined to use every resource at his command to find and conquer the city, come Hell or high water.

Einar Ibsen

"'There are no riches beyond my imagination—and
I will have them all, you can count on it.'"

VESTENMENNAVENJAR

STRENGTH	INFLUENCE	RANK
5	10	15

Advantages

An Honest Misunderstanding (151),
Connection: corrupt Vesten officials (149),
Disarming Smile (149), Large (148),
Reputation: shrewd (150), Rich (152), Streetwise (150)

Virtue: The Beggar

Insightful. Activate your Virtue to discover a Brute
Squad's type, or to know a Hero's Advantages.

Hubris: Reunion

Bitterness. You receive a Danger Point when you bring
up old grudges or bad feelings when doing so will lead
to trouble.

Servants and Underlings

Assassins, Duelists and Guards are those who Einar
finds the most useful. Thieves are only trusted when he
knows he has them under his thumb completely.

Redemption

Einar is too far gone for redemption, but he is a
coward. He is not a Villain who is willing to fight to
the death and will happily take a prison sentence if it
means saving his sorry hide.

Roleplaying Tips

Einar Ibsen is a coward at heart, one who overcom-
pensates by buying everyone and everything he
cannot be or have. He knows his cowardice, and
each time he is confronted about it, his reaction is
as violent, cruel and monstrous as his twisted mind
can imagine.

He avoids physical contact as much as possible and,
when nervous, compulsively caresses his nonexistent beard. He can wield a sword if need be, but
he has not been forced to fight in years. As such,
a physical confrontation would be a last resort for
him. He prefers ruining his opponents from afar.

Mother Guineu

History

The streets of Castille are full of unwanted children in need of aid, starving mouths to feed with no parents to look after them. It is a good thing then that Mother Guineu is there to feed and clothe all her lost kits. All she needs in return is their undying devotion, and their eyes and ears in every corner of Castillian society.

Eloise Sibyleigne was the eighth daughter in a minor noble family that could not possibly find eight good matches for their children. While her elder sisters were married to other members of the nobility or wealthy merchants, Eloise knew that when her time came there would be no dowry left and no chance for a suitable match. Instead she dedicated herself to the Church. Eloise believed that given time, she could become one of the most powerful women in the church in San Cristobal.

Ruthless in her manipulation and masterful in her guile, Eloise's machinations were soon spotted by Clara Santoval, the recently named Madre Clara of El Esperanza Chapel. The pious Madre Clara did not believe Eloise's claims at holy intentions and investigated the young woman. The Madre soon uncovered a plot by Eloise to blackmail a local wealthy nobleman into supporting her. There was a minor scandal and Eloise was ejected from the church.

By that time, Eloise had become quite the political animal. She used her connections within the city to cover up the reasons for her ejection. Instead, Eloise had given up her pious life to marry count Bernado de Balbo. Upon his untimely demise, she inherited his name, and Countess Eloise de Balbo settled into a quiet life of polite society. However, behind the scenes, the schemes for power continued, and Eloise's enemies could never discover where she got her information.

The secret lay in her charity work. Eloise created a program of feeding, clothing and even educating the lost children, who she called her "kits." Every child who came under Eloise's care found himself in a better situation than before. All that was required in return was a little spying now and then. The children brought her information from all over Castille, allowing Eloise to reach across the country and even into the politics of all of Théah itself. She used an alias in her dealings, calling herself Mother Guineu.

Now, Mother Guineu stands as a powerful force behind much of the power grabs in San Cristobal. Still, there are those that would stand in her way. Her eldest sister Marjorie's husband, the Count Didacus de Roja is a formidable opponent. Marjorie and Eloise never liked one another in their youth and Eloise has tried to destroy her sister's happiness.

When the count realized Eloise meant to destroy Marjorie, he launched a campaign to stop her by discovering her secrets and dragging them out into the light. He is the closest to discovering the connection between the genteel Countess de Balbo and the mastermind Mother Guineu. Mother Guineu has warned her little kits of the evil Count de Roja, who might take her away from them. The kits all know his name, and will not give up until he is stopped. After all, they would do anything for their Mother.

Schemes

(1) Recruit a secret weapon: a child with magic.

Few things could tip the scales of power in Mother Guineu's favor like having a child with magic on her side. Since magic is largely frowned upon in Castille, the whole endeavor will need to be kept secret, but Mother Guineu knows she needs a weapon up her sleeve that no one will suspect.

(3) Expand her spy ring into the house of Didacus de Roja.

Mother Guineu's kits are all over Castille, but so far they have been unable to penetrate into the house of Count de Roja. She must find access into his household and learn all his secrets.

(5) Blackmail Father Monserrat to gain a position of power within the Church.

Everyone has some weakness that can be exploited. Father Daniel Monserrat blocks any influence Mother Guineu has in the church. She could discover blackmail material and use it to drive the Father out of her way and expand her authority and prestige.

Mother Guineu

"It is well known that the most innocent are the ones that most suffer; I make sure that suffering is not in vain."

CASTILLE

STRENGTH	INFLUENCE	RANK
4	4	8

Advantages
Connection: San Cristobal aristocracy (149), Disarming Smile (149), Lyceum (153), Time Sense (148)

Virtue: The Moonless Night
Subtle. Activate your Virtue when you act behind the scenes, from the shadows or through a proxy. For the next Risk, when you determine Raises, every die counts as a Raise.

Hubris: The Witch
Manipulative. You receive a Danger Point when you try to get someone else to do your dirty work for you, and it backfires.

Servants and Underlings
While she has enough wealth to purchase the loyalty of Guards and the like, the majority of Mother Guineu's underlings are children. These children are almost always Thieves, who avoid a fight if at all possible.

Redemption
Mother Guineu has no interest in being reformed. Even if she is placed in jail, she will most likely find people there to manipulate and control. Only death will free her victims from her clutches.

Roleplaying Tips

As Countess de Balbo, Eloise is the very picture of proper and retiring Castillian nobility, the epitome of charity and grace. Too bad that beneath the surface lies the steely, manipulative heart of a dangerous political animal. Mother Guineu always speaks in kind voices, especially to children, and would fight to the end to protect any of her kits. Her gentle exterior hides a deft and ruthless mind, ready to do anything for power.

Reinhard Vogel

History

Once upon a time, there was a boy whose father was a beloved stage magician. The father did not want a child. For a creature so expensive as a babe was bound to be, he wanted a work of art, something perfect, beautiful and otherworldly. So he trained his son to be a master mimic.

The boy watched others in mirrors for the first few years of his life. He listened to other voices. When he could speak, he never spoke except in echo. His father mixed paints, poultices and potions, taught him to apply new faces. He did not realize the growing boy would learn to mirror others' desires as well.

One day, when his son was exactly as tall as him, he spun the young man to face the mirror. "Become me," he said. So the boy put on his father's face.

His father's name was Reinhard Vogel. The boy had not had a name before this; imitations do not have names. But when he painted his father's face upon himself, he became someone who existed. And this was new, and real, and exhilarating and terrifying.

It might have occurred to another man to use his newfound existence to take what he wanted. But this-person-who-currently-was-Reinhard was merely a mirror; he had no desires of his own. So he took what his father wanted, because what other desires were there? There was a girl his father wanted to seduce. This-man-who-was-now-Reinhard made love to her. Afterwards, he wasn't sure if he enjoyed it.

He returned that evening expecting his father's pride. He had been a superb imitation. His father's face was distorted in fear and rage. "You're going to Hell," he said.

Reinhard took a step back. "No," he said. "You are." His father was holding a knife. A body was found backstage that night. No one knew if it was father or son, except Reinhard Vogel.

Reinhard Vogel escaped into another life. He grew angry, despising people for their own hypocrisy. He became a coffin-maker, a sentinel, a sailor. Being loved was intoxicating—so he became those who were beloved. He wrapped himself in their desires—it had not occurred to him that he could have desires of his own.

He adores all his victims. He lives out their wildest fantasies for them and can never understand why they do not adore him. When they reject him, he discards their lives and moves onto a new one. He has made a game of becoming those who seem most beloved until those who love that person learn to despise him. He drugs his victims, binds them, recites to them their litany of desires, sins he is committing in their names. He lets his victims go when he is done with them, but they never return to their old lives.

He wonders sometimes—on haunted evenings, when he is no-one else—if there is a person he could become who he would not break. He sometimes wonders if the sins he commits in the name of others are really his own.

Schemes

(1) Replace a Hero and ruin their reputation.

If asked, Reinhard will say he thinks people are just a catalog of sins waiting to be committed, but in truth he is fascinated by goodness. He only imitates people he thinks are "good," or at least "beloved" and when he has a Hero in his clutches, he is determined to prove that the Hero is a monster—like Reinhard. Why are Heroes beloved, while he is despised?

(3) Unlock the secret of becoming a true doppelgänger.

Eisen folktales tell of *doppelgängers*, mimics supernaturally empowered to find and replace "real" humans; Reinhard wants to call himself a *doppelgänger*, only there is no magic to his tricks. Tales of such creatures have gone out of fashion in recent years, and perhaps there are no longer any to be found—but then the best *doppelgängers* would not be found, would they?

(5) Successfully capture and replace the ruler of a Nation.

The catalog of sins for a king or queen must be monstrous—but the forgiveness afforded to a ruler, even a self-indulgent one, more monstrous still. Replacing a Hero sounds fascinating; replacing a monarch even more so.

Reinhard Vogel

"You will always love me. I represent to you all the sins you never had the courage to commit."

EISEN

STRENGTH	INFLUENCE	RANK
11	1	12

Advantages, Virtue and Hubris

Unlike other Villains, Reinhard has no Advantages, Virtue or Hubris of his own. Instead, he has all of the Advantages of whatever character he is impersonating.

Servants and Underlings

Reinhard uses the servants and people around the person he is impersonating as his underlings.

Redemption

Reinhard emulates his targets as perfectly as he can manage, physically as well as psychologically. While this is only his warped perception of their psychology, under the right circumstances (and while he is imper-sonating the right person) Reinhard might be turned to a better and brighter path. Another method might be to encourage Reinhard to finally gain his own identity—challenging, but more likely to meet with permanent success.

Roleplaying Tips

In disguise, facing someone he means to fool, Reinhard is in every way the person he mimics. His terrifying training gives him the gait, the stutter, the parts of speech—all the externalities of his target. The person he is disguised as will seem to have her skills diminished, her sins magnified, her virtues hesitant.

Out of disguise, Reinhard is no one. Uneasy when people acknowledge him as a human separate from his masks, he stutters and stumbles, forgets his words. Reinhard will go to great lengths to find someone new to mimic rather than acting as himself. He is surprisingly desperate for affection.

Stavros Sarris

History

Many participants in Captain Küçük Metaxas's war for Numan independence were surprised to find, upon their success, that they did not all agree on what to do with the Numanari government. One of the most disappointed was Stavros Sarris, a successful Numanari businessman who used connections and sleazy deals to make life difficult for foreigners trying to invest in a not-so-free Numa. He positioned himself as a counter-revolutionary figure with the ability to help Vodacce and Crescent investors in the island keep control; but when the foreigners put money and resources into deals with Stavros, everything slowly went to hell.

Contractors worked slowly on-site, materials and employees went missing, things were built according to the wrong specifications—everything that could possibly go wrong went wrong. At every turn, an apologetic Stavros promised that the barracks for their garrison were just a little behind schedule and if they only put a little more money in, surely they could build something that would end the revolution. Over. And over. And over.

To a casual observer, Stavros played a small part in the revolution for Numa; but to Stavros himself, he was integral to the cause. Stavros was appalled to see the diversity of governmental systems that emerged in the wake of the revolution. They were a mess, and he wanted to rule them, but could not figure out how. He made the rounds of his Numanari contacts during the revolution, but all of them gave noncommittal answers and weak offers of support, rather than the love and gratitude he felt he deserved.

As Stavros turned away from politics, and back to his business, he was distressed to find that many of his contacts in Vodacce and Crescent territory actually trusted him more than the Numanarians! The Vodacce in particular were quite understanding (the Vodacce, as a rule, do not take betrayal and treachery personally). Every deal he broke and every building he sabotaged was for Numa, and what were the thanks he got? Mistrusted and held at arm's length by his own countryfolk, despite his political ambitions.

Stavros hatched a plan, interacting with his Vodacce contacts, to get control of Numa back from the ungrateful wretches who used his help and discarded him. The plan involved getting Numa back into the clutches of a much more powerful Nation, which then could strangle Numanari foreign trade and squeeze the life out of it, until Stavros could stand atop Numa's corpse. Stavros had once dreamed of a free Numa, that he controlled, but if his Nation must be in chains to be ruled—so be it.

Stavros next targets the Senate; but he aspires to even greater things. After all, should Numa fall into Vodacce hands again, the islands will need a Merchant Prince, and Stavros has a good idea who it should be.

Schemes

(1) Smuggle ancient Numanari pottery to Vodacce to gain influence.

Numa's resources fetch excellent prices on mainland Théah. Vodacce, the capital of conspicuous consumption, has a lot of money for rare and prestigious items. Of course, after centuries of other nations scavenging their artifacts, Numa now calls for all the world to return the Numanari handicrafts stolen over the centuries—they will not take kindly to Stavros' attempt to get in good with Vodacce at their expense.

(3) Get a law passed allowing Merchant Princes to own land in Akragosus.

Numa is still exceedingly suspicious of Vodacce, Crescents and even Sarmatians coming to Numa to do business. Stavros will rise in standing with the Merchant Princes if he gets an ordinance passed which allows a Vodacce legal recourse against anyone who denies him property for a fair price.

(5) Poison Delia Nikas of the Akragosus Senate and take her place.

Stavros eventually wants to be Merchant Prince of a Vodacce Numa, but in the meantime he needs to accumulate political power and influence. A seat on the Senate is the best way to achieve that, but his lack of charisma makes a fair election an unlikely prospect for him. If a seat suddenly empties off-cycle—such as that held by Delia Nikas—he might have a chance of filling it through his Numanari contacts.

Stavros Sarris

"It was my money, my work, my neck on the line in the revolution. If you are not going to pay me back for what I did, then I will damn well take it from you."

NUMA

STRENGTH	INFLUENCE	RANK
3	10	13

Advantages
Barterer (149), Connection: Vodacce politicians (149), Linguist (148), Rich (152)

Virtue: The Emperor
Commanding. Activate your Virtue. The GM gains a Danger Point for each other Villain or Brute Squad in this Scene.

Hubris: The Beggar
Envious. You receive a Danger Point when your Villain covets something, and does something unwise to get it.

Servants and Underlings
Stavros has deep pockets to hire a multitude of individuals to do his dirty work for him. He regards these people as disposable, however, and so has a high turnover rate and no loyal or long-time minions.

Redemption
Stavros is an entitled megalomaniac. He will never change.

Roleplaying Tips
Stavros Sarris sees himself and his efforts as the lifeblood of the Numanari Revolution. He was important, but he did not make it all happen by himself. Stavros is sleazy and spiteful, always looking for the loophole that will gain him an advantage in any deal. He is a furious ball of angry energy: feet tapping, fingers drumming, pacing back and forth in the room as he bubbles over with resentment. He dresses well, but he always looks like he rushed his clothes on in 60 seconds when he needed five minutes to get them looking perfect.

Tassine Bullet

History

"The argent crescent of the autumn moon shone mysteriously down through the swaying trees, highlighting the muscular yet curvaceous figure of the infamous highwaywoman, expert duelist and fashion icon, Tassine Anastasia Jade de la Croix Bullet. 'How bittersweet,' she thought, 'a tempting prize must stir me from my meditation on the tragic years of my youth!' Nevertheless, she boldly leapt astride her chestnut courser, Chanson-de-Minuit, and galloped swiftly after the coach."

—Excerpt from Tassine Bullet, Queen of Thieves, by ~~Modestine Porcher~~ Tassine Bullet

After a brief affair, Modestine's mother found herself with an inconvenient child. She endured parenthood about two years before she left little Modestine on her father's doorstep, along with a note saying Modestine deserved far better than her mother could give her.

Modestine's upbringing was staid and mundane. Thanks to Monsieur Porcher's trade as a scrivener, she at least had a lot of books to read. She devoured adventure novels, developing a romantic figure of her mother as a dashing antiheroine to contrast with her dull father. When she turned 13, she ran away and joined the notorious Gold Ribbon Girls. Named for the ornamentation on their sword hilts, this all-female gang of bandits preys on highways outside Charouse.

As she worked her way up through the ranks of the gang, she wrote a never-ending torrent of stories based on popular fictional characters. Her pieces were plagued by passive voice; adverbs and adjectives inelegantly bloated her purple prose. Yet, Modestine reckoned that the lack of original content, rather than her lack of talent, prevented her from getting published.

Only after her ascent to leadership of the Gold Ribbon Girls did things reverse. She changed her name to "Tassine Bullet," beating up anyone who called her Modestine. She changed the Girls' methods: Instead of preying on the easiest targets, they went after high-profile ones, who were sure to share reports of the robberies with the papers when they returned home. Tassine has now become the greater Charouse area's most notorious criminal, entirely by design.

The Girls also dabble in kidnapping as an easy way to build the narrative, keeping individuals whom they catch on the road in their secret forest lair. Tassine tortures her victims with hours of dramatic readings of her adventure stories, then forces them to memorize exaggerated descriptions of the gang's talent, so when they return to society, they can spread the world about Tassine Bullet and the gang.

Any time she hears of another criminal gaining notoriety, she finds him and throttles him until he seeks early retirement. If Tassine hears of an interesting Hero or Villain growing to prominence in Charouse, she becomes obsessed with his fame and taking it for herself. She antagonizes interesting Heroes just so she can engage in high-profile rivalries with them. The question, "What could I do right now to make myself more popular?" dominates all of Tassine's actions.

Schemes

(1) Destroy her birth certificate, the last proof of her real name.

Of all Tassine's parents' crimes, naming her "Modestine" was most tragic. She does not care how many guards she has to bribe, knock out or set on fire to infiltrate the Imperial Archives and destroy the proof that she was ever anyone other than Tassine Bullet.

(3) Seduce Musketeer Captain Cailloux to her side.

Captain Cailloux, musketeer liaison to the highway patrol, is as corrupt as he is sexy. With him in her pocket (and her bed), the Gold Ribbon Girls can run rampant. But he is already in an affair with the sympathetic Talia Besson! It would be a shame if something happened to Talia.

(5) Kidnap Aron Pons, the head of the highway patrol.

Tassine envisions a Montaigne where travelers pay tolls to bandits rather than government agents, where her robberies make her a folk hero. Aron Pons is one of the last good highway guards incorruptible and resistant to Tassine's numerous charms. Pons' removal from the highways will leave them open for the Gold Ribbon girls to coerce, extort and rob to their hearts' content.

Tassine Bullet

"Which brings out the luscious colour of my hair more, the sabre or the pistol?"

MONTAIGNE

STRENGTH	INFLUENCE	RANK
7	4	11

Advantages
Camaraderie (151), Fencer (151), Joie de Vivre (154), Leadership (149), Staredown (150)

Virtue: Coins
Adaptable. Activate your Virtue to take your first Action before anyone else in a Round.

Hubris: The Lovers
Star-Crossed. You receive a Danger Point when you become enamored with someone you really should not.

Servants and Underlings
The Gold Ribbon Girls are Guards, Duelists or Thieves. While some chafe under her leadership and might be turned against her (perhaps even becoming a Trusted Companion to one of the Heroes), most enjoy the prestige, pageantry and mean-spirited sisterhood that comes with membership.

Redemption
Tassine's Villainous exploits are borne from a romanticized view of the world. Showing her that she could just as easily accomplish this as a Hero is most likely to lead to success. Such Heroes should be prepared for what a Heroic version of Tassine would be like, however...

Roleplaying Tips

Tassine Bullet takes many Heroic and Villainous tropes to their logical, insufferable extreme—on purpose. If she had a mustache, she would twirl it. No cliché scheme, one-liner or wardrobe choice is beneath her. She frequently embodies exaggerated versions of Heroes' traits. If a Hero has a tragic, tortured backstory, Tassine monologues about her own tragic history, to win at misery poker.

The Gold Ribbon Girls are Tassine's greatest strength and clearest weakness. The Girls like the life of adventure and indulgence Tassine promises (and delivers), but she is tiresome, overbearing and patronizing.

Thora Ulfborn

History

The world was once an ideal paradise, where everyone could live and die in freedom and with dignity. This is the core belief that drives Thora Ulfborn in her battle against the twin oppressors at the heart of the world's corruption. Born to a peasant couple in Korren, a tiny town inside the Jarl Forest, Thora grew up largely ignorant of the difficulties of the world.

As Thora grew, local carl levied tax after tax, all but bankrupting Korren. Soon Korren was a ghost town, and those that remained behind starved. One particularly cold winter, there was simply not enough food for everyone. Thora's parents boiled tree bark to eat while she was given the last of the cheese. One morning, her parents did not wake up. Thora tried to wake them for two days, until a tax collector arrived and found her beside her parents' bodies.

The tax collector brought Thora to an orphanage in Kirk. Thora's hungry mind picked up everything quickly, from reading to history, her lessons teaching her more about the illness fueling the world. War, corruption, intolerance—all seemed driven by two things: the nobility and the Church. It was no surprise then that when she heard about the Rilasciare, she fled the orphanage and never looked back.

By the age of 16, Thora was a major member of the Rilasciare in Kirk. She believed as they did, that the Church and the nobility were destroying the world. Each time she returned to Kirk, she would wonder when all the talk would finally turn into revolution. She waited—and watched people starve, lose their land, lose all hope—and her anger grew.

The breaking point came when Thora was 19. A local power struggle between church luminaries disrupted all charitable works in Kirk, including the orphanage which had sheltered Thora. As funding dwindled and she saw the children there suffer without food as a cold winter approached. One night, several of the children started a fire to keep warm and the sparks ignited a mattress; the entire children's wing went up in a blaze that lit the night. In all, 46 children and ten matrons died.

Thora watched helplessly from the crowd, unable to save a single one. Seething with rage, she went to the homes of both church luminaries, blocked all the exits and set the buildings on fire. In one night she killed two major members of the Vaticine Church in Kirk, and their 15 servants and family members, trapped inside their burning homes.

Thora believed that her actions would spark a revolution, and was horrified when the other members of the Rilasciare condemned her as a radical. She had done more with two fires than two years of secret meetings and clandestine whisper campaigns. So Thora has taken a radical stance from the larger body and gone on a one-woman crusade against the Two Tyrannies herself, intent to cleanse Vestenmennavenjar from within with most powerful tool of her obsession: fire.

Schemes

(1) Organize secret meetings to spread messages of resistance against the nobility and the Church.

The people of Vestenmennavenjar are ready for a revolution, or so Thora thinks. She must spread the story of the coming uprising wherever she goes, organizing meetings to recruit members to her radical version of the Rilasciare. It does not matter how great the opposition. The message must continue.

(3) Conduct a brutal raid on Castillian diplomats to discredit Jarl Reinn Sigurdsen.

Local jarl Reinn Sigurdsen is the latest target of Thora's ire. Sigurdsen oversaw the city during the orphanage fire, and Thora blames him for the tragedy. His political career is based largely on fostering trade with Castille, and his diplomats are his treasures. Their brutal deaths will discredit him and upend his power once and for all.

(5) Burn down the meeting of the jarls at Ketil Hall.

A major meeting of the jarls has been called to discuss the dispensation of taxes and the raids along the coast by pirates. There will never be such a perfect time to destroy the oppressors of the people all in one place. Once everyone is inside, Thora intends to bar the doors and set the entire place ablaze.

Thora Ulfborn

"The fire is stoked. The oil is spilt. The flames will burn the corruption out—once and for all."

VESTENMENNAVENJAR

STRENGTH	INFLUENCE	RANK
7	3	10

Advantages
Connection: Vesten revolutionaries (149);
Legendary Trait: Panache (153); Psst, Over Here (150);
Second Story Work (150), Staredown (150)

Virtue: The Sun
Glorious. Activate your Virtue when you are the center of attention. For the next Risk, when you determine Raises, every die counts as a Raise.

Hubris: The Prophet
Overzealous. You receive a Danger Point when your Villain strongly defends one of her opinions when the time or place is inappropriate.

Secret Society
Rilasciare

Servants and Underlings
As a member of the Rilasciare, Thora can summon a Mob made up of local commoners and workers. Because of her connection to the Rilasciare any Brute Squad she creates with her Influence has its Strength increased by half—if she pays Influence to create a Strength 10 Brute Squad, for example, it becomes Strength 15.

Redemption
Thora is a revolutionary. While she has gone far beyond what the Rilasciare find acceptable, the goals she pursues are at their root, noble. Remind Thora that the purpose of revolution itself, is to protect those who cannot protect themselves.

Roleplaying Tips
Thora is a political zealot and a serial arsonist. Her brilliant mind is turned towards the bloody business of popular upheaval and she will not stop until the Two Tyrannies are overthrown. Thora's youth often makes people underestimate her, a fact that Thora uses to her advantage. Quick and cautious, she walks on cat-like silent feet and sneaks as quiet as death when committing arson. But when called upon, she can rally a group with stirring speeches like few others, preaching about the freedom long lost to the people of Vestenmennavenjar, soon to be reclaimed in righteous fire.

Mastermind Villains

"Oh. You brought a weapon. There you are with your
sword, and here I am, a noble with a wig and fan.
Still, I fear you overestimate your chances of success.
You see, you still think you are fighting only me."
—Adeliadis Petronilla Fassequele

Masterminds are always *popular*. Many Masterminds
are, incidentally, charismatic and charming,
masterful conversationalists. But that is not why the
Mastermind's company is sought—at least, it is not
the only reason. A Mastermind has something other
people want and he is willing to milk that advantage
for all it is worth. This loyalty and adoration that
Masterminds enjoy from others, while it may seem
genuine, is completely forced. No one loves having to
grovel for information or taking the fall for something
he has not done.

Want access to what the Mastermind has? Well, you
will have to do him a few favors first. Learn to dance
to the Mastermind's tune and you will fall so deep
into his schemes that you will no longer be innocent,
and no longer willing to see him fail, because the
Heroes are coming to take you down, too. That is
what comes of getting involved with a Mastermind.

Masterminds crave *power*. Oh, a Mastermind often
wants something else too—beauty, love, the thrill
of the hunt. But these things are all subordinate to
power. For what is bedding a beauty or winning a
gamble, except a show of power? A Mastermind
adores power. He caresses it. He covets it.

Sometimes this can be exploited. A Mastermind can
render himself vulnerable, ironically, when he risks
displaying his power in order to experience the pleasure of control. It is not uncommon for a Mastermind
to let himself be suckered into a monologue, into
tormenting a victim a little longer, or into one final
gamble, because, after all, one of the pleasures of
having power is experiencing it. The more sensual
Masterminds will say that it is the entire point of the
game—the rush from feeling the power in your hands.

The Mastermind likes to surround himself with
people. People are his puppets, his pawns, malleable
pieces in the great game of life. Moreover, people are
his audience and armor—a Mastermind's weakness
is he cannot work alone. The Mastermind depends
on others to do his dirty work, and without others to
manipulate, he is at a distinct disadvantage.

The brave Hero must beware, lest he come to believe
that the "others" the Mastermind can manipulate
only include those loyal to the Mastermind: Many a
Heroic party has fallen this way. Surrounded, without
his followers, the Mastermind may seem vulnerable.
However, it is not only his friends the Mastermind
manipulates—Heroes are people, too.

Core Aspect: Manipulation

The Mastermind knows that people alone are powerless. A person alone can kill or die, but a person alone is nothing compared to ten, a hundred, a thousand of the same. Power comes from pluralities working in concert; the Mastermind wants to be the conductor.

The mastermind sees people as tools. She uses those she can manipulate to accomplish her ends. These may be far reaching and political, or they may be as cheap as the next thrill. The Mastermind's goal could be an apocalypse—or to make a noble court more vibrant, interesting and thrilling. But whatever motivation and consequence intended, the Mastermind feels no remorse when she ruins lives to get what she desires.

Many Masterminds started their careers as Tacticians, those who move people and set schemes in motion, but in the service of a greater good. While the Tactician works for a cause outside himself, a Mastermind works for herself.

Where this transformation is born varies from person to person. Perhaps, there was a moment in the Mastermind's past when she viscerally learned that alone, she was powerless—only by keeping others in awe of her, could she stay safe. Her manipulations act as a security blanket, keeping a wall of bodies between herself and the world. Or perhaps, she simply got bored with being good.

A View of Heroism

Deft
They spin lovely lies, I create the truth.

Indomitable
They fight well. I have armies for that.

Steadfast
They think grit and guts will get them what they want? All the willpower in the world cannot overcome the fact that each one of them is alone.

Tactician
Oh, the naïve fools—do they really think they're supposed to *care for* the people they use as tools?

Trickster
They embrace chaos because they are too short-sighted to plan. Pathetic.

Playing the Mastermind

The Mastermind has optimized himself for manipulation, meaning that more often than not, he is a delight in company. He may be sharp, wicked and witty, a bit intimidating to be around (as popular people often are). Catch the interest of a Mastermind and suddenly he is funny—he knows what will amuse you. He is thoughtful—he always knows what you want. And, he is caring—the things you care about, in the deepest core of your soul, you will find he cares about, too. Mourning for your lost child? The Mastermind understands, and will bare his soul to you with his story of tragedy. Married to a woman you loathe? The Mastermind will tell you it is not so bad to start an affair.

Sometimes, however, Masterminds will not tell you what you want to hear. Sometimes, he will merely tell you what you expect, and what you fear. Maybe he will lie to you, say your husband died in yesterday's massacre. Those gambling debts? They are worse than you think. Your terrible illness? You haven't got much longer—not unless you do what he says. The Mastermind can always save you—or at least keep you distracted.

Mastermind Schemes

Below is a list of example Schemes you could use for your Mastermind Villain. Do not take them literally! They are jumping off points for you to write Schemes unique to the Villain you are creating.

+ Use leverage you have over someone to get what you want.
+ Seduce someone powerful or important.
+ Destroy someone's confidence or position.
+ Spread gossip about your enemies.
+ Find a patsy to take the fall.
+ Assemble a squad of loyal minions.
+ Seize land and assets from a weaker foe.
+ Pit friends against one another to weaken their bonds.

Adeliadis Petronilla Lassequele

History

Adeliadis has everything. Charouse nobility, born and bred, she grew up suckling at the teat of courtly intrigue, rather than drinking the milk of human kindness. Her father, Etienne, was a famous rake of the court, with a long string of beautiful mistresses. Her mother, Genevieve, was a celebrated prosecutor with a flawless record of convictions. Her parents rarely had time for each other, but Adeliadis always made sure they made time for her, through whatever antics she could.

Taking inspiration from her mother's ruthless legal endeavors, her first intrigues were to manipulate her father's mistresses, maneuvering their relationships to suit her. Etienne despaired of his romantic failures and, instead of disciplining his child, wrote volumes of self-indulgent poetry. Genevieve quickly realized that Adeliadis' own keen mind was the only thing that could keep her in check. Genevieve taught her daughter how to navigate courtly politics safely, but died of consumption before she could temper Adeliadis' devious urges. With the loss of her mother's restraint, Adeliadis became an unstoppable force of brilliant cruelty.

Her father attempted to remarry, but Adeliadis sabotaged each and every betrothal. Now Etienne is a bitter old hermit, living on the family estate far from Charouse, receiving perfumed letters from Adeliadis every day, full of elegant descriptions of her adventures. She encourages him to write his memoirs, as all enlightened men should in their twilight years, and promises she will see it published once it is properly edited.

Her clique, Les Papillons—"The Butterflies"—is a troupe of young courtiers who follow her every whim, happily engaging in social savagery at others' expense. Adeliadis also pits her Papillons against each other, to ensure her own prime position is never threatened. She sets them tasks—expose a gambler's shame, embarrass young lovers in front of their peers, steal private and damning correspondence—and flutters prettily around her victims as they fall.

Having developed into a beautiful young woman, and receiving the attention of scores of men, she has discovered how useful it is to be rid of the annoying ones by setting them to duel each other. Having young fools dying on each other's blades for her is a delightfully amusing pastime. Her murderous habits have started to catch the notice of the Lightning Guard, who frequently hear her name associated with this illegal fighting.

Schemes

(1) Bribe a master duelist to kill her enemies in a duel.

Her current enemies are a group of young women in the Court—The Pleiades—who have begun targeting her and her Papillons with witty mockery and social sabotage. Their leader, Giselle, is a trained Valroux swordswoman, and Adeliadis feels she is on the verge of being called out. Knowing she needs to be prepared, she has set her sights on Master Rodolphe de Saint-Nectaire, who she knows has extensive debts and may be persuaded to end this matter before it begins.

(3) Gain social standing as l'Empereur's mistress.

L'Empereur is planning a spring garden party, where he traditionally spends time with his mistress. Adeliadis wants to "arrange" for his current favorite to be ill that day, and then to do all she can to stand out among the other young ladies of the court. L'Empereur has spoken several times with her lately, and she has flirted with him—sending notes and gifts—and she feels he has responded favorably.

(5) Destroy the Impératrice's reputation with lascivious rumors.

Adeliadis wants to destroy the Impératrice's reputation so that she herself, as l'Empereur's mistress, will become the most powerful woman in the court. However, the Impératrice is Sorte Strega, so destroying her reputation is both extremely difficult and extremely dangerous. Adeliadis has charged her Papillons to arrange a widespread series of unfortunate and alarming mishaps to befall the Impératrice's daughters and weaken the Sorte Strega considerably.

Adeliadis Petronilla Fassequele

"Let us see how red we can make the lily-white face of that obnoxious Fronsac girl! I want her cut down a few notches before the Spring Ball..."

MONTAIGNE

STRENGTH	INFLUENCE	RANK
4	10	14

Advantages
Come Hither (149), Friend at Court (149), Lyceum (153), Time Sense (148)

Virtue: The Sun
Glorious. Activate your Virtue when you are the center of attention. For the next Risk, when you determine Raises, every die counts as a Raise.

Hubris: The Witch
Manipulative. You receive a Danger Point when you try to get someone else to do your dirty work for you, and it backfires.

Servants and Underlings
Adeliadis has a small contingent of Guards that protect her in any situation that she feels may be dangerous. She may hire others on a case-by-case basis, but the majority of her power comes through her social circles—Adeliadis is more likely to attack her enemies with blackmail and secrets than with swords or bullets.

Redemption
Adeliadis has always been manipulative and untrustworthy. There is no redemption for her, but she would work with Heroes for a time if it served her own selfish purposes.

Roleplaying Tips

Adeliadis is gorgeous, has a searing intellect and she knows it. If she chose, she could be a great scholar or a brilliant general, but these things do not matter to her. What matters are the delicate and devastating machinations of the powerful. She speaks in a lilting, carefree tone, and will not reveal her cruelty until she has her victim exactly where she wants him. She often has a small, over-primped animal leashed at hand, such as a monkey. The way she treats these creatures provides an excellent guide to her emotional state, for she does not conceal her true feelings from those she utterly controls.

Agafya Markova

History

Twins are a gift from the Leshiye, they say, maybe that is why both children were born with the green eyes that signify the chosen of Grandmother Winter. Agafya Markova was the firstborn and Viktor followed swiftly after. Technically, as the firstborn, Agafya would inherit her parent's land, but she could not see herself ruling without her brother by her side.

Agafya always liked those mornings when she awoke to find a fresh blanket of snow covering the world in serene beauty. As children, the twins would sneak out to disturb the perfect layer of white. On one of these perfect mornings, many years later, Agafya decided she would go out and hunt. She walked downstairs and found Viktor waiting in his red fur-lined boots.

She tried to convince him to stay in that day. He was not feeling well, but he insisted on coming along, for old times' sake. A blizzard caught them on their way back, and the only thing they could do was dig a shelter. The storm raged for hours; Viktor's hand, clutching hers, turned ice cold. A soft shudder passed through her brother's body as his last breath passed his lips.

Suddenly, a wrinkled hand pulled her through the snow and Agafya knew it was Matushka who saved her. She begged for her brother's life to be restored, terrified of being left truly alone. The woman clucked her tongue, reaching into her muddy boot and pulling out a small vial. Agafya grabbed it, not caring about the vial's dire price—that she must learn to stand on her own.

She never told Viktor he died that day. He did not understand when she had to banish him, but if she let him stay she could not keep her promise to the Mother. Her mind twisted and turned over the Mother's words and the only way Agafya could think to keep her promise was to be free of her brother.

Agafya's heart ached, fighting against her very nature, but like a river changes course so did she adapt to life alone. The constant heartache became the fuel for a cruel persistence. She came to see that emotion merely muddled the clarity of the logic she needed to rule.

Focused on maintaining utter control of her lands, she disguised herself with Matushka's Gift to mingle with the peasantry and hear the sentiments among them. If she caught scent of rebels or insurgents, she had them lifted from their beds and publicly executed. All was going well until "the Hero" came.

Viktor had come to free the people from Agafya, but her forces quickly subdued him. When he was brought before her, Agafya did what she swore she would never do again—she spared her foolish brother's life. Burning away the last shred of compassion in her heart, she chased Viktor of her domain. He was long gone when she realized she had lost the Mother's Gift.

Schemes

(1) Groom a trustworthy villager as a spy.

Without her Gift of Disguise Agafya is unable to infiltrate and spy on her populace. Having a trustworthy villager spy on his own people would make it much easier to keep track of any undesirable developments. Since the banishment of her brother and creation of the work camp, Agafya's image has suffered terribly and the populace no longer trusts her.

(3) Destroy the rebel group opposing her rule.

Recently a rebel group has launched several guerilla attacks in her domain. Secretly, Agafya hopes her brother is the one behind them, so she can do her penance and regain her Gift. Gathering information will be her first step. Her guards have given word there is a merchant in town, Sergei. Questioning him will be her first step.

(5) Fill her prisoner work camp with the remaining dissidents.

Agafya believes total control is a necessity for efficient leadership. To that end, she has created a prison camp to send all dissidents who oppose her rule. Without villagers opposing her rule and rallying behind those who would seek to overthrow her, her brother will have a near impossible time dethroning her.

Agafya Markova

"The only way to lead is by absolute control of your subjects. How can I protect my people if they will not follow my orders blindly? Resistance must be struck down hard, lest it spread."

USSURA

STRENGTH	INFLUENCE	RANK
8	8	16

Advantages
Indomitable Will (149), Leadership (149), Rich (152), Second Story Work (150), Sorcery: Mother's Touch (217)

Virtue: The Beggar
Insightful. Activate your Virtue to discover a Brute Squad's type, or to know a Hero's Advantages.

Hubris: The Thrones
Stubborn. You receive a Danger Point when you are stubborn and refuse to change your mind in the face of evidence.

Sorcery
Agafya has the Gift of Resurrect. Her Restriction is Dignity. (See Appendix)

Monster Qualities
Agafya has the Quality of Shapeshifter, with the limitation that she can only change her form to that of another human. However, this Quality is tied to her Lesson from Mother's Touch (see Appendix: Sorcery: Mother's Touch, Dignity (Restriction)). Until she completes her Penance, she cannot access this Quality.

Servants and Underlings
Agafya has no shortage of Guards and Duelists willing and eager to serve her. Her lack of access to reliable spies is notable—if she were to gain such allies, they would be represented by Thieves that answer directly to her.

Redemption
Agafya believes that the act of sparing her brother's life is the reason she has lost her magic. While she is not wholly wrong, her understanding of this is flawed—it is not that she spared his life, but why. Agfya asked Matushka to spare her brother for selfish reasons—she was afraid to be alone—and then refused to honor her word for the same reasons. If Agafya can be shown the error of her way of thinking, learn to truly care rather than thinking only of herself, she might be turned away from her dark path.

Roleplaying Tips

Agafya's adherence to logic may seem sensible from a distance but up close and personal her icy personality and cruel tendencies are not so appealing. Agafya rarely smiles, and when she does, her grimace is so insincere it makes your skin crawl. She is very controlling and has little patience for any misguided fools who try to tell her how to rule her lands.

Anatol Akalewicz

History

At one time many believed that Anatol Akalewicz was going to become one of the greatest labor leaders in all the Commonwealth. Born to a businessman and his wife, Anatol was raised listening to political speeches supporting the power of commoners to fight for a better future for themselves. Anatol believed he would become part of that legacy, and exercise his beliefs through where he spent and generated his money. He worked closely with his father and upon the old man's death, inherited the business.

Once Anatol became a businessman, he came to understand the levels of corruption that prevented the commoners from becoming truly equal with the nobility. Not everyone embraced the Golden Liberty; many of those with wealth used their privilege to keep the people in their place. He tried to be a good citizen, all the while becoming more frustrated by how corruption disenfranchised the poor all around him.

Anatol decided to stand up and advocate with the Sejm for better transparency of the internal politics of the country. He believed that should the people gain access to information, they would be better able to interact with the system. Anatol spoke passionately and eloquently, at rallies and in private rooms, vehemently defending his position.

For that reason Anatol's business was burnt to the ground. Furious, he watched as his workers died in the blaze and a man snuck away from the fire. Anatol caught the arsonist, intending to take him to the authorities, but the man laughed and said he would beat any charges, because of who protected him.

Incensed, the rage inside Anatol flared and he beat the arsonist to death, right then and there. Certain that he would be caught, he hid in a local tavern, where he was contacted by a local underworld broker named Berchik Russalek.

Berchik explained that Anatol could be safe against his political enemies, escape a murder charge and could even rebuild his business. All he needed was protection from the politicians, protection that organized crime could give him. Anatol quickly agreed.

Over the next few years, Anatol became a member of the Commonwealth's underground criminal network. All his built-up passion and rage became the fuel he used to overpower any opponent. Whatever squeamishness Anatol might have once had disappeared, and he became a brutal criminal player. Soon, he ran his own criminal organization, predicated on one idea: The common man could not depend on any support from the government. Anatol's protection rackets and smuggling under government tariffs, along with raids to seize weapons for resale targeted nobility.

To this day, Anatol uses his criminal connections to wriggle his way into the political sphere. Come what may, Anatol has dreams of turning his criminal empire into a viable alternative to the Sejm, a branch of the merchant class that has the resources and the guts to face down the noble's corruption.

Schemes

(1) Uncover the mole in his criminal organization.

Members of the Sejm have tried to pull apart Anatol's criminal empire for years. Now, important secrets only his inner circle would know have gotten into the hands of the authorities: there is a mole in Anatol's operation. Anatol will find and destroy the mole before she corrupts everything he has built.

(3) Blackmail or bully Curonian nobleman Adomas Valdas out of power.

Adomas Valdas is not a good man. The nobleman is responsible for half-starving his peasants while signing plenty of contracts to produce weapons to the military. Find information to blackmail Adomas out of that position of power. It would be even sweeter if those weapons produced could be co-opted to the Anatol Alkalev empire, too.

(5) Call for a vote repealing the rights and powers of Sejm's upper house.

The Sejm held on to far too much power even during the establishment of the Golden Liberty. Many have enjoyed the idea of making the people more powerful in the balance of the Commonwealth, but that movement has met with resistance. Perhaps it is time for Anatol to step out of the darkness and into the light to make that political move a reality.

Anatol Akalewicz

"You think the Golden Liberty revolutionized everything. But down here, very little has changed."

THE SARMATIAN COMMONWEALTH

STRENGTH	INFLUENCE	RANK
3	7	10

Advantages
Connection: Sarmatian underworld (149), Legendary Trait: Wits (153), Reputation: Philanthropist (150)

Virtue: The Prophet
Illuminating. Activate your Virtue to know whenever any other character lies to you until the end of the Scene.

Hubris: The Emperor
Hot-Headed. You receive a Danger Point when your Villain flies off the handle and loses his temper, causing trouble.

Secret Society
Rilasciare

Servants and Underlings
Guards, Assassins, Duelists, Thieves and Pirates all call Anatol "boss."

Redemption
Anatol has become an unrepentant criminal and plans to stay that way. He would rather fight to the death than be locked away by a failed system.

Roleplaying Tips

Anatol may once have been a pleasant man with simple ideals, but that day has long passed. Though he keeps up appearances as a charismatic man of the people, Anatol has become a ruthless criminal, willing to do what needs to be done to ensure he can get ahead. Anatol prefers to be considered a simple man and surrounds himself with tasteful, well-made appointments rather than lavish belongings. Fearless and outspoken, Anatol never backs down from a fight and loves a good political argument. He never goes anywhere without a bodyguard or two.

Facio Contarini

History

Facio Contarini was always good with numbers. Raised the unobtrusive son of a minor factor in Porto Spatia, Facio eschewed the decadent pursuits of that great city in favor of ledgers and balance sheets. While his friends spent their days lazily watching exotic ships and people enter and leave the harbor, Facio was hard at work in his father's counting house. Numbers did not simply speak to Facio, they sang operettas, and he was their conductor.

Always watching, always calculating, always keen to find any advantage, Facio's efforts in his father's back room began to bear fruit. For every republic he invested, he earned three in return. By the time Facio was old enough to take over his father's business, it had been transformed from a minor factor into one of the wealthiest banking houses in Vodacce.

For all his wealth, Facio grew restless. Making money came easily to him, and his austere nature and lack of vice failed to assuage his boredom. An advantageous marriage to Luciana Sforza, a wealthy shipping heiress, earned Facio a cold marriage, but a hot ledger. With his capital and her shipping interests, the *Banca di Contarini* quickly opened branches in every corner of Théah.

Facio was now the patriarch of one of the wealthiest banks in Théah, if not the world, and had earned the trust and respect of the Merchant Princes of Vodacce. But this simply was not enough. Facio quickly realized the money and the trappings of wealth it purchased meant nothing to him. It was not the accumulation of wealth that mattered—it was its manipulation that brought him pleasure.

Having long vanquished any worthy challengers in the financial arena, Facio set his sights on the great Merchant Princes of Vodacce themselves. Only they could provide the challenge he sought. Facio would participate in their "great game," if for no better reason than it amused him to do so. Possessed of all his father's empathy, but little of his moral compass, Facio manipulated the threads of commerce to earn the trust and respect of the great Princes. Bernoulli, Villanova, Caligari and more sang his praises and could find no fault in his judgement.

With their reputation beyond question, Facio and the *Banca di Contarini* quickly became the preferred choice among the Princes to organize their holdings and settle convoluted trade disputes. It is from this lofty precipice that Facio indulges in his most secret of joys: defrauding the powerful. Left unchecked, Facio will drain the vassals of the great Princes dry and set events into motion that will orchestrate their ultimate downfall, simply because he can.

Schemes

(1) Bankrupt Gespucci Bernoulli's sons and sell their debt to the Villanova.

Facio works night and day to ensnare Gespucci Bernoulli's decadent sons in an expensive web of vice they will never escape. "Uncle Facio" uses his proxies to ply the boys with Terra's most expensive courtesans, the finest steel, and the most exotic pharmacopeia. Only when they are most desperate will Facio sell their debts to the Villanova and enslave them to their most hated enemy.

(3) Get hold of the Vendel League's private ledgers.

Far from limiting his schemes to the shores of Vodacce, Facio has set his sights on the Vendel League. Facio has dispatched his most trusted agent, Antonio Peruzzi, to acquire a copy of the Vendel League's private ledgers. Posing as a sympathetic wine merchant, Antonio has paid the debts of his new Vendel "friend." It is only a matter of time before Antonio asks his friend for the "honor" of viewing the League's private ledgers.

(5) Bribe pirates to divert the Caligari treasure fleet into his hands.

Facio was informed of a treasure fleet that is straining under the weight of Syrneth treasures recovered from a haunted isle in Ifri. The fleet may even contain the secret to eternal life. Plagued by strange weather and disturbing apparitions, the Caligari treasure fleet is limping its way from port to port. Facio has dispatched his corsairs to divert the fleet to his private island.

Facio Contarini

"Avarice is for amateurs. Why waste one's wealth buying a pawn when you can buy the player?"

VODACCE

STRENGTH	INFLUENCE	RANK
3	13	16

Advantages
Lyceum (153), Spark of Genius: mathematics (154), Time Sense (148)

Virtue: The Moonless Night
Subtle. Activate your Virtue when you act behind the scenes, from the shadows, or through a proxy. For the next Risk, when you determine Raises, every die counts as a Raise.

Hubris: Coins
Relentless. You receive a Danger Point when you refuse to leave well enough alone or quit while you are ahead, and it gets you into trouble.

Servants and Underlings
Facio's underlings come in all forms. Guards, Duelists, Thieves and Pirates are all under his employ in various numbers. Whatever it takes to get the job done.

Redemption
Very little could turn Facio away from Villainy. One sliver of hope is to convince him there is more profit to be made on the right side of the law. Even then he will never be a good person, and the moment he senses a profit to be made somewhere else he will be back to his old tricks.

Roleplaying Tips

Facio is a masterfully forged painting of austerity, respect and professional detachment. His foes have spent a fortune searching for some small evidence of vice and have always walked away disappointed. Beyond a predilection for having a glass of Odissean port after dinner and collecting antique coins, Facio does not duel, gamble or visibly manifest the native decadence of his countrymen. Facio is the physical embodiment of mirthful avarice clothed in the banal raiment of a banking genius. He always looks his victims in the face, smiles, then suffocates them in a complex web of intrigue.

Fritjof Larsen

History

Anita Larsen was of low birth. Her family were housecarls of a minor noble family in the Kirk region, but were set adrift when the nobles they served were dispersed or killed after raiding the wrong town in the Highland Marches. Anita's parents became manual laborers who rarely did the same job two weeks in a row; but Anita aspired to higher goals, wanting something better for herself, and her parents. She was tough, trustworthy and personable, working her way up through a coachmen's guild's ranks until she became liaison to the Vendel League itself.

Anita's brother Fritjof shared his older sister's ambition, but not her social graces. Fritjof spent his childhood trying to be bigger, louder and better than his sister, to get more attention from his parents or the people around him. It did not work. Worse yet, his sister was infinitely kind and understanding about it. He felt unloved and like a gremlin whom everyone simply abided.

As they got older, Fritjof became more cerebral and Anita more social. Fritjof enrolled in a university and received an expensive education. At the same time, Anita was working as a coachman, the first step towards a political career. Fritjof delved deep into political theory books, trying to understand what it was his sister had that he did not, and what was giving her the kinds of success he craved.

He got through Cristoforo Scarovese's *Ends and Means*, but did not realize it was a satire of bad rulers; and he did not read Scarovese's *Disciplines* at all. So he decided to adopt the methods of some of Vodacce history's worst rulers, and set about murdering all his enemies. Whatever power he wanted, he would seize, and kill anyone who opposed him.

Fritjof was met with great initial success. He goaded Arvid Holt, his best friend from university, to arrange for Fritjof to join the shipping wing of the Vendel League. Then he arranged accidents, poisonings and other treachery to sicken or eliminate his rivals. Violence favors the aggressor, and Fritjof was already the favorite choice for carl of a major business district in Kirk before anyone started to catch on to him.

When Anita started campaigning for carl against him, Fritjof was completely blindsided. He tried to talk to her, but she was cold and firm, unwilling to back down unless he repented his ways. Fritjof used Anita's trust in him against her, poisoning his own sister and removing the last meaningful obstacle to his election as carl.

Fritjof has only gotten more careless since then. He throws lavish parties and hobnobs with political actors as well as crime bosses. The Vendel League wants him gone, but Fritjof is swiftly surrounding himself with physical and political bulwarks against any challenge. The League saw this happen once before with the Atabean Trading Company, and they are not going to let it happen again.

Schemes

(1) Burn his sister's house to destroy proof of his deeds.

Fritjof's plan to kill Anita was clever. Over the course of many visits and with the help of some bribed servants, he filled the house and his sister's food and drink with small quantities of poison which caused her to sicken slowly over the course of many weeks. The problem is that the house and all the poison are still there for investigators to find.

(3) Usurp control of Kirk's "Werebear Army" organized crime outfit.

Even the Vendel League is not sure what to do about the Werebears, who have their claws in every racket in Kirk from smuggling to human trafficking to counterfeiting. Fritjof likes the way the Werebears do business, and hopes that a clandestine association with them will provide enough muscle and leverage for all of his evil schemes.

(5) Poison his closest friend, Arvid Holt, and steal his shipping company.

Arvid and Fritjof roomed together at the university and stayed best friends well after graduation, but Arvid's unchecked success as a shipping magnate has made him soft. The increasingly solicitous and moralizing tone of Arvid's letters makes Fritjof worry Arvid's on to him. Oh well—if the poison plan worked once, it may well work again.

Fritjof Larsen

"You come into my house, and expect you can just do business without paying your respects to me? Perhaps a swim in the ice-cold waters of our harbor will clear your mind."

VESTENMENNAVENJAR

STRENGTH	INFLUENCE	RANK
3	3	6

Advantages
An Honest Misunderstanding (151), Inspire Generosity (149), Rich (152)

Virtue: The Road
Friendly. Activate your Virtue when you meet a character (even a Villain) for the first time. She treats you as friendly for one scene.

Hubris: The Hanged Man
Indecisive. You receive a Danger Point when you take an Action to pause in hesitation, doubt or uncertainty before making a move.

Servants and Underlings
Guards and Thieves make up the majority of Fritjof's enterprise, although he's got a few Pirates on payroll as well.

Redemption
Fritjof is beyond redemption and very little will stop him aside from imprisonment or death.

Roleplaying Tips

Fritjof is the classic corrupt politician. He always wears clothing that is a little more expensive and flashy than necessary. When he speaks, he does so with relaxed, casual ease, like he is everyone's friend. Fritjof thinks he is much subtler than he actually is. Once upon a time he may well have been, but after his initial successes with poison and blackmail, he has become overconfident and complacent. If you butter Fritjof up, he may well begin to monologue about his ambitions.

Gabriella Angelo

History

Gabriella Angelo learned to play cards for pennies as a six-year-old prodigy; by ten she was a novelty, and Gabriella's mother pulled herself out of poverty by renting her brilliant daughter out for games by the hour, games against the self-proclaimed finest gamblers in Vodacce, eager to test themselves against this pre-teen genius.

Gabriella remembers those years fondly.

At age ten, games and gambles were a challenge; her mother's money (and her money) always rode on the outcome and they lost the pot more than once. Being brilliant does not mean every game is won. But as clients paid up and coin kept rolling in, Gabriella's mother happily stashed her money away in a bank, married a florist and stopped renting Gabriella out for games.

Gabriella kept playing. By the time she was 16 she was addicted to the thrill, or to what the thrill should have been, but the intensity wasn't there any longer—not with money stashed safely in the bank. So she gambled the money in the bank away and took to the road—leaving her mother and stepfather suddenly destitute—seeking out underworld gambling hells, depraved dens where men could bet with blood as easily as money.

Gabriella lost her two middle fingers her first night in a hell; what she remembers most from that night is the thrill, even amidst all her pain and terror. The very next evening, she forfeited her life to a roll of the dice, but when the time came for her killer to collect, she found him dead in a ditch—apparently he had bet his own life the previous evening, then fled the debt, but his murderers had found him. Understanding this, staring at the corpse, she laughed and laughed and laughed. Afterwards, she staked her life six days in a row on those same dice, and never lost.

But now even these bloody bets are beginning to lose their savor. Most opponents, after all, can recover from the loss of a finger, and bets that end with loss of life are sadly getting rarer. Gabriella's thrills now come from stripping her opponents of what they adore; she refuses to bet for anything less than the ruination of her opposite number.

She has won spouses, parents, children, vast estates and merchant fleets and she is willing to put it all again on the table, provided her opponents are willing to bet the best of themselves in return. For many, the temptation proves too much. And so Gabriella gambles.

Schemes

(1) Obtain the perfect poison for lacing her cards.

Gabriella started experimenting with ruses desperate men have deployed against her from time to time, but all the poisons she has tried lacing her cards with have proved insufficiently subtle; any poison that she can detect post-application, she refuses to use. The infamous courtesan Giulia Tofana invented a paper poison that is undetectable once applied. Gabriella would stake a lot to get her hands on that.

(3) Extort the local Guard chief by winning everything he owns.

Francesco Sforza, the local Guard chief, is that rarest of things: a prudent man in Vodacce. He gambles little and he never bets more than he can afford to lose. Gabriella's fixated on him: If she could entice him to throw caution to the wind, she could get leverage on him—by winning whatever he owns, and by wrecking his precious reputation for prudence.

(5) Control a gambling house, to play games forever.

Ultimately, Gabriella wants to create a hell where clients can only bet things that, if they lost, would destroy them; clients would leave either having had their lives ruined, or having ruined others' lives. The Golden Moon, Vodocce's most infamous, most dangerous gambling hell would of course be the best place to obtain. If that fails, she has heard of a haunted hell that has opened in Eisen.

Gabriella Angelo

"Nothing to bet? Do not be silly, sweet girl. Nobody ever has nothing to bet."

EISEN

STRENGTH	INFLUENCE	RANK
7	2	9

Advantages
Barterer (149), Brush Pass (151), Disarming Smile (149), Fascinate (149), Quick Reflexes: Hide (152)

Virtue: The Sun
Glorious. Activate your Virtue when you are the center of attention. For the next Risk, when you determine Raises, every die counts as a Raise.

Hubris: The Hero
Foolhardy. You receive a Danger Point when your brash, cocky or reckless actions cause trouble for you and another Villain.

Servants and Underlings
Thieves and Duelists make up Gabriella's underlings.

Redemption
Gabriella's Villainy stems almost entirely from the thrill she gets from gambling with high stakes. Showing her a way to do this while serving a Heroic purpose would perhaps change her.

Roleplaying Tips

Gabriella is *fun*. Her eyes sparkle, she has a wide smile and she wants to *play*—and what kind of fool would refuse a stake with a girl so game? She does not come off as malicious so much as reckless. Gambling with Gabriella is a heady and intimate experience. She will start the night betting shaved ducats and asking her client what he adores. By night's end, her mark will have mostly bet and lost the best of himself; he will drink and cry and Gabriella will smile. Gabriella has several sneaks and groups of roughnecks in her debt; they help her collect, and Gabriella does not believe in making bets she cannot collect on.

Lotje Abbing

History

Lotje Abbing was born during the War of the Cross to a minor noble family with extensive forested lands at the feet of the Drachenberg Mountains. She was raised strictly and indoctrinated into the family tradition of hunting the bandits and monsters that threatened the family lands.

As a young girl, Lotje savored the hunt. After fighting in the War, and mastering the versatile Drexel *zweihänder* style, it became more important for her to not simply catch and slay her quarry. Instead, her enemy had to know he was beaten when she delivered the death stroke. She realized humans, more than any other creature, were able to appreciate their doom with exquisite clarity.

The War killed all her family save her twin brother, Lothar. Inseparable, the two kept each other alive through all the horrors that beset Eisen, and they returned home set on rebuilding. Lothar assumed the lordship, and assumed Lotje would support him. Instead, she arranged a Grand Hunt in his honor, releasing a majestic stag, and while he celebrated over the body of the stag, she shot Lothar and took his head as a trophy.

Now Lotje's home is a menagerie of pelts, taxidermy and trophies both exotic and ghastly. She has hunted all over Théah to bring its predatory marvels back for her enviable collection of the monstrously macabre. Hidden from prying eyes, her private suites hold the mounted skulls of her human prey, with Lothar in pride of place. Someone who proves their dedication to the hunt, convincing her they are her equal—without being a threat—could get quite the tour of this collection, and solve many unexplained murders.

Despite her bloodthirsty tastes, Lotje is fiercely protective of the Bauern on her lands. While punishment for crimes is becoming the prey in one of Lotje's hunts, the Bauern who follow their obligations to their lady are treated with grim respect. Though neighboring lands still suffer hardship, and frequent missing persons in the forest, she and her huntsmen bring back enough meat to keep her own people surprisingly well fed.

In return for this safety, her baueren report to her any vagrants, foreigners or other strangers that pass through. Some are invited to stay, and some are even seen again. Her public reputation has been maintained with care, and an invitation to her estate to hunt is still considered a treat by many Adel, despite the occasional unfortunate accident.

Schemes

(1) Capture and hunt Valentin, the Ussuran ambassador.

At a gathering of the Adel in Starke, Lotje met Ussuran Ambassador Valentin, and they discovered a shared love for the hunt. Intrigued, Lotje followed him when he left the city and saw him transform into a wolf. She is excited by the idea of hunting a beast with the mind of a man, and has invited him to visit her estate soon with the lure of a potential alliance.

(3) Invite Heroes to a hunting contest, but hunt them instead.

Lotje has heard of the exploits and the valor of Heroes. Jaded at the notion of high ideals, she wants to test whether their instinct for survival is stronger than their friendship and morality. She intends to release a group of Heroes on her lands, along with a gang of cut-throat criminals, informing them all that only one person will be allowed to walk free. Regardless of who would be left standing, it would be interesting for her.

(5) Release a drachen, and hunt it once it has feasted on rabble.

Lotje has found a reference in the most ancient records of her family to a drachen, supposedly trapped in its cave by an avalanche. With modern explosives and mining equipment, it may be possible to free the beast. She will need surveyors and engineers, and a small city's worth of fresh human prey for it to feast on, once restored to strength it should prove to be the greatest quarry Théah has to offer.

Lotje Abbing

"It is not enough to kill. Anyone can kill. To be a true predator, you must embrace the prey. Being my prey is a privilege; understand your place in the natural order."

EISEN

STRENGTH	INFLUENCE	RANK
11	8	19

Advantages
Academy (153), Bruiser (151), Duelist Academy: Drexel (237), Rich (152), Staredown (150)

Virtue: The Devil
Astute. Activate your Virtue after a Hero spends Raises for an Action. That Action fails. The Hero still loses the Raises she spent.

Hubris: The Tower
Arrogant. You receive a Danger Point when your Villain shows disdain, contempt, or otherwise looks down on a Hero or someone who could cause harm to friends.

Servants and Underlings
Guards, Duelists and Thieves serve as spies for Lotje with a surprising level of loyalty. Those who serve her well are rewarded, and her underlings know this.

Redemption
There has been a seed of darkness in Lotje's heart ever since she was young; she cannot be redeemed.

Roleplaying Tips

Lotje is a robust and forceful woman. She speaks in a clipped manner, without hesitation or doubt, and expects the subordinates around her to act according to their station. Her tone remains measured even when she should show anger or other strong emotions, as if something dead is hiding behind her eyes.

She firmly believes she is an apex predator, and is brutally disciplined in order to remain at the top. She trains many hours a day to stay in peak condition and is likely to fixate on the most physically capable person in any group, or casually kill the weakest to cull the herd of waste.

Luck, The Fool

History

Lucian Thompson's final project at the Wandesborrow Academy of Circus Arts, better known as Fool School, was an elaborate miniature circus. Brindled rats, ants, spiders and centipedes were its clowns, jugglers, acrobats and ringmasters. One prominently featured surprise was an insect called a cockroach, which Luck had discovered during an exchange program. Thanks to the panicked riot that destroyed Luck's vermin circus at the end of his presentation, the cockroach is now a common household pest throughout Avalon.

Luck still graduated from Fool School, but his final stunt, which came at the end of a long series of similar works—high-concept satires of things no one thought needed satirizing; jokes played for shock and offense rather than humor—made it difficult for him to get a job after graduation. He was reduced to the lowest common denominator of foolery: an itinerant entertainer traveling Théah, putting on shows in town squares to earn enough coin to get him to his next gig.

He did not enjoy it. The public did not appreciate the high level of humor which Luck himself preferred, forcing him to resort to the usual physical comedy and scatology. Over the next few years, Luck's lifetime goal of using humor to spur intellectual discourse self-destructed. Nothing had meaning anymore for him.

As nihilism and spite replaced his artistic principles, Luck had one trick remaining that he could rely on: He could communicate with vermin. Roaches, rats, gypsy moths and other hated creatures could pass information to him when he called them, and followed his orders if he asked. The beasts were easier to relate to than people; their world had an order, made sense to Luck. That world was not full of idiotic lowbrow humans who did not understand real art.

So, as Luck traveled from place to place, he collected a retinue of creatures whom humanity hated as much as Luck hated humanity. They were his eyes and ears, his fingers on the pulse of the world. As they brought him secret after secret, and as Luck gained access to higher circles and noble entertainments, he used the knowledge he had gained to poke and prod at Théah's elites, turning them on one another and watching them ruin each other's lives. Now this…this was entertainment.

Luck has now performed in every country in Théah. Wherever he goes, a tide of scurrying creatures accompanies him, moving through gaps in walls and between grass blades like a moving shadow. In his wake, he leaves a tide of broken hearts and lives, harmonious courts split by lies and betrayals and mistrust. This, he knows, is his true calling, a comedic exploration of chaos and destruction. Soon it will be time for him to return to the land of his birth, where he will take aim at his Nation's greatest hero.

Schemes

(1) Kill Avalon's royal court jester and take his job.

Fauntleroy and Luck were classmates at Fool School. Fauntleroy was not anywhere near as intelligent as Luck, but Fauntleroy got better marks and more adulation from teachers, because he relied on safe, lowbrow humor instead of Luck's avant-garde satires. Now, Fauntleroy is the darling of the Avalon court. What good fortune that Luck both hates him and needs to get rid of him to further his next plan.

(3) Ingratiate himself with Avalon nobles who resent Queen Elaine's rule.

Queen Elaine represents the triumph of the heroic spirit, the affirmation of all the positive values and high-minded ideologies Luck despises. But her rise to power has also attracted numerous detractors, envious of her power. If anyone can find and unite these dissenting voices where they hide in the Avalon court, it is Luck.

(5) Blackmail the Queen to make him an official advisor.

The perfect, flawless symbol of Avalonian hope and supremacy must have some skeletons in her closet. No one has found them so far, but no one has used rats and roaches as spies yet. As much fun as it would be to control Elaine with the threat of scandal, Luck knows Elaine might resist…and he is just as excited to see what would happen to the Glamour Isles in the event of such a revelation.

Luck, the Fool

"I am power without limit; I am chaos made flesh. And I am doing this because I think it is funny."

AVALON

STRENGTH	INFLUENCE	RANK
3	7	10

Advantages
Perfect Balance (150), Slip Free (150), Small (148), Virtuoso: comedy (152)

Virtue: The Moonless Night
Subtle. Activate your Virtue when you act behind the scenes, from the shadows, or through a proxy. For the next Risk, when you determine Raises, every die counts as a Raise.

Hubris: The Witch
Manipulative. You receive a Danger Point when you try to get someone else to do your dirty work for you, and it backfires.

Servants and Underlings
While Luck has a great deal of Influence, he does not employ others unless absolutely necessary. He prefers to wield his Influence to gather information and secrets through his ability to commune with and control vermin, most commonly rats and cockroaches.

Redemption
Appealing to Luck's vanity and entertaining him with interests other than the sick form of art he practices may quell his sociopathic tendencies; however, he will never be truly redeemed.

Roleplaying Tips
Luck exhibits a sliding scale of personae ranging from capering fool to his true self, a smart, self-possessed sociopathic man. He is full of social commentary and biting criticism, delivered with a low, even and relaxed tone. He builds nothing and tears everything down. Relationships are among his favorite targets. If a Hero confronts him, he will observe her and point out the weaknesses in her friendships and her treatment of other Heroes.

If and when Luck enters a story, he will do it as a minor side character, as comic relief or background color. He does so by design. He wants the world not to see him coming, to discount him.

Juggernaut Villains

"You track me down, you seek to confront me, and now you expect you will end my experiments. But I will tell you, your arsenal is lacking; there is nothing in your rhetoric I have not heard before. Threats of violence? Promises of public spectacle? Appeals to my better nature? You truly are naive. I fight for the future of Heaven, Hell and Earth."
—Elena Grigori, the Ebon Doctor of Voruta

Biting her lip, tasting blood, the Juggernaut rises stronger after every defeat—after all, cracked bones heal. Years of hard-won victories and painful, sapping losses have taught her that pride is a luxury; a battle won is no victory if it means subsequently losing the war. To win a war—and only to win a war—a Juggernaut will fall back with her tail between her legs, lick bloody wounds and accept defeat rather than fight on.

Dark tales swirl of those sorry Heroes who underestimated the Juggernaut. The hunter who left a wounded werewolf dying in the snow, the detective who assumed a disgraced noble was a defeated one—perhaps the Hero believes she is being merciful, but what is mercy to a Juggernaut? Just another chance to strike.

Heroes who are unfortunate enough to fight a Juggernaut would do well to remember this: The Juggernaut gets what she wants.

This sounds like a trivial statement. It is not. A Mastermind may tell herself she desires something lovely, wicked and arcane, but really she just wants power; likewise, a Beast may talk a good game, but all he really wants is bloodshed. Chameleons want the satisfaction of having fooled someone, the Deranged wants the world to be part of his story—Juggernauts have desires as varied as fruits of the forest. What distinguishes the Juggernaut as a Villain is that her will burns so deep that she is willing to pare away any decency, any sentiment, any humanity from that core desire, in order to get what she thinks she has coming.

Unlike any other type of Villain, a Juggernaut cannot be distracted or redirected from her aims. There are only two ways to defeat a Juggernaut: Give her what she wants or annihilate her completely. Sometimes the former is possible; some Juggernauts merely want "simple" things—old heirlooms, new fortunes, specific political positions. Other times, the only sane way to defeat the Juggernaut is utter destruction—no half-measures will do.

Core Aspect: Desire

The least frightening Juggernauts are the ones who are no longer human. Vengeful spirits, evil *Leshiye*—it does not seem so strange when a creature of darkness comes purpose-built, discounting decency, affection, even comfort, in its zeal to fulfill some sinister purpose. A creature of darkness may claim to be complicated, rarely is it so conflicted as a mortal. No, it follows its hungers with a singularity of purpose that most humans can only envy.

Encountering a Juggernaut who appears human but turns out to be the result of a curse or possession is often a relief for Heroes. Not because the Juggernaut is easier to defeat, but because his existence does not imply disturbing things about humanity. Those Juggernauts that are not supernatural at all, but purely human, are perforce a good deal more disturbing.

No one is born a Juggernaut. What does it take to make a person deliberately pare himself down, until only a single desire drives him? Humans are by nature conflicted, and that is a comfort, even a mercy. Even the coldest killer can be made to hesitate when a beloved is in danger, can be redirected, somehow undone by his own contradictions. Every human is inconsistency incarnate, but not Juggernauts.

A View of Heroism

Deft
They lack staying power and break easily.

Indomitable
Impressive in combat, but off the battlefield they are inconsistent. A sharper blade does not mean you live to fight another day.

Steadfast
Their desires are naïve, but at least they know what they want—and are willing to commit.

Tactician
Too dependent on others to carry out their plans. Fools, their ploys and their people will always fail them.

Trickster
All that panache cannot conceal a confused child who does not know what to fight for.

Playing the Juggernaut

Juggernauts are difficult to get along with; obsession makes few friends and mighty enemies. As stated above, most people find the Juggernaut's singleness of purpose disturbing, and it is the rare Juggernaut who manages to hide her obsession for any length of time. Any attempt at small talk will end up becoming about the Juggernaut's obsession; most pleasantries, unless they contribute to the Juggernaut's goals, are a waste of time.

Likewise, unless the Juggernaut is determined that appearance is important to her work, her appearance is likely to be disheveled at best. Comfort and pleasure no longer matter to the Juggernaut; many forget to eat, forget to sleep, forget to change clothes. When a Juggernaut decides that appearance is somehow important to her aims, she tends to look just a little too perfect.

In her most vulnerable moments, the Juggernaut tends to look tired, hollow, haunted; a life of endurance, of pursuing goals she knows will not come easy, takes its toll on even the hardiest survivors. The Juggernaut often takes no pleasure in her quest. She is goaded on by harder emotions, a twisted sense of duty, searing anger or choking fear. She might say she would stop if she could.

But would she?

Juggernaut Schemes

Below is a list of example Schemes you could use for your Juggernaut Villain. Do not take them literally! They are jumping off points for you to write Schemes unique to the Villain you are creating.

+ Use someone innocent to further your goals.
+ Consume power from another so you may keep going.
+ Abduct the loved one of your foe until he gives in.
+ Destroy something your opposer loves.
+ Strike first, but withdraw quickly to test your foe for a final battle.
+ Wear down a Hero by sending minions to harass her every movement.
+ Steal what you need; leave nothing in return.
+ Intimidate someone who opposes you.

Anselet

History

Stone walls. Stone floors. No hope. No escape. This was the life Anselet lived, and it is her reality, her constant companion, now that she is free. The daughter of wealthy Castillian merchants, Anselet was born Anna-Lucia Espiranza, though that is a name to which she no longer answers. The guards that kept her a prisoner in a Montaigne tower called her Anselet, and that is the name she will carve on the tombstones of all of her enemies.

What Anselet remembers of her youth are memories played over and over during the years of her captivity, moving pictures frozen in crystal clarity. She remembers the day the Montaigne came. Anselet's father, Edwardo, was a Castillian merchant who often traded with the military for supplies, secretly carrying their messages across the war-torn countryside. His spy activities drew the first soldiers to Corasone. The soldiers' orders were to turn Edwardo to their side, make him a double agent to spy on the Castillians. The captain who led the attack, Francois LeRoux, took Anselet hostage. If Edwardo would serve as a double agent, said LeRoux, his daughter would be returned.

Anselet's father agreed to the hostage situation. He promised Anselet that she would come home soon. The last image Anselet remembers of her home is her mother and father standing in the doorway of the house, waving goodbye as they watched Anselet, tied to the back of LeRoux's horse, ride away.

Then came the years in the tower. Anselet's tower was in the northwest of Castille, in territory held by the Montaigne. The structure was old and the tower room the perfect cell to keep the little girl isolated. For years, Anselet lived inside this room, with only the barest necessities to keep her alive. She survived despite her meager treatment. Her imagination bore her through the hardest of the cold nights—she imagined herself safe and far away, in her old home.

Then, one day, Anselet awoke to find the door to her cell open. Confused, the weak young woman wandered into the nearest town to find war was over. Overjoyed, Anselet found a cart and driver to take her home. When she reached the house, she saw them through the window, everyone alive and happy and

well. Even little Jeannate was all grown up. Anselet was perplexed at why they had not come for her. As she watched them eat dinner, all her years of fear and despair twisted into hatred.

She slipped into the house and confronted her family, silent as a wraith. Horrified at her appearance, Anselet's parents tried to explain themselves, but to no avail. Furious and betrayed, Anselet grasped a kitchen knife and slashed her mother's throat. The rest fled in terror at the screaming monster that had once been Anna-Lucia and they have been running ever since. Anselet swore over her dead mother's body that she would find every single person responsible for her years of hell and would make them pay.

Schemes

(1) Find where her sister Jeannate is hiding.

Her family went into hiding after her first attempt on their lives. Find where the family has sent Jeannate and make her suffer for being the safe, innocent, lucky youngest.

(3) Pass judgement on the town of Corasone for letting her be captured.

The townsfolk of Corasone knew Anselet had been taken and yet did nothing to rescue her. The town must be judged, sentenced and punished for their inaction. And where better to start than with their most precious prizes: the beautiful daughters of the town. If Anselet could not have a peaceful life, none of them will, either.

(5) Destroy the LeRoux family, including the servants and animals.

Captain Francois LeRoux was the one responsible for Anselet's capture. Now every member of the LeRoux family must be found and destroyed, their estates utterly obliterated. It might take some time, but Anselet's vengeance must be carried out to the bitter end.

Anselet

"I was all alone for ten years. You did not come rescue me. Now, no one can rescue you."

CASTILLE

STRENGTH	INFLUENCE	RANK
9	1	10

Advantages
Indomitable Will (149), Legendary Trait: Finesse (153), Perfect Balance (150), Quick Reflexes: Weaponry (152), Second Story Work (150), Small (148)

Virtue: The Moonless Night
Subtle. Activate your Virtue when you act behind the scenes, from the shadows, or through a proxy. For the next Risk, when you determine Raises, every die counts as a Raise.

Hubris: The Moonless Night
Confusion. You receive a Danger Point when you fail to understand an important plot element and that misunderstanding leads to danger for yourself.

Servants and Underlings
Anselet works alone, though she may intimidate others along the way into temporarily doing her bidding.

Redemption
There is no redemption for Anselet. Her pain and anguish runs too deep. The only way she will stop is in death.

Roleplaying Tips

Anselet is a delicate bird of a woman, with thin limbs and sharp, haunted eyes. Yet underneath her frail looks beats the heart of someone who will never be caged again. Nimble on her feet and always quiet, Anselet prefers not to be seen or heard until she chooses to be. She flits from shadow to shadow on gentle feet, a whisper between eyeblinks that is gone before anyone can guess. Anselet feels no pity, no remorse, and instead focuses on the wrongs of the past and the endless need for vengeance that spurs her on.

Deargh Kilgore

History

There are places in the Highland Marches where fierce believers still hold onto the old gods and their ancient, often bloody traditions. One of those people is the deathless captain, Deargh Kilgore, speaker for the gods beneath the waves.

A dedicated follower of the old gods, Deargh flies the deep grey banners of the endless ocean above his decrepit ship, the *Deathless Depths*. He sails up and down the Avalonian coasts in search of sacrifices for the old gods in the hopes of bringing them back to glory, and eventually joining them in eternal power. To that end, Deargh and his crew travel from town to town, raiding where they can. Once he takes a town or a vessel, his offer is simple: Cast away your old beliefs and join his crew as a servant of the old sea gods, or perish.

Those that manage to escape tell stories about the screams of those who have agreed to join the crew, as Deargh initiates them into his service. The cost of joining is a body part, sacrificed in supplication to those under the ocean's surface. The crew of the *Deathless Depths* are known by their mutilated bodies and missing limbs.

To many, Deargh's beliefs seem like lunacy, but the captain is anything but insane. Despite his raiding ways, Deargh respects the rules of parlay and will allow parties aboard to reason with him. He speaks like a well-educated man, despite his obviously humble beginnings. He quotes from the Church of Avalon scriptures as well as the Vaticine texts, and can debate any theological topic over a wicked game of chess.

Deargh claims he was once a captain in the Avalonian navy, whose ship was left to founder, abandoned by the admiralty, in the heat of battle. Surrounded by his sinking ship and dying men, Deargh swore his undying service to whatever gods or powers, old or new, would help save his crew. The old gods answered, and Deargh worships them with a zealotry born only of someone who has seen a true miracle. From that day onward, Deargh became the old gods' champion on land and sea, dedicated to maintaining their truths across all Avalon.

Especially high in Deargh's eyes is the Queen of the Oceans herself. Deargh is known for sacrificing one pair of youths every full moon cycle to the Sidhe Queen Maab, tying the youths' hands together and dumping them overboard off the coast of the Banesidhe Shoals. Like a man serenading his beloved, he recites the old songs to the Queen of the Sea.

This tenderness, however, disappears when it comes time to bring new recruits into the crew. Deargh's rituals to the old gods are devastating, meant to bond the crew to their new destiny and to one another. Deargh believes his sacrifices and constant dedication to the old gods will reawaken them and bring them to the surface.

Schemes

(1) Kidnap new crewmembers to replace those who have died.

Reaving in the name of the old gods is dangerous. Many crew die—some in battle, some from infection after sacrificing a body part. Replacements must be taken by raiding and pressed into service.

(3) Lead a grand sacrificial ritual to bless his ship.

The blood of the unbelievers drives the power of the old gods and will bring their blessings to the *Deathless Depths*. First, spill the blood of the innocent aboard ship and paint the railings from bow to stern. Then seek a pious person and make them renounce their faith, then bind them to the prow of the ship before battle.

(5) Become a prophet by discovering the name of the old gods beneath the waves.

The old gods' names have long since been lost to legend. Track down the ancient artifacts of the old gods in the Banesidhe Shoals and use these artifacts to find the names of the old gods. Only then can Deargh himself find the path to walk among them beneath the waves.

Deargh Kilgore

"The old gods lie beneath us, waiting to be reborn, and they see you. Do not worry. I am sending you to meet them."

THE HIGHLAND MARCHES

STRENGTH	INFLUENCE	RANK
13	4	17

Advantages
Duelist Academy: Sabat (239), Leadership (149), Lyceum (153), Married to the Sea (150), Survivalist (148), Signature Item: coral-encrusted saber (152),

Virtue: The Magician
Willful. Activate your Virtue and target a Hero. Until the end of this Scene, you cannot spend Danger Points and the Hero cannot spend Hero Points.

Hubris: The Prophet
Overzealous. You receive a Danger Point when your Villain strongly defends one of his opinions when the time or place is inappropriate.

Servants and Underlings
Guards, Duelists and Pirates make up the crew of the *Deathless Depths*.

Ships
The *Deathless Depths* is a Ship with the Origin of Avalon and the Background of Prominent Battle.

Redemption
There is very little that will redeem Deargh. Because of his warped beliefs, only death, or a solitary prison cell, will stop him.

Roleplaying Tips

Deargh is a true believer, a zealot and a ruthless killer. Anyone that gets in the way of his plan to find the old gods and become one of them will be destroyed. Anyone who he must use, is fair game. Even the bodies of his crew and his own flesh are not inviolate in the search for a way to eternal glory. Deargh operates in two modes: as the almost dapper, well-spoken sea captain, and as the heartless murderer. When calm, Deargh's voice is steady, almost charming. When whipped into a frenzy, his voice rings out over the waves, full of mania and religious fervor.

Elena Grigorii

History

She stalks the streets of Vortua at night, wrapped in a black cloak, seeking subjects for her hellish experiments. In her laboratory the indigent unfortunates will be installed as medical experiments amidst the wailing jars and vats of human ichor. The luckiest subjects will be murdered quickly, their hearts extracted and stored, still beating, in glass tanks. Unlucky souls will have their blood drained by hollow-point needles, or see their own vivisection reflected in a mirror—they will die screaming.

They say the Ebon Doctor is a victim of her own experiments; that a swallow of elixir left her unfathomably strong, but always in pain. The Ebon Doctor exists. All the tales are true. But there is much more to her story than that.

The Ebon Doctor, out of disguise, is a brilliant theologian named Elena Grigorii. Elena Grigorii, brilliant theologian, is terrified of Hell.

Elena Grigorii entered seminary skeptical of Hell—after all, it seemed uncharacteristic for an omnibenevolent deity to punish even the worst sinners eternally. But she had not realized just how skeptical she was, until in the course of theological study she was given access by a kindly professor to a newly found proof of Hell's existence, straight from the desk of the Inquisition. This proof worried her.

This proof worried her because, where all the other proofs of Hell had struck her as flawed, this was airtight. Elena was terrified, because she knew this to be true: No finite life of sin deserves infinite suffering. Infinity is too terrible to contemplate—and yet the proof was on Elena's desk, and after her seven sleepless midnights, she wept, because she did not have it within her anymore to pray. Elena felt betrayed by the Creator of the Universe.

If Hell existed, then Theus' omnibenevolence was more alien than she could accept. She had learned to twist her mind around Theus' mysteries, but this was not mere intricacy that ate at her now—this was something much more deadly. She could not serve a god who tortured the sins of a finite lifetime eternally, and if Theus had indeed built death so that it might lead to an infinity of pain—then the only thing to do

for it, by her own over-simplified morality, was to see to it that death stopped existing.

And so, she started her experiments. It has been three years since Elena began these experiments, and she thinks she can see the path to immortality. However, her great project is in danger: Ambroży Czyżyk, a retired Hussar, has tracked the tales of vanished slum dwellers, and nearly caught Elena when she tried to take a young girl. Ambroży fought Elena—she screamed her purpose at him—he barely escaped alive. The girl got away; but since then Elena's experiments have halted. Elena is sure that Ambroży is an instrument of Theus. And he *would* appear just as Elena is approaching immortality—but can she still find eternity while facing her Creator?

Schemes

(1) Loot the local morgue for fresh material.

Ambroży Czyżyk's City Watch now patrols the streets, but they have not yet posted guards on the morgue. If Elena is to continue her experiments, she needs new subjects, badly. Live bodies would be better, but she fears any kidnappings will surely bring Ambroży down on her. However, if an opportunity arises to obtain some corpses, she will surely take it.

(3) Seek the Akwanse rubies from Ifri that concentrate essences.

Elena has some ideas for how to build her Elixir of Eternal Life, but in order to test her most promising formula, she needs rubies. The Akwanse rubies can be used to reduce the soul to its essential salts—allowing a scientist to extract a soul from a still-living body and remanifest it inside sturdier casing—a custom-built homunculus, for instance.

(5) Perfect the Elixir of Eternal Life.

This is Elena's ultimate goal. The process she is currently aiming for would achieve replicable immortality by reducing souls to their essential salts and remanifesting them in immortal bodies—but she is willing to try other tactics to create the elixir, if other options seem more promising.

Elena Grigorii
"The Ebon Doctor"

"Please do not scream, I am trying to hear what you are saying. And do not thrash—I know from experience it will hurt more if you do. Now hold open your eye for me..."

THE SARMATIAN COMMONWEALTH

STRENGTH	INFLUENCE	RANK
8	2	10

Advantages
Signature Item: Inquisition Treatise (152), Spark of Genius (154), University (154)

Virtue: The Tower
Humble. Activate your Virtue to gain 2 Danger points instead of 1 when you activate your Hubris or trigger a Quirk.

Hubris: The Hanged Man
Indecisive. You receive a Danger Point when you take an Action to pause in hesitation, doubt or uncertainty before you make a move.

Monster Qualities
Elena has the Quality of Powerful.

Servants and Underlings
Many of Elena's experiments have created Monsters out of animals and humans alike. Her specimens most often come away with the Qualities of Chitinous, Powerful, Tentacled, Regenerating or Fearsome.

Redemption
Logic and reason are Elena's salvation. Prove the falsehood of the existence of Hell, or somehow assure Elena that not only can she avoid such a fate, but she could aid others in doing so, and she might be convinced to turn from her wicked path.

Roleplaying Tips

Elena's been consumed by her determination to defeat death even though it damns her. If confronted, she will argue passionately for her choices—yes, people died, and more will keep dying if she continues her workings, but on the other hand—eternity!

Elena's obsession has hollowed her out; she does not eat regular meals, and likely looks it. She is wildly intelligent—before she dropped out, she was the Seminary's most promising student. Even stooped by obsession she is cuttingly logical, a tremendous debater. Elena views theology not as philosophy, but as science. She keeps the Inquisition's proof of Hell on hand always.

Isentrud der Chegir

History

Isentrud is a woman of implacable will. Born the daughter of a poor iron miner in the war-ravaged village of Unterhaid, Isentrud was forced to help her father in the mines after the death of her mother and brothers in the war.

Isentrud was frequently forced to hide in the mines to avoid the periodic raids of reprisal from nearby Pösen, but her father's love kept her strong in the face of adversity. As time passed, she began to speak to the darkness...and it began to answer. The darkness became her friend, her mentor, her confidant in those times of hardship.

Everything changed one day. Responding to an attack from Unterhaid, mercenaries from Pösen arrived to seek the assailants. Isentrud fled before the mercenaries advanced, and her father was shot trying to get her to safety. He died slowly in Isentrud's arms and she ran deep into the mines to hide her tears. She prayed to the darkness to make her strong...and it did.

Isentrud emerged from the mines reborn. Her dark rhetoric of vengeance incited a general rising in Unteraid and the surrounding towns, against Pösen. It was not long before Isentrud's mob stood before the gates of Insel itself, Pösen's nigh-impregnable capital. Staring at the hated fortress, Isentrud led the charge across the marshy land leading to the fortress. A colossal disaster, the guns of Insel massacred Isentrud's host with cannonade after deadly cannonade. Isentrud did not break stride until she came face-to-face with the armored form of Elsa Pösen herself. She never felt the shot that felled her, nor the hours it must have taken her to crawl through the blood-soaked marshes of Insel to rest in the swamps of Salzsumpf.

Isentrud sank into darkness as the last of her lifeblood spilled into the Salzsumpf. There in that dark place, among shadow-haunted ruins and the distant wailing of sirens, Isentrud embraced the cold, the mud and the frigid waters as they flowed over her head. So much pain, so much blood, so much hate and despair had seeped into the murky soil of Eisen over the last 30 years. Isentrud embraced it all and rose up, once again reborn.

Months passed, and Isentrud recruited followers from among the broken and hopeless of Eisen. Raiders, mercenaries, criminals and the faithless were drawn to her by the promise of purpose and a chance at immortality. Calling her "The Unbroken," Isentrud deemed her followers "The Unbroken Circle," and welded them into an iron band of suicidal fanatics.

Isentrud plans to purify herself and her followers of weakness, and what better test could there be than facing the only person to ever truly hurt her, Elsa Pösen. Isentrud kills patrol after patrol in hope of luring Pösen into the Salzsumpf. If that does not work, Isentrud will simply have to pay Pösen a visit at Insel itself. Isentrud will never be weak again.

Schemes

(1) Goad a city official into becoming a member of the Unbroken Circle.

Insel's watch captain recently lost his wife during one of Isentrud's raids. Isentrud intends to seduce the heartbroken captain to join the Unbroken Circle through demonstrations of power and the promise of his wife's resurrection, in trade for the keys to Insel.

(3) Lure members of the Pösen family to her deadly "proving ground" trap.

Not a single member of the Unbroken Circle has risen like Isentrud. Undaunted, her hope now lies with the only person as unstoppable as herself, Elsa Pösen. Isentrud intends to lure the Pösen family into the Salzsumpf and force them to endure her "tests" until Elsa comes to the rescue, where Isentrud will face her in single combat, kill her and watch her rise as her equal.

(5) Mount a frontal assault on the cannons of Insel and take the city.

For all their success in defeating Pösen's patrols, Isentrud's followers still reek of weakness and the fetid bonds of mortality. When she assembles an adequate force, she will finish what she started, assault Insel, and take it by storm—no matter the cost. Only the pure will remain.

Isentrud der Chegir

"I will never bow down like you. Be small like you. Be weak like you. I am the hand of darkness. The broken, reforged. I am Eisen."

EISEN

STRENGTH	INFLUENCE	RANK
7	6	13

Advantages
Bruiser (151), Hard To Kill (153), I Won't Die Here (154), Indomitable Will (149)

Virtue: The Emperor
Commanding. Activate your Virtue. The GM gains a Danger Point for each Brute Squad and each Villain in this Scene.

Hubris: The Prophet
Overzealous. You receive a Danger Point when you strongly defend one of your opinions when the time or place is inappropriate.

Monster Qualities
Isentrud has the Quality of Chitinous. This Quality represents her super-human stamina, granted to her by the darkness in the mine. However, she looks like a normal human and does not appear to have a hard outer shell.

Servants and Underlings
Isentrud's band of murderers is made up almost entirely of Duelists, although a handful of Guards also serve her.

Redemption
There is no way to remove the darkness in Isentrud. The only way she will stop is if she is killed.

Roleplaying Tips

Isentrud is Eisen's shadow, a dark reflection of a proud and resilient people. Her withering gaze resigns itself to disappointment and few live up to her exacting expectations. Isentrud's glacial temperament and relentless demeanor pervade her every action. Fear is beyond comprehension. Mortality is an anecdote to coddle the weak. Isentrud is the glacier, the mountain, the implacable march of time. She does not flinch, she does not flee, and she definitely does not die.

Jorunn Snø

History

They say once a person is lost to the cold in the frozen north of Vestenmennavenjar, there is no way back. The body will be found, bleached white by the frost, the eyes glassy and empty. Those are all good ways to describe Jorunn Snø. One problem: Jorunn is not dead.

Jorunn started life growing up in the town of Vorlenjarl. He was the smallest and sickliest boy in town, interested more in caring for small animals inside the barns then going out to rough-house with the other children. Town legend said his mother was a great warrior that sailed off in a raiding boat one day and never returned. The boys used to say his mother took all the strength in the family and left none for her son.

For the most part, Jorunn did not let the bullying get to him. He found safety among the elder women of the village, who taught him how to weave and sew, as a trade. By the time Jorunn was a man, he had started his own tailoring business and was very successful.

It was that success, rather than his good nature, that attracted Mara Orlunsdatter. Mara was a red-haired beauty who married Jorunn more for his business potential than for love. The quiet Jorunn was head over heels for his wife and now had everything he needed in Vorlenjarl; however, he also had jealous enemies. Several of the local men, including innkeeper Bjarni Rossiek, grew up hating the meek Jorunn. When Bjarni started up an affair with Mara, he conspired with his friends to get rid of Jorunn once and for all.

Jorunn had just turned 26 when the men of the village invited him for a hunt. They explained they wanted to put the past behind them. Jorunn, good natured and forgiving, agreed. The next morning Jorunn met Bjarni and the others in the woods. They plied him with wine, laced with a drug that knocked Jorunn unconscious. When he awakened, snow was coming down so thickly he could not find his way; and all his supplies were gone.

He wandered the woods, slowly dying, whispering prayers to the old gods and whatever else might hear him. A frost spirit found Jorunn and inhabited his body, twisting the innocent man's soul with vengeance and wrath.

Only three nights later, Jorunn walked out of the woods and returned home. His body was bleached white as the snow, his eyes flat as glass. He found Bjarni in his home with Mara, locked in a passionate embrace. When Mara saw Jorunn, she fainted. The frozen man caught his wife in his arms—but the instant he touched her she froze solid, and shattered. Her lover screamed and fled, leaving Jorunn behind in the ruins of his life.

Bjarni has been running ever since, because Jorunn is on his trail. Jorunn feels that the bullies are who made him what he is, and woe to anyone who gets in his way. Wherever they go, just when they believe they are safe, he appears, followed by the bitterest frost and the mournful, howling wind.

Schemes

(1) Freeze Bjarni and his bullying friends.

Bjarni set Jorunn up to die out in the woods so he might have Mara for himself. Now Mara is dead, but the frozen man's vengeance is not yet complete. Bjarni and his friends are on the run, and Jorunn is close behind, inevitable as the winter storm.

(3) Stalk a Hero until he can freeze him solid.

Good people make Jorunn furious—his heart is frozen, bitter and the good he sees in others enrages him, reminding him of what he lost. Drag off a Hero to freeze, to prove their virtue is not strong enough after all.

(5) Find the most innocent person in the land to trade for his release.

The spirit that holds Jorunn's body will make a deal. It will release Jorunn if the most innocent person will take his place instead.

Jorunn Snø

"Please, can you hear me? It is so cold out here...hello?"

VESTENMENNAVENJAR

STRENGTH	INFLUENCE	RANK
5	5	10

Advantages
Eagle Eyes (149), Hard to Kill (153), Indomitable Will (149), Masterpiece Crafter: tailoring (151)

Virtue: The Tower
Humble. Activate your Virtue to gain 2 Danger points instead of 1 when you activate your Hubris.

Hubris: Reunion
Bitterness. You receive a Danger Point when you bring up old grudges or bad feelings when doing so will lead to trouble.

Monster Qualities
Jorunn has the Qualities of Chitinous, Elemental (Ice), Fearsome and Swift.

Servants and Underlings
Jorunn has command over many creatures and malevolent spirits that roam the wilds of winter. Wolves, spirits of wind and ice, and the wraiths of those who have been trapped in the mountains follow his quest for vengeance.

Redemption
The vengeful spirit of winter that dwells within drove Jorunn to villainy. Displays of loyalty, true friendship, and other similar shows of Heroism are required to reawaken the good man who lies at Jorunn's heart, trapped in chains of ice.

Roleplaying Tips

Jorunn Snø was once a kind, decent man. Now, he is a monster that comes out of the cold and drags people away to freeze in the storm. Jorunn moves with glacial slowness when confronted, but once on the hunt can lope like an animal. He remembers his old life as a distant memory, frosted over by his hatred for those that left him to die.

Perrote Églentier

History

Perrote was born the only son of Damiene and Phillipa Églentier, a pair of entertainers that traveled Montaigne plying their trade to the highest nobility in the land. The Églentier family were the foremost experts in making ghost mirrors, trapping the souls of the deceased inside at the moment of their deaths.

The Églentier family used their Porté magic to bind spirits, then displayed their menagerie at salon parties in the employ of the nobility. For years Perrote did not understand what his parents did for a living. It was not until magic manifested inside him that his parents sat him down and explained the family business.

Perrote was a quiet, decent boy who desired nothing more than to become a painter. The boy became depressed, so much so that Phillipa grew concerned for his health, and convinced Damiene to send their son to her brother for a while. Perrote grew into a man in a small apartment over his Uncle Bertrane's tailor shop in Prevoye, and would have stayed there had not his mother grown ill. At 20, Perrote rushed to his mother's side in Charouse to help his father nurse her back to health. Perrote even tried to use his meager Porté magic to help her, Marking all his family members to try and channel health into his flagging mother.

Damiene, in desperate need of money for medicine, allowed his mirrors to be rented for a party by the nobility despite Phillipa's illness. During the party, the exhausted Perrote heard a voice calling out to him. He followed the voice to a corner of the lavish gallery and found a gilded silver mirror. Inside was the ghost of a man in a physician's garb with a long plague mask, his throat savagely cut. The ghost told Perrote he could help Phillipa, if only he could be free.

Perrote tried to resist, but his fear for his mother overwhelmed him—Damiene and the guests heard a horrible shattering and raced down the hall to find Perrote standing over the smashed mirror, his body jerking like a puppet's. He raised a shard of glass, and went after his father. The older man used his own Porté magic to fight off his possessed son, and in the end, Perrote ran away—even as he screamed for his father's help.

Now the possessed body of Perrote is on the loose, murdering his way through the capitol and transferring the souls of his victims into a single mirror. On the walls over the bloody murders he paints the word "J'accuse" in blood, a hint to his bloody identity. What this means even Perrote does not know. Whenever confronted, he tries to plea for help while at the same time his body attacks anyone that might find out his secret. The trouble is, though the spirit controls the body, Perrote has been able to keep control of his mouth—so the spirit caused Perrote to sew his own lips shut.

Schemes

(1) Steal blood from a sorcerous Hero to maintain his strength.

The spirit inside Perrote's body requires a substantial amount of magic to keep it going. The blood of a Hero can fuel the spirit's hold on the body. The spirit craves more time in the mortal world, and if it means bleeding a Hero for whatever it can get, then bleed him it will.

(3) Kill Perrote's familial Major Marks, then cut out his vocal chords.

Perrote's family is searching for him. The spirit inside Perrote knows that if it is not careful, Perrote's relatives will find a way to set him free. Their connection with Perrote through Porté magic is keeping him at least nominally in control, and still aware. The spirit must destroy them and finally slice through Perrote's vocal cords.

(5) Bind his victims' souls in a mirror prison.

A mirror once held the spirit prisoner for untold scores of years. Now it will reap as many souls as it can to include in a new mirror, and make a silent chorus only it can hear.

Perrote Églentier

"The shards are too many to count,
and it is too late to go back…"

MONTAIGNE

STRENGTH	INFLUENCE	RANK
8	2	10

Advantages
Bar Fighter (151), Legendary Trait: Finesse (153),
Signature Item: mirror shards (152), Sorcery: Porté (219)

Virtue: The Fool
Wily. Activate your Virtue to escape danger from the
current Scene. You cannot rescue anyone but yourself.

Hubris: Reunion
Bitterness. You receive a Danger Point when you bring
up old grudges or bad feelings when doing so will lead
to trouble.

Monster Qualities
Perrote has the Qualities of Fearsome and Swift.

Servants and Underlings
The ghost within Perrote keeps him isolated and alone.

Redemption
Perrote is a slave inside his own body. He is not a
Villain himself, but he is possessed by a wicked and
vengeful spirit that thirsts only for blood. Expelling the
spirit from Perrote's body is required to save him.

Roleplaying Tips

Perrote is not really a man anymore, but a soul
trapped inside a possessed body, mouth sewn shut
to keep from begging for help. Perrote's body moves
on its own, driven by the spirit, its limbs jerking in
uncoordinated motions, and with a loping, quick
gait. Perrote hums eerie songs wherever he goes
as he savagely attacks others and harvests their
souls into mirrors. His fingers constantly twitch and
his face is slack with a kind of mute horror as he
slaughters his victims.

Slepa Miskovna

History

By the time Matushka caught up to her, it was already too late. Slepa Miskovna was gone; the woman she was, abandoned; the wolf-nature impure. Slepa left a trail of kills behind her, uneaten, abandoned. She had become half-human, half-wolf, but her form had a fearsome asymmetry, her head larger and more lupine on one side, sunken and human on the other. Abusing the powers given to her by Matushka, using them to murder and terrorize, corrupted her form into something unnatural. Even as Matushka watched, Slepa's form shifted and morphed like an insect that had just emerged from its chrysalis, but it never reached equilibrium. Matushka shook her head and walked away. Some problems were beyond even Grandmother Winter's immense powers.

Slepa saw Matushka turn away. She lunged after the old crone—but the sprinkling of snow had become a sudden storm, and Slepa lost sight, sound and scent of her in seconds. No matter, she thought. She would catch up with her eventually.

Ever since that night, five years ago, Slepa has wandered Ussura in search of prey, sport and ideological satisfaction. It pleases her to fight and win against renowned hunters, giant beasts and even squads of soldiers. But her ambitions have grown beyond mere killing. After all, she chose this life because she knew she was something greater than a mere human. Slepa sought out Matushka in the forests so many years ago, to show Grandmother Winter her speed and strength, prove that she really was the best. If Matushka will not help her assert that and reward her with a fitting Gift, she reasons, perhaps she can do it herself.

Slepa now has a small cult of modern primitives, petitioners whom Matushka has turned away. Slepa comes to them in their despair and offers them a second chance, not as shapeshifters, but as her worshippers. They abandon the trappings of civilized life, clothing themselves in animal skins and hunting in the wilderness with makeshift weapons. Few of them survive for very long, succumbing to cold or illness; but their brief lives and honorable deaths in a struggle against nature itself give them meaning they could not find in the cities and on the farms, and they contribute to the greater glory of Slepa Miskovna.

Slepa wants to see Ussuran society collapse. She wants to see buildings burn and farms go to seed. She wants the Ussuran people to rediscover the strength that allowed the first of them to survive in the hardest land in the world, before the modernizers and city-dwellers erase everything worthy about themselves. She herself, she knows, is the finest of them; but she is beginning to realize she needs to influence the world beyond the shivering savages who follow in her footsteps. Shapeshifters are the future. If she just finds a few more of them, if she can open a few eyes with her foolproof ideology, then perhaps she can prepare for her ultimate target: the hunt for Grandmother Winter.

Schemes

(1) Kill hunting dog Miron the Giant, who never forgets her scent.

Die Kreuzritter has hunted Slepa multiple times, and each time she has barely escaped with her life. The massive, indefatigable hound, Miron the Giant, has been at the forefront of the chase the past few times, tracking her through heavy snowfalls, over rivers and other seemingly impossible conditions.

(3) Assemble a pack of Ussura's deadliest shapeshifters.

A wolf needs a pack. Slepa knows that many of Matushka's touched are more like Slepa herself than like humans or beasts. Her first stop is Pavtlow, to see about this "Pavel Toe-Biter" she has heard of. Next, the Borovoi Forest, to find the owl-woman.

(5) Hunt down and kill Matushka herself.

Grandmother Winter has forsaken her truest and finest children. She uses the powers of the wilderness to protect and coddle the humans, who do not deserve her attention. If she will not acknowledge true power, she will feel power's teeth from Slepa and her pack.

Slepa Miskovna

"You all know deep in the base of your minds that the humans who cower behind their walls and their tools and huddle by their fires can never understand who we are and what makes us strong."

USSURA

STRENGTH	INFLUENCE	RANK
10	5	15

Advantages
Boxer (151), Cast Iron Stomach (148), Direction Sense (148), Leadership (149), Reckless Takedown (150), Reputation: Savage (150), Strength of Ten (155), Survivalist (148)

Virtue: The Beggar
Insightful. Activate your Virtue to know a Hero's Rank in any Trait or Skill, or to learn a Hero's Hubris.

Hubris: The Magician
Ambitious. You receive a Danger Point when you chase after power and the deal you are after is dangerous or causes trouble.

Monster Qualities
Slepa has the Qualities of Relentless, Shapeshifting and Swift.

Servants and Underlings
Slepa has many followers, but few of them are distinctive enough to bear any mention.

Redemption
There is no longer a way to separate the beast within Slepa from the woman; there is no saving her.

Roleplaying Tips

If Slepa corners you, you might not be lucky enough to receive a quick death. Instead, she will talk at you first. Slepa has come up with a complicated and often self-contradictory ideology which maintains that modern humans are worthless, but that Ussurans retain the best qualities of mankind in conquering the wilderness. Nonetheless, Ussurans should submit to the wilderness and the wilderness should submit to Slepa. Everything she does and everyone she meets becomes a way to make her feel stronger and more secure. In spite of her pretensions to murderous self-sufficiency, this lone wolf is nothing without the adulation of others.

Venerio Barleto

History

To supplement his poverty, minor noble Venerio Barleto made the circuit of the Merchant Princes' lavish parties, but even leaning on their charity could not keep him fed and housed permanently. Then he wooed Lucita Bosque, a party planner and arbitrator in noble disputes. When Vodacce nobles needed a neutral zone to discuss business, Lucita provided it. As part of the wedding terms, Lucita's assets became Venerio's assets; her business became his business. That is the way it is done in Vodacce.

Lucita's half-sister Bianca saw her chance to take what was Lucita's for her own, slowly turning Venerio against his wife. What right had a mere woman to run a business as an equal to her husband? Never mind that Lucita had started the business herself and had much more experience in it. Soon Venerio discovered Lucita had been taking his money—which should have surprised no one, as Lucita needed Venerio's money—until recently, *her* money—to run the business. Tricked by Bianca, Venerio slit Lucita's throat as she slept.

Now, Venerio's successful partnership with Bianca has inflamed his already-inflated ego. Why not use his privileged position as a neutral arbitrator for his own gain? Why not sell advantage to one or the other party, forging connections to the highest Signori in Vodacce until Venerio himself is positioned to become a Merchant Prince?

Venerio has changed lately. Once he was affable and diplomatic. That veneer is still there, but suspicion, mistrust and mounting ambition have changed what is underneath. His speech is different now—clipped, rhythmic, measured—ticking like a clock. He jumps at shadows, or spends lost moments talking to people who are not there. However, now that he controls negotiation in Vodacce, there may be no stopping him.

The rest of Vodacce's social and political scene is worried, because Venerio has begun to dispense with subtlety. By Vodacce standards, Venerio is a loud, arrogant, boastful man who relies on his privileged social position to bully others. As of yet, he is not important enough to scare real Merchant Princes, but his stubbornness, riches and connections allow him to run roughshod over everyone in society below him.

Vodacce society is not sure what to do about Venerio. He seems untouchable. Every social event he attends—you can be sure he will appear at anything major—is tense at best, and a social catastrophe at worst. Venerio demands the attention and adulation of everyone present, bullying his way into a share in every deal, threatening to use his social clout to upend the affairs of anyone who doubts him. Violence or assassination might be an option if Bianca, a Fate Witch, were not constantly on watch, ready to summon Venerio's bodyguards if she detects any threat to their interests. He grows more powerful and more insane with every night he is unchecked.

Schemes

(1) Hire, convince or coerce a sorcerer into banishing Lucita's vengeful spirit.

Venerio's murdered wife Lucita is a particularly vexing ghost, in that she appears only to Venerio, and often at the worst possible times. He needs to find a sorcerer well versed in dealing with ghosts, to banish someone no one else believes exists, even in a world where ghosts are relatively commonplace.

(3) Run a secret coven of illegally educated Fate Witches.

The prohibition on teaching Fate Witches to read means nothing to Venerio. He plans to draw a number of Witches into his web via Bianca with the lure of education, then keep them under his control by threatening to expose their illegal skills if they stray from his grip. He will need to improve security on his dwelling to keep them safe.

(5) Usurp a Vodacce Merchant Prince's throne.

With the help of the aforementioned Fate Witches, Venerio plans to worm his way into a Merchant Prince's good graces, discover his weaknesses, and then strike him down. He hopes that if he strikes fast enough, he will have control of the Prince's organization before others suspect him, keeping him safe from their retribution.

Venerio Barleto

"Begone, foul ghost! How shall my legend swell while you despoil my dreams and wake my wrath? I slew you for your trespassing—yet Hell has spat you back onto my destined path."

VODACCE

STRENGTH	INFLUENCE	RANK
3	**11**	**14**

Advantages
Linguist (148), Rich (152), Trusted Companion: Bianca (154)

Virtue: The Wheel
Fortunate. Activate your Virtue to delay an Opportunity or a Consequence by 1 Action.

Hubris: The Tower
Arrogant. You receive a Danger Point when you show disdain, contempt, or otherwise look down on someone who could cause harm to friends.

Servants and Underlings
Guards and Duelists make up the majority of Venerio's hired staff. His most valued ally is his slain wife's half-sister, Bianca. In addition to the typical capabilities of a Trusted Companion, Bianca is also a Fate Witch, meaning that she can activate Sorte powers by spending Danger Points on behalf of Venerio.

Redemption
Venerio is a weak, cruel, selfish man. He cares for no one aside from himself and that is not likely to change anytime soon. Because of his self-centered nature, if confronted and bested, he will easily surrender to save himself from oblivion.

Roleplaying Tips

Venerio is outwardly diplomatic, inwardly scheming and theatrically mad—unstoppable in his pursuit for power. Most people only see Venerio's outward veneer of tact, diplomacy and respect. Bianca is almost always by his side, so that Lucita's husband and sister can comfort one another in their time of need. When he is alone, around people he trusts, his speech takes on a repetitive cadence as he dramatically monologues about ambition, destiny and hate. He yells at Lucita's ghost, or talks to the walls as if they were people with whom Venerio must share his thoughts.

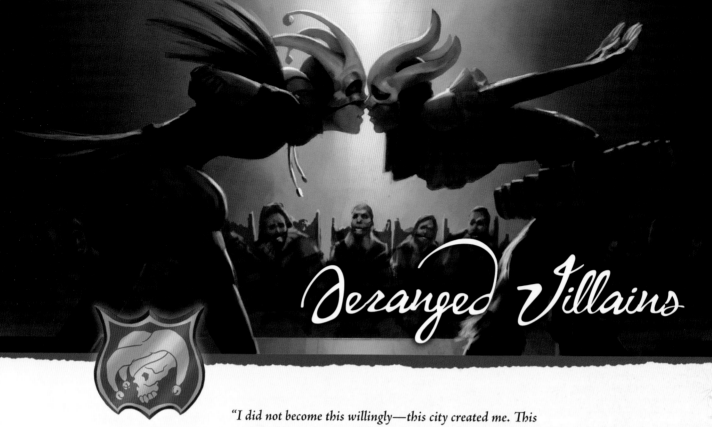

Deranged Villains

"I did not become this willingly—this city created me. This
city told stories of the Rat-King's rise. This city told the
story of the sewers and the swarms, of the midnight and
the moonlight and the sickness and the plagues. You ask
me who I was before this—I daresay I have always been
this. Even before I walked these streets, I was their story."

—Pavel Toe-Biter

Every madman lives in a world where his actions make sense. That world is not the world anyone else lives in. The Deranged, fundamentally, *do not make sense*. The man who wants to destroy his abusive parents? He may be scary, but he makes sense. The man who wants to destroy his abusive parents and will only do so by turning them to stone? There is something Deranged about him.

The Deranged lives out his life as the Hero of his own story, a story he tells himself, and no one around him understands. This can make a Deranged a terrifying opponent; you do not know what he will do next because what he will do next is never obvious. To those living in the real world, the actions of Deranged seem terrifyingly inconsistent and nonsensical.

A Hero who wants to predict a Deranged Villain will have to learn the story he believes he is living, the story that paints his vision with cruelty. The Hero will have to twist her own mind enough to understand that the world the Deranged lives in is not quite the same as her own—and in the process she may go a bit insane, too. But one need not predict the Deranged to defeat him.

Others may fear the Deranged, may need the Deranged, may love the Deranged, but it is rare—even for allies—to understand him. Even those who protect a madman often fear him. The Deranged are isolated. And, conversely, very rarely does a Deranged understand his opponents perfectly. After all, he is not living in the same story as his opponents, so why should he?

Reassuring as that may be, it is hardly reason to underestimate the Deranged. A Hero may take it upon himself to pity a Deranged, but such pity may be deadly if it provides the Hero with false reassurance. This Villain is unpredictable, volatile and set on crushing any part of the world that does not fit his unique vision.

Core Aspect: Isolation

Some Deranged are simply born out of sync with the world. This Deranged has always been mad, haunted from birth by strange obsessions, childhoods full of so-called kindness that is less than kind, and cruelties the horror of which she genuinely cannot understand. Other Deranged—well, she once lived in the same world as everyone else did, and maybe it even made sense, until suddenly it did not. Suddenly she knew things no one else did—she was full of genius, kindness and cruelties and saw meaning no one else could see.

The Deranged may be confused, almost childish, when confronted with the consequences of her actions; she does not realize that her actions are Villainous, per se. Or she may laugh, cackle madly, try to explain why what she is doing is good or necessary—or why she need not care for what is good and necessary. She herself is the only important factor in what she is doing. Many Deranged are philosophical; many are quite intelligent. Many have elaborate schema, and can be quite clever. Just as madness isolates the Deranged, so too does her insanity, making it obvious to her that she must perpetrate horrors no sane person would consider, or leading her to make intuitive leaps beyond the bounds of logic.

A View of Heroism
Deft
They know they cannot depend on the world. They shift it themselves with their finesse—so why are their visions of what it could be still so narrow?

Indomitable
Tremendously talented at the boring sort of violence.

Steadfast
What a shame, that such commitment should be wasted on such conventional aims.

Tactician
They make plans as though the world of tomorrow will be the same as the world of today.

Trickster
Why act strange and fantastic without trying to turn the world into a strange, fantastic place?

Playing the Deranged

When playing a Deranged, before settling permanently upon a portrayal, it pays to decide exactly how it is that this particular Deranged has managed to avoid being institutionalized, or murdered, for as long as he has. Does he hide his derangements well? Does he have terrifying supernatural powers? Is he charismatic, even in his madness? Can he, or will he, provide some valuable service to powerful people?

As Villains, above all, the Deranged are *strange*. Sometimes his insanity is obvious; he cackles, he spits, he talks to taxidermied animals, he talks to himself. Playing an obvious Deranged is an exercise in melodrama, picking out speech tics and twitches to make the portrayal as appropriately unsettling as possible.

But not all insanity is so easy to spot; a Deranged might seem perfectly reasonable right until you kiss him, or criticize his paintings, or break into his super-secret workshop. For this kind of Deranged, it may be helpful to decide on his affects when he is lucid, and mark the change when the crazy comes to the surface. What mannerisms change in the non-obvious Deranged when you trigger his madness? Does the kissed Deranged begin a choking embrace, does the painter's speech become staccato, does the workshop maven weave elaborate half-sensical explanations to justify his appalling experiments?

Deranged Schemes

Below is a list of example Schemes you could use for your Deranged Villain. Do not take them literally! They are jumping off points for you to write Schemes unique to the Villain you are creating.

- Betray an ally to gain a temporary advantage.
- Lie about your plans to throw people off your trail.
- Corrupt others into seeing your unique view of the world.
- Bribe local authorities to ignore your habits.
- Terrify someone important and keep her in your pocket.
- Haunt a victim so he spreads your tale.
- Manipulate another Villain into taking the fall for you.
- Unleash your Brutes to cause havoc out in the streets.

Guiomar Palomino

History

Guiomar is a woman of unrestrained energy. All her life she found her heart beating to the thrum of the guitar, and felt freedom in the swirl of moving figures, and now those she touches succumb to a painful parody of dancing. Her ambition, to succeed and be admired for her skill, has transmuted into a sick addiction and now she revels in the contortions of her victims.

Guiomar was the regional champion for dancing the traditional Malmignata, a frenetic dance said to originate from the bite of a terrible spider. She devoted her entire life to practice, and was not above putting sand in her competitors' dancing shoes or drugging their wine so that she would remain the prima donna of every show. Her jealous feuds with other dancers were town gossip for weeks after a performance, which pleased her greatly.

After a particularly grueling performance, Guiomar, delirious with fatigue, wandered out into the fields and encountered one of the Malmignata's namesake spiders, dancing in the moonlight. Fascinated, she let it climb onto her hand. Its bite should have killed her, but the adrenaline rush from her dancing allowed the painful venom to work its way through her whole body—keeping her moving long enough for a transformation to take place.

The power she has now comes from the bite that drove her mad. Rather than killing her, it infused her body, seeping into her sweat and saliva. She is able to pass her madness onto others with a touch or kiss; her nights always end with tragic results for her dance partners.

Guiomar is feverishly manic, living in a world colored by the poison and her own delusions of passion. She believes she is on a great adventure, bringing joy wherever she goes, always heading toward a far-off city where she will dance under a star-lit sky, forever. Her normal day is dancing to exhaustion, and then the dance continues in her dreams, only for her to wake and dance again. Guiomar cannot entirely tell the difference between dreams and reality any more, and is all the more terrifying for it.

She stays on the road, travelling from town to town at random to find people who will keep up the dance with her. Those left in her wake mourn their dead, care for the comatose bodies of those who survived, and pray that they will someday recover. The towns she passes through also lose much of their sense of community, as public dances and celebrations offer only a bitter reminder of the mad, spinning woman.

Those lucky enough to realize what is happening around them when she appears might be able to appease her by dancing, though they are in for an ordeal. Eventually she may wander off, allowing them to attempt to rescue those she touched. Many without the stamina or patience to wait her out also succumb to her, as she poisons them for spoiling her rhythm.

Schemes

(1) Obtain the deed to a bar, to host uninterrupted parties.

The Vino del Corazón is a dancing tavern where Guiomar spent a lot of time in happier days. Since her change, she has been expelled from the venue many times because of her disorderly behavior. The current owner is a jovial man called Esteban who wants to fill the tavern with happiness and community.

(3) Abduct Camila Montoya, one of Castille's best guitar players.

How can one dance without music? Camila Montoya is playing in Zepeda and is famed across Castille for her dance music. Guiomar believes that, if she can get her hands on Camila, with her touch she can compel the guitar player to play forever, so Guiomar can dance to constant music and be truly happy.

(5) Force the local mayor to dance himself to death in front of everyone.

The local mayor, Jimon Del Oro, has gone from thinking of her as a poor afflicted girl to a dangerous threat. Guiomar wants to punish him. She will get to Jimon through his son, Raul, with whom she shared a burgeoning courtship before she was bitten. The young man still cares for her and follows her, trying to convince her to rest, though he seems immune to her commands.

Guiomar Palomino

"You have to dance because that is what I want, and why can't you see that dancing is beautiful and just get back on your feet, you worthless lazy killjoys!"

CASTILLE

STRENGTH	INFLUENCE	RANK
8	1	9

Advantages
Brush Pass (151), Poison Immunity (150), Quick Reflexes: Perform (152), Virtuoso: Dance (152)

Virtue: The Hero
Courageous. Activate your Virtue to add Bonus Dice to your Risk equal to the Fear rating of your target.

Hubris: The Wheel
Unfortunate. You receive 2 Danger Points when you choose to fail an important Risk before rolling.

Monster Qualities
Guiomar has the Quality of Venomous. Her venom causes its victims to wildly flail and convulse, which Guiomar's shattered mind interprets as a dance. Uniquely, Guiomar can also apply her venom with only a touch, rather than an attack. This causes the victim to lose two Raises from their pool rather than 1, but they suffer no Wounds.

Servants and Underlings
Guiomar has no underlings and lives a solitary life aside from the people she manipulates to dance on a nightly basis.

Redemption
Guiomar's "gift" has turned her insane, if there was a way to remove her Venomous Quality, she would stop her murderous ways. Then, it might be possible to get her the help she desperately needs.

Roleplaying Tips

Dance! Muttering and singing to herself, Guiomar occasionally lunges at people to whisk them up into her world. She is desperately feverish, almost a phenomenon rather than a person, a natural force to be avoided. She is constantly coated in a sheen of sweat, and smells odd—not the rank sweat of an unwashed person, but a kind of sickly sweet and entrancing scent from the venom that courses through her. She may pick out particularly graceful or fit people from a crowd to dance with her, an experience survivors describe as akin to staring down a deadly snake while riding a bucking bull.

Kolbjorn Wyrm

History

Even from a young age, Bjorn Magmarsson was an odd child. Unlike many of the children in his village, he was lazy and stand-offish. His father sought to teach little Bjorn the merit of hard work, but the boy resisted. Bjorn was sent away to live with his uncle, Malor, down by the cliffs. He and his father never spoke again.

By the time Bjorn was a teenager, he was considered one of the wastrels of the village. Malor was not much better, and the two lived off of Malor's inheritance. Still, something began to bother the boy. He felt adrift, with no purpose of his own.

One night when he sat down to a meal with his uncle, he confessed to his feelings. Malor put down his mead and went to a low, long cabinet. Bjorn guessed, later, that his uncle gave him the Scrolls of the Great Wyrm just as a way to shut him up. But once he saw the emblem of the Great Wyrm on the illuminated scrolls, Bjorn was hooked. Reading about the Wyrm and its inevitable return kindled something in him, filling the hole inside him. He arose with new meaning and decided he, Bjorn, would be the one to resurrect the Great Wyrm to its former glory.

Bjorn left his uncle's house to begin his crusade. All of the ancient texts Bjorn found stated that only through blood would the Great Wyrm return, and so Bjorn sought out the greatest teachers to become a proper warrior. A group of Vestenmennavenjar mercenaries, the North Wind's Sons, took him on and taught him to fight. It was not an easy task for a boy so lazy, but his newfound dedication drove Bjorn to become a wild, ferocious killer.

This impressed the Sons, but not half as much as Bjorn's preaching of the Great Wyrm. Before long, many of the Sons came over to Bjorn's way of thinking. The head of the mercenaries wasn't too happy and tried to kill Bjorn in the middle of the night. But the boy bested the elder mercenary, crushing his skull. The mercenaries renamed him on the spot—Kolbjorn Wyrm, the Bringer of the Great Wyrm's Resurrection.

It has been years since that night, and now the Sons are all dedicated to Kolbjorn. Worse, they have attracted quite a following. The lost and confused, the disillusioned and destitute flock to hear Kolbjorn's message when one of his speakers visits a town. The speaker always precedes an attack by one day, presenting the chance for neighbor to turn against neighbor and sacrifice to the Great Wyrm in advance of Kolbjorn's coming. Anyone that does is spared the slaughter to come. Anyone who survives may join the worship of the Wyrm.

Schemes

(1) Raid a nearby settlement in the Wyrm's name.

The towns along the western coast have long since become comfortable and weighed down by the riches of Vendel League ships. Attack the towns and make sure the peasants understand the power of the Wyrm is still strong in Vestenmennavenjar.

(3) Find remains of an ancient cult of the Great Wyrm.

There are rumours of a cavern, deep within the ruins at Costa, where ancient documents were secreted away, relics of an ancient cult to the Great Wyrm. Find the cave and discover the ancient relics that explain the cult's practices and what power they can convey.

(5) Destroy the fleet of Avalon in the Great Wyrm's name.

The Avalonian fleet is only part of this decadent era that has long forgotten true worship to the ancient days. Take a ship to confront the Avalonians, and utterly destroy their ships in the name of the Great Wyrm.

Kolbjorn Wyrm

*"No longer will you suffer, for death is here.
The Great Wyrm will rise and set you free!"*

VESTENMENNAVENJAR

STRENGTH	INFLUENCE	RANK
12	6	18

Advantages

Bruiser (151), Duelist Academy: Leegstra (238),
Extended Family (149), Leadership (149),
Reputation: Fierce (150), Signature Item: Scrolls of the
Great Wyrm (152)

Virtue: The War

Victorious. Activate your Virtue the first time you
Wound a Hero during a fight to make her take a
Dramatic Wound in addition to the Wounds you
normally deal.

Hubris: The Magician

Ambitious. You receive a Danger Point when you chase
after power and the deal you are after is dangerous or
causes trouble.

Servants and Underlings

Kolbjorn's followers are mostly Duelists, with a handful
of Assassins. Kolbjorn favors aggression in his underlings, and so tends not to employ those who concen-
trate on defensive tactics or those who use subtlety.

Redemption

Now that Kolbjorn finally has a purpose, there is
nothing that can dissuade him from Villainy.

Roleplaying Tips

Kolbjorn is a bearsarker in the truest origin of the
term, dedicated to destruction while in devoted
supplication to something greater than himself.
Kolbjorn believes that while he is in battle, he channels the power of the Wyrm to smite his enemies.
Nothing gives Kolbjorn more joy than this notion. In
fact, he utterly eschews any other concerns besides
the return of the Wyrm. Kolbjorn is a powerful
looking man, with wild eyes and a terrifying grin
once he gets talking about the Wyrm. That smile
does not leave his face when he goes into battle. If
anything, it only gets wider.

Ludwika Krzyżanowska

History

The story of Ludwika Krzyżanowska is that of rags to riches, a true success story of the Sarmatian Commonwealth. Ludwika grew up the child of a war orphanage. Ludwika and the other children scraped to survive. Children died often. Ludwika was repeatedly sick due to malnutrition and would have succumbed to her illnesses had she not been adopted at age 12.

The older couple were members of the old nobility, looking for a companion for their young daughter, Nora. Ludwika charmed her way into the couple's hearts by singing folk songs from her village in a clear, beautiful voice. Entranced by the pretty girl's charms, the couple bundled Ludwika in furs and carried her that very day to their estate in the small town of Kazetzk.

Ludwika's life transformed in a matter of days. Gone were the long, sleepless nights when her stomach would ache from hunger. She was given her own room and beautiful things, from dresses to toys. It was a dream come true at first—except for Nora. The girl often stole or ruined any gifts the couple gave Ludwika, and blamed her for any wrongdoings in the household. All the while Ludwika, obsessed with becoming the picture-perfect daughter of Sarmatian nobility, kept herself immaculate and clean.

The simmering hatred between the two girls came to a head over the gift of a small gold locket. The couple gave the locket to Ludwika for her 15th birthday, with the promise that they would always care for her. Nora stole the necklace and ran to throw it into the river. Ludwika managed to grab it back, and in a rage shoved her sister into the river, instead, turned and left Nora to drown.

The couple was heartbroken. But whenever their sadness was greatest, Ludwika was there, to sing to them and bring them solace in their pain. By the time Ludwika was 18 years old, she inherited the family's small fortune and manor house in town. But the young woman was not satisfied just living as a rich land-owner. She invested the family's money into beautification projects to improve the town, earning the respect of many of the families and business owners.

Within five years, she was a major power in the village. Within ten, she was the mayor, and Kazetzk transformed from a sleepy hamlet into a gorgeous pastoral paradise. Gone were the squalid houses and scrambling peasants. The people were well-fed and strong, their homes beautiful as a picture. All this was done by Ludwika, in the name of making Kazetzk the most perfect place in all the Commonwealth. Of course, such perfection comes at a price.

Ludwika now rules Kazetzk like a petty tyrant, and has rigged the election three terms running to keep her stranglehold on the town's future. Locals who do not fall in line find themselves frozen out of business or driven out of town—or worse.

Schemes

(1) Issue and enforce town beautification standards.

Nothing is ever perfect enough for Ludwika, and her new plans for the continued revitalization of Kazetzk demand new and stricter policies for dress, cleanliness, architectural design and more. The town guards have been briefed on the new standards and have been given leave to enforce these rules by any means necessary.

(3) Discredit any opposition running for mayor.

A new opponent is challenging Ludwika in the next election. Mila Yudkovitz has plans to loosen Ludwika's grip, and that cannot be allowed. Mila must be discredited, but she seems to be a perfect angel with no skeletons in her closet. Ludwika is prepared to do whatever it takes to remove her competitor.

(5) Destroy the ugly Karolżka orphanage.

The Karolżka Orphanage holds many bad memories for Ludwika, who wants nothing more than to see the horrible place burnt to the ground. The orphanage houses nearly 80 children without families, but the mere sight of the ancient building is enough to send Ludwika into a terrifying rage. She has hatched a secret plan to burn down the orphanage and blame brigands for the crime.

Ludwika Krzyżanowska

"Pick up that child and place him in the dungeon until he learns how to wash his hands properly. Honestly, it sometimes feels as if I am fighting this battle alone."

THE SARMATIAN COMMONWEALTH

STRENGTH	INFLUENCE	RANK
4	7	11

Advantages
An Honest Misunderstanding (151),
Cast Iron Stomach (148), Fascinate (149), Rich (152)

Virtue: The Road
Friendly. Activate your Virtue when you meet a character (even a Hero) for the first time. She treats you as friendly for one scene.

Hubris: The Emperor
Hot-Headed. You receive a Danger Point when you fly off the handle and lose your temper, causing trouble.

Servants and Underlings
Guards, Duelists and Thieves make up the majority of Ludwika's hired underlings. She might employ Pirates to abduct a particularly troublesome individual who starts meddling in her affairs.

Redemption
It would be difficult to redeem Ludwika, because she utterly believes there is nothing wrong with what she is doing. The best thing would be to lock her away in a very clean, orderly prison.

Roleplaying Tips

Ludwika grew up in a place of abject poverty and the tell-tale signs of that early deprivation still haunt her features today. That said, Ludwika takes great pride in her appearance and will never leave the house with a single hair out of place. Her temper is also legendary. When doing business, Ludwika is even-tempered, genteel, even charismatic. But should anyone breach the niceties of society or defile her town in any way, Ludwika flies into a rage so severe that her guards are known to scatter before her in terror for their lives.

Madame Illuminata

History

In Vodacce, women are seen and not heard, until a young woman steps out of line. Then she is warned that if she is not careful, Madame Illuminata will come and drag her off into the dark. This might sound like a bedtime story to frighten young girls into obedience, but the terrifying figure of Madame Illuminata is a horrible reality.

Once she was a Hero. Raised in the capitol of Vestini, Isabella Lorenzo was the proud eldest daughter of her family and a perfect specimen of Vodacce breeding. Gorgeous and intelligent with perfect manners and charm, Isabella was married off at a young age by her father to the Count Roberto Delaga. She produced for him three beautiful sons and a daughter named Viola, and on the outside, the family looked perfect.

Behind the mask of polite society, the family was a mess. Count Roberto was harsh and abusive to his family. When Isabella sought aid from her father, he told her to be a good wife and sent her back to her husband. It was then that a member of Sophia's Daughters contacted her, and helped her plan her escape from her husband. In the meantime, Isabella helped other women get help.

Her allies had booked passage for her and her children aboard a vessel heading for Numa. However, as she bundled up Viola, her eldest son appeared, with the Count in tow. Her husband had Isabella arrested for attempted kidnapping, and she was locked away in chains. She never saw her children again. At least, not as she was.

Isabella was kept in chains for three weeks. Her ankle was badly broken during an escape attempt and never properly set, leaving her in constant pain. Then the Count came to see her, with several men wearing dark cloaks. Dragging her into a room they promised that she would feel better soon. Then, as Isabella fought, the men lobotomized her. The last thing she clearly remembers is her daughter's crying face, burnt into her memory for all time. The rest is lost to the lobotomy and the subsequent years of programming.

What was left afterwards was not Countess Isabella Delaga, but a masked nightmare...Madame Illuminata. Isabella's terrifying transformation took years. The servants of the Merchant Princes aimed to create a perfect weapon against Sophia's Daughters. They convinced the lobotomized Isabella that she had once had a family and a life, all of which were betrayed by her immoral behavior. In her weakened state, Isabella was programmed to believe that her sacred duty was to root out this decadent behavior wherever it took hold.

Once they were sure of her loyalty, Madame Illuminata, as she was now known, was gifted with a terrifying mask that hummed lightly with power and whose eyes were pure darkness. Her position as a beloved, if mysterious, guest of the Merchant Princes, gave her access to all corners of society. And from there, she began her awful, one-woman inquisition against indecency.

Schemes

(1) Humiliate a socialite by enumerating their flaws.

There are none who are free of fault and the women of Vodacce must work constantly to achieve perfection. Dafne Corti has fallen below Madame Illuminata's standards and she must be made to see the error of her ways. Publicly. And painfully.

(3) Bribe the Guards of Sophia's Daughters to work for her.

Sophia's Daughters have many protectors, but no one is without a price. Find those Guards that can be bought and make them work for the Madame, so they might deliver the names of those women bound to step out of line.

(5) Find her runaway granddaughter and lobotomize her.

Viola's granddaughter Clarissa has run away from home to join Sophia's Daughters. The Madame remembers Viola as a perfect little girl, so how could her grandchild go so far astray? She must join Madame Illuminata in her holy work to cleanse Vodacce of improper behavior.

Madame Illuminata

"My, such a disappointment."

VODACCE

STRENGTH	INFLUENCE	RANK
6	7	13

Advantages
Come Hither (149), Direction Sense (148), Indomitable Will (149), Staredown (150), University (154)

Virtue: The Glyph
Temperate. Activate your Virtue to prevent any magical effect (Sorcery, artifacts, monsters, etc.) from affecting you.

Hubris: The Hanged Man
Indecisive. You receive a Danger Point when your Villain takes an Action to pause in hesitation, doubt or uncertainty before she makes a move.

Servants and Underlings
Madame Illuminata wields a great deal of Influence, but employs no servitors directly. Instead, she commands the forces of whatever Merchant Prince currently serves as her benefactor.

Redemption
What happened to Isabella was tragic and irreversible. The best a Hero can hope for is to put her out of her misery. Heroes who look into her past could make right some of the wrongs the Madame performed, for the sake of Isabella's memory.

Roleplaying Tips

Madame Illuminata is a nightmare given form, a monster that lurks in the night to frighten young women into better behavior. A product of mutilation, years of physical torture and mental reshaping, Madame Illuminata hides her malevolence behind a blank mask. She travels through society as an understood threat against improper action, a tolerated horror that helps the Merchant Princes keep the women in line. Her wooden shoes make a soft, dragging sound across stone floors as she drags her damaged leg behind her with every slow, painful step.

Pavel Toe-Biter

History

Once, Pavel Toe-Biter merely was a story used to scare children. "Tuck your feet under the covers or Pavel Toe-Biter will get you!"

Pavel Ivanovich (no relation) grew to the age of 17 with his mother telling him to beware this other Pavel. Pavel's mother was a fanciful creature, wispy and sickly and given to stories. Most others in their village considered her more than a little eccentric. But the tales she told—of milk by the bedside and the monstrous Pavel, who could shift himself from man to rat and back again—fascinated all who heard her tell them.

Pavel adored her, and when she died, he was devastated. He was a little sickly himself, and like his mother a little eccentric, so when he was sent to live with the miller and his seven strapping sons, it was decided by his uncle that the best way to cure him of his mother's strangeness was to shame him. At night, he was given blankets that, no matter how he turned, he could not fold his limbs under, and his cousins laughed at his thrashing. They pinched his toes until he wet the bed in sheer terror, then told their father, who forced Pavel to wash the sheets in a cold stream, and then sleep, shivering, in damp bedclothes.

When Pavel realized he was not being haunted by a phantom from a tale, but merely being tricked by his cruel cousins, he decided to take revenge. His cousins soon woke with bites on their feet—not tiny pinches, but punctures made with sharp teeth. Then rats were found in the walls, and the eldest cousin admitted that perhaps Pavel had been right to fear the Toe-Biter after all.

Pavel should have stopped at that point, but he was already too far gone. His mother had believed in Pavel the Toe-Biter—so why couldn't Pavel the Toe-Biter be? Why couldn't he, Pavel, make the fiction fact? And so the hauntings continued, moving from Pavel's house to other village homes, until the hysteria became so great that the no-nonsense miller and his seven sons decided to move to Pavtlaw. Pavel followed, ecstatic, for Pavtlaw was the city where Pavel Toe-Biter was said to originate.

In Pavtlaw's taverns, wicked stories of the Toe-Biter abounded; he was said to live in the sewers, so Pavel slipped from his uncle's house and learned to live in the sewers. He started hearing the whispers of rats in his ears and he was still sane enough to be amazed.

Before this, some small part of Pavel still doubted that he could really be his mother's monster. Now he knew he was the Toe-Biter in truth; the cost was his hope of living a human life. For the Toe-Biter, said his mother, hated all humankind, and though Pavel had pledged himself to a life of toe-biting, he had never pledged himself to hatred before. Now he threw hate over his shoulders like a ratty cloak.

Schemes

(1) Find the lair of the God of Rats.

Ratcatchers tell the tale of how Pavel became the King of Rats by finding and eating an elusive Leshiye named the God of Rats. The rats Pavel talks to tell him that the God of Rats exists, but they are under its command not to tell anyone where it is. When Pavel is not terrorizing humans, he is hunting for the Leshiye's lair.

(3) Devour the God of Rats to steal its power to command rodents.

Finding the Leshiye is one thing; devouring it is a whole different story, for who knows what supernatural forces it may command? Pavel can turn from rat to man and back, but that alone is unlikely to defeat the Leshiye. If Pavel hopes to eat the God, he will need to be wily.

(5) Use diseased sewer rats to start a plague.

The ratcatchers say that, come a year of two blue moons, rats will swarm out of the sewers and spread plague. A year of two blue moons is not far from now, and the citizens of Pavtlaw have begun attributing the Toe-Biter's increased activity to that coming event. Pavel feels if he does not start a plague then, he will be failing his narrative imperative and the stories of the Toe-Biter will fade.

Pavel Toe-Biter

"You know the stories of me, don't ya? The rats in the sewers, they will tell ya—if you can hear 'em. Nobody hears 'em. Nobody hears 'em—nobody but me."

USSURA

STRENGTH	INFLUENCE	RANK
6	1	7

Advantages
Boxer (151), Perfect Balance (150), Reckless Takedown (150), Second Story Work (150), Small (148)

Virtue: Coins
Adaptable. Activate your Virtue to take your first Action before anyone else in a Round.

Hubris: The Hanged Man
Indecisive. You receive a Danger Point when your Villain takes an Action to pause in hesitation, doubt or uncertainty before he makes a move.

Monster Qualities
Pavel's transformation into a Monster is not complete, but he is no longer fully human either. Pavel has the Quality of Nocturnal.

Servants and Underlings
At the moment Pavel only has rats to keep him company, and no underlings.

Redemption
Pavel's Villainy comes from a place of pain, betrayal and torture. Redemption of such a figure would require compassion and kindness, and reminders that there are people in the world like his beloved mother.

Roleplaying Tips

Pavel has forgotten human manners; he is filthy, blows his nose on his sleeve, eats crud from his eye, hunches, twitches and chitters. He spits when he speaks and repeats himself constantly. He has no concept of personal space, which means he is usually standing uncomfortably close or awkwardly far from any human he is with. Catch him off-guard, though, and you will note that his mannerisms are still somewhat affected. He was raised by a gentle mother, and keeps an echo of this in the moments when he forgets he is supposed to be a creature from a tale.

Sakse Tryggvasson

History

As a child Sakse was a bully, thief and a bitter braggart, embarrassing his family. Bitterness became rage became obsession. The only point of clarity in Sakse's rising tide of anger was his longtime obsession for his childhood friend Snorri, the daughter of the village carl. Snorri's hair was like gold and her soothing voice burned the darkness from Sakse's soul, if only for a time.

As Sakse grew from a bitter child into a bilious man, his obsession for defying his wyrd grew in proportion to his unhealthy "love" for Snorri. Watching her from afar, he knew a simple fisherman could never impress a carl's daughter—but what if he were something more? Taking up his skinning knife, Sakse abandoned Kopingsvik and signed on as a Vendel privateer.

Sakse was more pirate than privateer, embracing greed and bloodlust in equal measure. He seldom took prisoners, and was cruel to those he did. One fateful day, his vessel sighted a badly damaged Avalonian merchantmen drifting into Vendel waters. Sakse led the boarding party and found a wounded noble, a rebel lord seeking refuge from the rise of Queen Elaine.

Feverish and dying from injuries received in his flight from Avalon, the lord spoke deliriously of how he cunningly hid his family's gold at the edge of the mound where Elaine would never find it. As the lord died in Sakse's arms, he saw a new path unfold before him, one paved in foreign gold that led straight to Snorri. Sakse's first action after this was to stab the privateer's captain in the heart and pitch him overboard. His second was to bully his way into command.

Sakse's band raided deep into Avalon, spreading fire and terror until they reached Silverdale, razed it to the ground, and put its people to the sword. As darkness fell, Sakse and his band tore into the mound behind the lord's manse in search of the gold. What they found instead was the unalloyed fury of an ancient Sidhe. Only Sakse emerged from Silverdale, with barely discernible embers of his sanity intact. Half-scalped and cursed to never recognize another person's face, the Sidhe told him his only hope to break the curse was to scalp his obsession, Snorri, and bring her hair back to the Sidhe.

Limping back to Kopingsvik, Sakse broke into the carl's home under cover of night, seeking Snorri. Bursting into her room, he found two golden-haired beauties staring at him in horror. Looking confusedly from face to face, he desperately plunged his knife into the breast of the nearest, while the other fled into the night. Shouts from a man dressed as the carl startled Sakse into action, and he escaped out a window, with the village watch close at hand.

Sakse later discovered that the woman he killed was Snorri's sister. A simple mistake really. Snorri will understand; her love could be no less than his own. She will see when he returns to claim her radiant scalp.

Schemes

(1) Gather a crew to raid the Avalonian shores.

An unanticipated side effect of Sakse's curse allows him to sense those infused with Glamour. Renaming his ship *The Gyllen*, Sakse vents his fury up and down the coast of Avalon. *The Gyllen*'s new crew is a band of Vendel exiles who wear the golden hair of their victims as sashes about their waists.

(3) Steal the Sun-tears, Boucher Master Demarque's meteoric iron knives.

Demarque's legendary skill as a knife fighter is enhanced by his use of the "Sun-tears," a pair of meteoric iron daggers that fell to Terra in a rain of golden fire. Demarque single-handedly thwarted Sakse's second attempt on Snorri's scalp, earning his ire and igniting Sakse's obsession. Sakse will go to any length to murder Demarque and use the Sun-tears against the Sidhe who cursed him.

(5) Scalp Snorri to lift the curse, and kill the Sidhe in revenge.

Sakse will not rest until he scalps Snorri to lift his curse. His first attempt was thwarted by chance; the second by Demarque. Nothing will stop Sakse a third time. Not the carl and certainly not Demarque. Sakse intends to return to Silverdale with Snorri's scalp firmly in hand, have the curse removed, then claim his bloody revenge against the Sidhe.

Sakse Tryggvasson

"You understand the meaning of sacrifice, don't you my dear? A few golden locks? A small price to pay for a love such as ours..."

VESTENMENNAVENJAR

STRENGTH	INFLUENCE	RANK
10	2	12

Advantages
Bruiser (151), I'm Taking You with Me (154), Indomitable Will (149), Quick Reflexes: Weaponry (152), Riot Breaker (153)

Virtue: The Fool
Wily. Activate your Virtue to escape danger from the current Scene. You cannot rescue anyone but yourself.

Hubris: The Lovers
Star-Crossed. You receive a Danger Point when you become enamored with someone you really should not.

Servants and Underlings
Sakse has no devoted underlings, though he seeks a new crew for *The Gyllen*. He has the knowledge of where to find thugs willing to do nearly anything for money, mostly Pirates, Thieves or Duelists.

Redemption
Even before he met the Sidhe, Sakse was a terrible man, there is no redemption for him.

Roleplaying Tips

Sakse's downcast gaze, and what remains of his matted hair, conceal a visage that alternates between confusion, mirth, rage and madness. He avoids looking at faces at all costs, but has become a keen observer of clothing, mannerism, voice, and most importantly, hair. Sakse has long abandoned the concept of fear, and revels in the company of his murderous crew. His well-worn skinning knife is a constant companion, and the few who catch his attention give him a wide berth.

Stewart, The Swamp Goblin of Den Bog

History

From the moment little Stewart was born, all the residents of Bolger Falls in the Highland Marches knew that the boy was different. With his longer-than-normal limbs, and sharp, pointed teeth, he was an odd child. The bullying began shortly after his mother's death, as Stewart tried to take care of himself and live a normal life. He finally decided that if he was going to be treated like the monster of the town, then he would embrace the title.

From then on, Stewart was a full-blown mischief-maker. He would leave awful presents for the town girls and put insects into the beds of his neighbors. After the pranks Stewart would retreat into Den Bog, the nearby swampy marsh land that lay to the west of Bolger Falls. In the bog Stewart felt truly at home. He found an old cottage deep in the woods and Den Bog became Stewart's little fiefdom, and he its ruler from that day forward.

Stewart's pranks earned him the town's hatred, and he became the target of many bullies. That is when Lillian MacDowell stepped in. The daughter of the local crofter, Lillian's family held sway in Bolger Falls, and Lillian was known as one of the most kind-hearted girls around. She stood up for Stewart and defended him against the townsfolk.

The two became good friends and it was not long before Stewart fell head-first in love with Lillian, planning their epic romantic relationship. After all, if Lillian could see him as a good person, a real person, like anyone else, then of course she would want to be with him.

Stewart planned a lavish surprise for Lillian at the edge of the swamp one day, a gorgeous picnic with flowers and everything she liked to eat; she came, and he confessed his love. The surprised Lillian explained that she was his friend and nothing more, and the heartbroken Stewart flew into a rage. He believed Lillian just needed some convincing to love him back, and so he kidnapped her and took her to his little kingdom in Den Bog.

The town was in an uproar. Lillian's family, especially her elder sister, Deirdre, and Deirdre's fiancé, Fearghal, searched everywhere for her, and came up empty: Lillian was lost to the Bog.

In Den Bog, Lillian spent days trying to escape from Stewart, who plied her with sweet words and trinkets and screamed at her in rage when she would not give him so much as a smile. One night Stewart went out to continue his torment of the townsfolk, and Lillian finally escaped. Though now free, she decided she could not go back home until she stopped Stewart, so she hid in a den of ancient færie stones. When Stewart found Lillian gone, he went berserk. He hunted the bog for her, but the stone sheltered Lillian and masked her presence. Now, Stewart takes his rage out on the townsfolk; he'll lure Lillian out of her hiding place, one way or another.

Schemes

(1) Ruin Deirdre and Fearghal's wedding with a cow stampede.

Lillian's little sister is getting married to her beloved Fearghal, and it is going to be the town's event of the year. It is sure to lure Lillian out of hiding, especially if there would be a tiny disaster to draw her back. The wedding is right near the livestock paddocks, and Stewart has a plan.

(3) Harass villagers with traps, fires and dead pets.

Stewart grew up bullied by the people of the village, and so he is only doing it in return. Plague the village with every manner of bad trick, to pay them back for every slight done to poor Stewart.

(5) Make Lillian love him by abducting her baby brother.

As long as Lillian stays away from Stewart, she will never fall in love with him. But she will come to rescue her little brother, Colin, if Stewart takes him to the Bog. Once she is back, he is sure he will be able to convince her to love him forever.

Stewart, the Swamp Goblin of Den Bog

"The bog, the bog, the bog's our home. She will come to see that, eventually. I just have to make her love me, and that should be easy enough."

THE HIGHLAND MARCHES

STRENGTH	INFLUENCE	RANK
5	1	6

Advantages
Direction Sense (148), Perfect Balance (150), Quick Reflexes: Athletics (152), Survivalist (148), The Devil's Own Luck (155)

Virtue: The Fool
Wily. Activate your Virtue to escape danger from the current Scene. You cannot rescue anyone but yourself.

Hubris: The Emperor
Hot-Headed. You receive a Danger Point when your Villain flies off the handle and loses his temper, causing trouble.

Servants and Underlings
Stewart has no friends, and works alone.

Redemption
In a single word, compassion. Stewart needs friends and understanding, and perhaps even a cause, greater than himself, to believe in.

Roleplaying Tips

Stewart was a bullied child who turned into the very spoiled, bratty monster everyone pegged him for when he was young. He is the epitome of a bog monster, haunting the Highland bogs. Whatever warmth Stewart once had was directed at Lillian, and when she turned him away, that love twisted into obsession. Stewart is a horror to everyone, but when he sees Lillian he transforms into a cordial, if a little brutish, man who is desperate to convince a lady that he is worth her attention.

the White Lady of Hirschblut Tower

History

The White Lady of Hirschblut Tower was not always so. Many years ago she was simply Anne, the baker's daughter. One winter in Hirschblut, a small village in Eisen, food became scarce. So scarce that even for the baker there was nothing to eat. Desperate, Anne's father sent her out to collect firewood, and when she returned home she found he had killed her beloved hound, Arno, and served him for dinner.

Anne's fury was blinding. She picked up a kitchen knife and slit her father's throat. Grabbing Arno's charred carcass she ran deep into the forest. She stopped only when her feet were raw and her lungs could no longer bring in oxygen. She beat the ground over and over again until a madness crept into her heart, the melted snow mixing with blood, bathing Arno's corpse.

In a moment of enlightenment, Anne knew what she must do. Over the next few days, she killed small forest creatures and beasts sewing them to Arno's corpse, baptizing it in unholy life. She sang songs to the carcass and kissed it gently. On the seventh day Anne's creature rose from the snow.

The creature called itself the Groll, and pledged itself to Anne. They spent the rest of the winter slaughtering whatever stumbled upon their path. With each kill Anne's skin and hair grew fairer and the Groll's form became more twisted. The more power Anne sewed upon the Groll, the more magic it gave to her—and the deeper their bond grew.

So it came to be that by the time Anne came back to her old town she was unrecognizeable. Bandits plagued Hirschblut, and Anne and the Groll fought them—not for the townsfolk, but as sustenance. When the townsfolk lauded her efforts a scheme formed in the young woman's mind.

She performed more heroic deeds, enacting her dark arts only under the cloak of night. Soon, the people gave her Hirschblut Tower and named her its Lady. She then cast a spell on the town—each night, as they slept, their memories were wiped and they started fresh the next day. The town of Hirschblut became her beloved Groll's hunting ground.

One day, a man covered in mud came to Hirschblut claiming the Lady was not the town's savior, but a witch. The Lady and the Groll met the Schlammman in the town square and fought until sunrise of the following day. The Schlammman struck down the Groll, but could not bring himself to kill a lady so fair and left town to scatter the parts of the Groll to the four corners of Eisen.

Afterwards, the Lady healed herself and mourned the loss of her love, alone in her tower. The same rage she felt when her father had killed her hound sunk deep into her stomach. Death would be far too kind for the Schlammman; instead she cast a spell that stole the Schlammman's very identity. She cursed him to forever walk Théah ignorant of himself until her love was reconstituted and she and the Groll could devour him together.

Schemes

(1) Spread lies of the awful deeds of the Schlammman.

Ludwig Schlammman believes himself a Hero of Eisen. Having had his memories stolen by the Lady, he bases his actions off the folktales people tell of him. The Lady can think of no better punishment but to turn his deeds dark and evil. When she returns his memories to him, then he will see the monster he truly has become.

(3) Devour a peasant to stay young.

The Lady's youth is directly tied to the life force of others. Still scarred from the Schlammman's attack, she must devour a person each week if she is to remain young and powerful. The population of Hirschblut cannot sustain her hunger and the town provides an important cover for her to hide behind. She will have to find her meal elsewhere.

(5) Revive her great love, the Groll, by assembling its skeleton.

The Groll's skeleton was scattered to every corner of Eisen by the Schlammman. The Lady's magic was not powerful enough to stop him. Now, she sends her greatest knights to find the bones so she may reassemble them and revive her love. She hears its bones calling to her, the nearest one from the Wälder.

The White Lady of Hirschblut Tower

"Come sit, rest your weary feet. Tell me tales of the far-off lands you have traveled and the people you have met. I am dying to hear your story—I must have you for dinner."

EISEN

STRENGTH	INFLUENCE	RANK
6	5	11

Advantages
Lyceum (153), Rich (152), Trusted Companion: The Groll (154)

Virtue: The Road
Friendly. Activate your Virtue when you meet a character (even a Hero) for the first time. She treats you as friendly for one scene.

Hubris: The War
Loyal. You receive a Danger Point when you go back for a fallen comrade or refuse to leave a wounded ally.

Monster Qualities
Under most circumstances, the Lady appears as a pale and beautiful Eisen woman, the epitome of beauty and grace. When confronted with danger, however, she manifests the Qualities of Elemental (Ice), Fearsome and Regenerating.

Servants and Underlings
The townspeople under the Lady's control are mostly unremarkable, and act simply as Brutes. They avoid violence, focusing on spreading false tales of the Schlammman, or locating the pieces of the Groll so they can be rewarded. The Lady's most powerful servitor is the Groll. If she could find all of its parts and breathe life into it again, the Groll would be a terrifying creature who answers only to its Lady.

Redemption
There is no warmth left in the Lady's heart, save for the Groll, and no redemption for her. Perhaps even more of a monster than the Groll, her only end is death.

Roleplaying Tips
The Lady of Hirschblut Tower is kind and soft spoken. She never raises her voice, which lilts through the air like a bird song. For all the darkness within, the twisted hate crawling within her gut, externally the Lady is good and gracious. The only time she reveals herself, her true self, is in the darkest, most secretive places—before she devours a victim, or laments over the loss of her beloved. It is then that she transforms into the monster she truly is, twisted with rage and anger, driven mad by the years alone and her many horrible deeds.

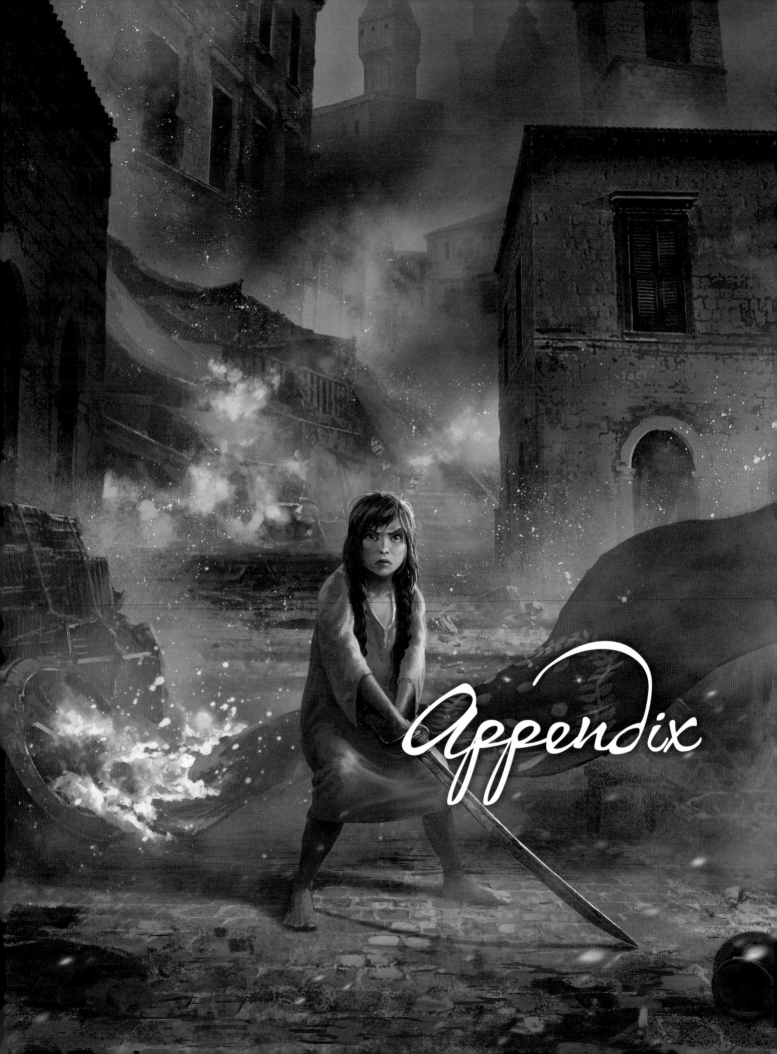

Appendix

New Mechanics

Advantages

2 Point Advantages

FLAWLESS EXECUTION

Must have the ability to perform Duelist Maneuvers. Choose one Maneuver you know. You can spend a Hero Point instead of a Raise to perform this Maneuver. All other rules pertaining to Maneuvers still apply (you can still only perform some Maneuvers once per Round, you cannot perform the same Maneuver twice in a row, etc). A Hero can only use this Advantage once per Round.

3 Point Advantages

LEARNED DUELIST

A Hero must have the Duelist Academy Advantage in order to purchase this Advantage. Choose another Duelist Academy Style to learn.

STUDENT OF COMBAT

You learn the Slash and Parry Maneuvers, as well as one non-Style Maneuver of your choice, and can perform these as a Duelist does. The Duelist Academy Advantage is considered a 3 point Advantage for you.

4 Point Advantages

SAVIOR [KNACK]

It is not enough to simply stop a Villain—you must change her. The greatest weapon against wickedness is to take an agent of evil and make her a force for good. When you take a Risk in the direct pursuit of redeeming a Villain and turning her toward a path of Heroism, you can spend a Hero Point in place of spending a Raise for any Action. If an Action would require multiple Raises (because of Improvisation, being Unskilled, being under Pressure, etc.) you only need to spend one Hero Point to accomplish it. Because you are not spending Raises for these Actions, it remains your turn—this means that, in effect, so long as you have Hero Points you can continue to take Actions back-to-back if every Action that you take is directly related to the redemption of a Villain.

Backgrounds

DOCENT

Is Théah worthy of the friendship of Numa? You will put them to the test.

Quirk

Earn a Hero Point when you push another character to live up to her potential, even when it means trouble or when it complicates the situation.

Advantages	Skills
Duelist Academy	Athletics
(LAKEDAIMON AGOGE)	Empathy
Team Player	Scholarship
	Warfare
	Weaponry

Brute Squad Type

INQUISITORS

Spend a Danger Point when the Squad's Strength would be reduced using Convince, Intimidate, Tempt, or any similar effect of coercion. Their faith is unshakeable, and the Inquisitors ignore the effect.

Dueling Style

LAKEDAIMON AGOGE STYLE

You can perform Dueling Maneuvers while wielding a bow. You use your Ranks in Aim to determine the effects of Maneuvers, in place of Weaponry. Your Lunge Maneuver is replaced by the Agoge Thrust. Agoge Thrust deals a number of Wounds equal to your Aim plus the number of Raises you spend, but you must spend your next Action this Round to recover and regroup, spending one Raise to do so (and gaining no additional effect). Full background to come in 7TH SEA: PIRATE NATIONS.

Sorcery: Mother's Touch

RESURRECT (GIFT)

Spend a Hero Point and lend aid to a character who has died in the last minute (such as giving him a drink of water, staunching his wounds, or literally breathing the life back into him). The character returns to life, but he remains Helpless.

DIGNITY (RESTRICTION)

Limit: You must always act with calm and logic, and never allow emotions to cause you to act rashly or without careful consideration for the consequences of your actions.

Penance: You must undo the decision that you made, and undo the consequences that resulted from your rash actions.

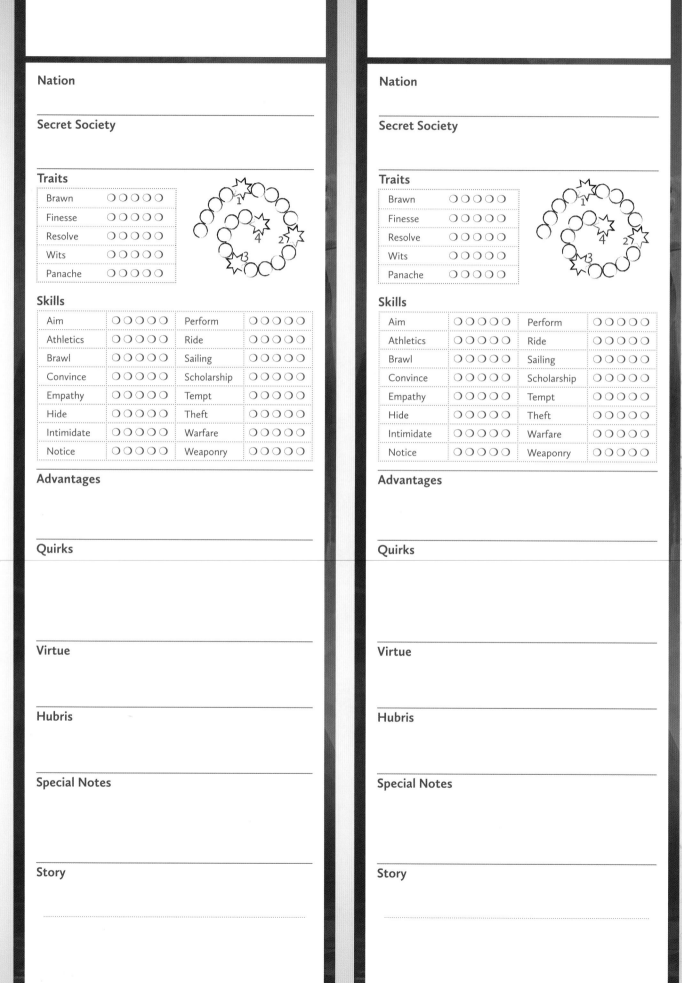

Nation

_____

Secret Society

_____

Traits

Brawn	○○○○○
Finesse	○○○○○
Resolve	○○○○○
Wits	○○○○○
Panache	○○○○○

Skills

Aim	○○○○○	Perform	○○○○○
Athletics	○○○○○	Ride	○○○○○
Brawl	○○○○○	Sailing	○○○○○
Convince	○○○○○	Scholarship	○○○○○
Empathy	○○○○○	Tempt	○○○○○
Hide	○○○○○	Theft	○○○○○
Intimidate	○○○○○	Warfare	○○○○○
Notice	○○○○○	Weaponry	○○○○○

Advantages

_____

Quirks

_____

Virtue

_____

Hubris

_____

Special Notes

_____

Story

....

Nation

_____

Secret Society

_____

Traits

Brawn	○○○○○
Finesse	○○○○○
Resolve	○○○○○
Wits	○○○○○
Panache	○○○○○

Skills

Aim	○○○○○	Perform	○○○○○
Athletics	○○○○○	Ride	○○○○○
Brawl	○○○○○	Sailing	○○○○○
Convince	○○○○○	Scholarship	○○○○○
Empathy	○○○○○	Tempt	○○○○○
Hide	○○○○○	Theft	○○○○○
Intimidate	○○○○○	Warfare	○○○○○
Notice	○○○○○	Weaponry	○○○○○

Advantages

_____

Quirks

_____

Virtue

_____

Hubris

_____

Special Notes

_____

Story

....

| STRENGTH | INFLUENCE | RANK |

Advantages

Virtue

Hubris

Servants and Underlings

Redemption

Special Notes

Schemes

| STRENGTH | INFLUENCE | RANK |

Advantages

Virtue

Hubris

Servants and Underlings

Redemption

Special Notes

Schemes

An Index of Heroes & Villains